ELIZABETHAN NARRATIVE POETRY

Elizabethan Narrative Poetry

LOUIS R. ZOCCA

1970

OCTAGON BOOKS

New York

ACKNOWLEDGMENTS

I SHOULD LIKE TO ACKNOWLEDGE MY GREAT
debt to Leicester Bradner of Brown University for his constant
guidance and interest in this work, and to Professor W. T.
Hastings also of Brown University for his painstaking criticism of the manuscript.

To the Modern Language Association of America I express
my gratitude for their generous grant which enabled me to
secure rotographs of all the material which lay inaccessible in
faraway libraries. My thanks also to all the libraries which lent
their efforts in securing texts or answering questions.

LOUIS ZOCCA

New York City
May 1950

Contents

PART TWO:
THE VERSE ROMANCES

PART THREE:
MYTHOLOGICAL NARRATIVE POETRY

INTRODUCTION

PERHAPS NO PERIOD IN ENGLISH LITERATURE has quite equalled the Elizabethan Age. The versatility of its poets, their boundless exuberance and especially the apparent ease with which they seemed to produce their works have amazed critics ever since. Today the world still marvels at the high level of their production and particularly at the multitude of the poets whose song made the reign of Elizabeth the golden age of poetry. Yet it was not always so. The Marlowes and the Shakespeares, the Spensers and the Jonsons are what they are, wrote what they wrote, because other men preceded them, men who wrote painfully, haltingly, men who had to retrace the paths to great poetry, traversing the morass into which the language had fallen since the days of Chaucer. These pioneers were beset by baffling linguistic problems; they had to carve out their own rules of prosody. Gascoigne, Sidney, Webbe and many others of their time were all troubled by the great metrical problems confronting the English language. Once more English poets had to learn to sing in numbers; once again they had to restore to English the fluidity of Chaucer's tongue. For the language of the Tudors was a far cry from the language of Edward III.

A large part of this experimentation was carried out in the

narrative poems written by unknown or forgotten versifiers. Their countless attempts, often miserable failures from a poetic viewpoint, scornfully referred to by contemporaries as "a gallimaufray of paphlagonian things," nevertheless enabled the greater poets tó avoid their mistakes. Many of these compositions may be the flotsam and jetsam of literature, yet they mark the course of the stream of poetry during the centuries between Chaucer and Spenser. For the stream never really disappeared during the years intervening between these two poets. It may have shrunk to a mere trickle; sometimes it ran underground where it was not to be perceived; but it always flowed, and these lowly narrative poems often helped to keep it from drying up.

It will be the concern of the following pages to record and evaluate some of these productions. Often their poetic worth will not stand a close examination; more than once the reader will become impatient at their immaturity. Sometimes only a single line will rescue them from oblivion. In many cases their sole merit lies in the fact that they are the first flights of fledgling poets trying out their wings. Occasionally, however, they turn out to be the first soarings of great eagles like Marlowe and Shakespeare. Taken as a whole, they are part of the great yeasty mass which will provide material for the more renowned poets who are to follow.

Most of the narrative poems of the sixteenth century fall within this range of popular poetry. Providing as they did a large part of the reading matter for the rising middle classes, they show all the vigor and the raciness of the people; but they also show the mediocrity and limitations of their outlook. In them we shall find the most varied aspects of life, with the most miserable hacks and the most gifted of poets treating the same stories. The loftiest of subjects will be found side by side with the most banal themes. Important questions of state will be coupled with the most trivial incidents. Not infrequently, however, hidden among them will be specimens of truly great verse which has gone to enrich the vast storehouse of Elizabethan poetry. Out of them will come the stuff for the greatest plays and the most sublime poems to be found in the English language.

Because of the vast output and varied character of this narrative poetry, the present study is restricted to three general classes of poems: 1) the historical, 2) the fictional, 3) the mythological. Many other subdivisions are possible, as for instance, pastoral poetry. But since these are special fields, which in many cases have already been thoroughly studied, we must of necessity confine ourselves to the specimens of purely narrative poetry.

Although this narrative poetry goes largely unrecognized, it is still one of the historically interesting products of the Elizabethan age. It flourished under the special conditions which existed during Elizabeth's reign. Not long after Elizabeth's accession to the throne, English literature experienced a definite quickening. Perhaps an even stronger reason than the new Humanism, begun under her father, the underlying cause of the phenomenon was the powerful feeling of nationalism which was perhaps the all-pervasive influence. The English Reformation, itself, was a sign of national unity, for though there were many dissenters from the reformed faith, the nation was in reality united. The movement was hardly new; in reality it went back to the twelfth century, to the struggles between Henry II and Thomas à Becket. It is true that there had been setbacks, recent ones, such, for example, as the reaction under Mary Tudor. However, Mary's adherence to Rome and her marriage to a foreigner had served only to unite the various political factions which had been squabbling. These groups continued to bicker, yet in times of stress they all vociferously joined in their denunciations of the Spanish hydra and the Wolf of Rome.

Foremost in this movement was the Puritan party, whose chief aim was to spread its doctrines far and wide over the kingdom. It is common knowledge how this rabidly Protestant group, beginning as a small intellectual nucleus in the universities, had proselytized among students who, in turn, had gone out as clergymen into the shires. Eventually, their beliefs seeped into the professions and secured for the Puritans a powerful hold upon the middle classes. Thus were their fundamental ideas implanted in the English mind, and, though the Puritans experienced temporary political setbacks under Elizabeth, they ultimately triumphed. The years of struggle to obtain recognition were filled with disappointments, exile and, sometimes, martyrdom. Often the strife threatened to split the nation into two factions. Frequently, because of the sudden shifts in policy, today's patriot found himself declared a traitor on the morrow. Nevertheless, under Elizabeth there was a definite feeling of national unity, one religion—English, one nation—English. England was insular and definitely proud of it. There was no more conclusive proof of this than the bitter opposition offered to the projected marriage between Elizabeth and Alençon. This tremendous sense of solidarity reached its greatest pitch during the threat of the Armada.

The pride which was bound to arise in a nationally conscious people brought definite results. Suddenly England became anxious to know all about English history and English heroes. Chronicle after chronicle was compiled for the benefit of the English masses. Fictitious histories, legendary accounts were piled up side by side with true historical records. The great heroes of the nobility were exalted, but also the good, solid burghers, the lord-mayors of London and other sturdy sprigs of the middle classes. Historical poems became increasingly popular. Before long the chronicle play made its appearance and was loudly applauded by both nobleman and citizen. The English people had discovered itself as a subject for poetry. One of the favorite means used in spreading the history of England was the *mirror*, a genre which goes back to the Middle Ages, but which now found new uses as the English pursued an intentional policy of combining the dissemination of this historical knowledge with the promotion of a definite political theory—the theory of the Tudor state.

PART ONE

The
Historical
Material

I

The Early *Mirrors*

ENGLISH WRITERS OF THE SIXTEENTH CENTURY, as was indicated in the Introduction, discovered in the medieval *mirror* the ideal medium for disseminating a knowledge of history and, through this knowledge, spreading political ideas. Thus the *mirror* came to play an influential role in the development of English poetry, as well as in the laying of ground work for the chronicle plays produced during the last decades of Elizabeth's reign.

The term *mirror* itself was quite elastic. During the Middle Ages, it became the English equivalent of the Latin *speculum,* and was applied chiefly to religious writings. Gradually, however, it came to signify any written work which pointed out a moral. There grew up a multitude of *mirrors* dealing with doctrine and morals, *mirrors* for princes and lovers, *mirrors* for fools.

Throughout the Middle Ages, the genre is put to many uses. It is employed for didactic works, for works of a devotional nature and to exemplify that contempt for the world which is typical of medieval religion. A good specimen of the didactic *mirrors* is the *Speculum Guy de Warewyk,* a homily of ap-

3

proximately five hundred couplets, written *circa* 1300. Taken principally from Alcuin, it demonstrates the manner in which the famous teacher showed to the Earl Guy how to distinguish between vice and virtue, when the latter came to him for advice on how to flee the world and its enticements.[1]

Besides the ubiquitous *Miroir du Monde,* which was translated into English as the *Ayenbite of Wit,* we find among the numerous works of devotional nature, John de Waldeby's *Speculum Vitae,* consisting of eight thousand short couplets. This treatise dwells upon the seven prayers of the *Paternoster* and holds up a glass in which everyone may see his life.[2] Of more secular character, but by no means unique, is John of Arderne's *Speculum Phlebotomiae,* which, like other medical works of this famous author, became extremely popular in England. Even a cursory glance at a medieval list of *mirrors* impresses the reader with the wide currency of this genre. Yet there is constantly present the didactic intent as well as a tendency towards asceticism, the desire to recommend a contemplative life in preparation for a pious death. Ever present in these works is the consciousness of a Day of Judgment and the insignificance of this life in comparison to eternity. Consequently, all this literature exhibits a contempt for the world and its joys, a typically medieval attitude.

This *contemptu mundi* literature may be conveniently divided into three main parts: first, the type illustrated by the works of Bernard of Morlaix and Innocent III; second, the works which are patterned upon the Dance of Death; and finally, the *De Casibus Virorum* theme as exemplified by Giovanni Boccaccio.[3] Only the last of these divisions concerns us, for it is in this group that the bulk of the historical narrative poetry naturally falls. The powerful influence exerted by

. . . . .

[1] J. E. Wells, *A Manual of the Writings in Middle English* (Yale University Press, 1916), p. 275.

[2] Wells, *op. cit.,* p. 348.

[3] Willard Farnham, *The Medieval Heritage of Elizabethan Tragedy* (Berkeley: University of California Press, 1936), p. 40.

Boccaccio on the *mirror*, as well as in the fictional element of narrative poetry, will become increasingly evident.

Quite early this type begins to be identified with *complaints*, *tragedies* or *lamentations*, all types which, though different in name, attempted to represent the same thing, the portraying of the penalties of sin and its consequences upon mankind.

It is in Boccaccio's Latin treatise, *De Casibus Virorum Illustrium*, composed in 1363, after he underwent his temporary conversion, that we see the *mirror* altering its character from the devotional to the historical. Through its translations into many languages, this work exerted a great influence on European literatures, forming for centuries the principal basis of Boccaccio's reputation. In Farnham's words:

> On its humanistic side it was a learned and eminently useful compilation from universal history; on its artistic side, it was a true innovation, in that it gave for the first time a definite form to the medieval conception of tragedy.[4]

Boccaccio was hardly an innovator in this genre, however, because Petrarch had preceded him years before with his *De Viris Illustribus*, a treatise dealing with the lives of the Romans from Romulus to Titus. In his orderly manner, Petrarch had already tried to deal soberly with history by pruning away the supernatural and, as in Caesar's sketch, by attempting to evaluate the varied testimony in order to demonstrate that all the fault lay not entirely at Caesar's feet.

But it was Boccaccio's *De Casibus* which appealed to the Renaissance. Its great attraction lay in its attempt to explain the vicissitudes of great men through the vagaries of that notoriously fickle lady, Fortune. This widespread concept, which had existed in Roman literature from the earliest beginnings, is developed by Boccaccio, who represents Fortune as the per-

. . . . .

4 Farnham, *op. cit.*, p. 71.

sonification of the instability of earthly things.[5] In his philosophical implications, Boccaccio concludes that men are brought low by Fortune because of their striving for honors or wealth. As a result of the first fall of man, Fortune holds great power over those in high places. Thus a great man's fall from high estate is a natural consequence, the tragic but inevitable result of the sin of Adam and Eve.

Boccaccio's work is at once a general compendium of mythology and history. It begins with Adam and Eve standing naked before the author, asking that their tale be told. With the common Renaissance disregard for chronological exactness, it mingles legendary and historical characters. It parades before us Saturn, Zoroaster, Hercules, Myrrha, Orpheus, Narcissus, together with the more historical Lucrece, Midas, Romulus and Remus, and Darius. Most of the Roman emperors appear in it, along with Alaric, Rosamund, Tancred and Guy de Lusignan. There is a reference to Count Ugolino, later to be used by Chaucer in *The Monk's Tale*. We are given a cursory view of the most notable tragedies of history, real or legendary, down to the days of King John II of France, who met his defeat at the hands of the English in 1356.

Through the familiar device of the vision, those famous men and women who have at some time or other been favored by the fickle Goddess appear before Boccaccio. Some clamor to have their tales heard; others engage in conversation with their fellow-sufferers. All of them loudly lament their woes. Occasionally, the author contributes a tale so as to illustrate a moral, while in several instances Fortuna herself narrates the story. But throughout the work, we encounter ironical remarks on the blindness of those who have been entrusted with the government of the world. One by one parade before us the great of the Earth; Agamemnon, proudly passing from triumph to triumph, achieving wealth and fame, only to be brought to an

. . . . .

[5] H. R. Patch, *The Goddess Fortuna in Medieval Literature* (Cambridge: Harvard University Press, 1927).

ignominious end, the ironic death at the hands of Aegisthus. Downfall, likewise, awaits Celtic Arthur, who is slain by the traitorous Modred.

The purpose of *De Casibus* appears to be, then, to describe the most memorable and crushing blows dealt by Fate to the illustrious personages of mythology and history. It was written, as the author tells us himself, "with the object of teaching princes the virtue of wisdom and moderation by holding up to them the example of misfortunes provoked by egotism, pride, and inordinate ambition." [6] Clearly then, the position that Boccaccio fills in the history of the *mirrors* is one of transition. He stands somewhere between the early *specula* and the final stages of the type as it ultimately developed in England. He shows both elements, yet the didactic dominates the purely historical, for it is obvious that in Boccaccio the moral element is very strong. The Florentine studied his princes from a hostile point of view. One senses a bitter scorn in Boccaccio as he portrays their excessive lavishness and pride, their greed and sloth, their hatreds and desire for revenge. It is the mood of his momentary revulsion from the world; consequently, he is primarily concerned with demonstrating the utterly fickle ways of Fortune and the need for spurning the joys and activities of this Earth. And the moral is clear: seek the honors of the world, but seek wisely and virtuously, accepting the sudden changes in Fortune as inevitable.

Chaucer's *Monkes Tale* also contains a series of brief *mirrors* which explicitly point out the dangers of trusting Fortune too far. Using the chief figures of antiquity, as well as those of his own day, as examples, he illustrates how brief are the joys of this world and how sudden and unpredictable is the spinning of the wheel of Fortune. In Chaucer's own day John Gower's *Speculum Meditantis* (ca. 1380-90), reverted to the original purpose of the genre. It is largely a mixture of allegorical and

. . . . .

[6] John Lydgate, *The Fall of Princes*, ed. Henry Bergen (*EETS*, 1924), I, xi.

devotional information, purporting to show the sinner the way to return to salvation.

The vogue of the *mirror* was continued in England by John Lydgate, who serves as an important link between Boccaccio and the Renaissance. Although Lydgate used Boccaccio as his basis for the *Fall of Princes*, a huge compilation of thirty-six thousand lines, it came to him second-hand, for he worked from a French version of Boccaccio by Laurent de Premierfait.[7] Not possessing the artistic vision of either Boccaccio or Chaucer, Lydgate appears to us plainly as the monk whose prime purpose is to reveal this world as a vale of sorrow and to advise his readers to flee its sinful mirage. Whereas the two preceding authors were inclined to attribute the downfall of their princes to human traits, Lydgate ascribes it solely to the sins of the persons in question. Therefore, he becomes one-sided. He draws the inevitable conclusions that sinful actions will be punished, and conversely, that virtuous behavior will be rewarded with happiness.[8]

Perhaps as a result of his long hours in a confessional, Lydgate exhibits a broad humanity and tolerance of certain sins. In contrast to the rather strident tone of Boccaccio, who composed his work while in the midst of his famous conversion, Lydgate seems inclined to gloss over the failings of priests and princes, although at all times he advocates morality and chastity. He softens Boccaccio's bitter attitude towards women. If unable to forego such censure, he apologizes for his satire. Only when confronted with heretics does Lydgate vent his wrath. This is, perhaps, natural, for, from his monastic perch, Lydgate must have regarded heresy as the foulest of crimes.

. . . . .

[7] The latter had made two versions of *De Casibus* using the first (unrevised) issue of this work. His first redaction was fairly close, while the second, issued in 1409, is extended by moralizing and other medieval interpolation. Thus Lydgate's *Fall of Princes* (1430-40), which followed this second version, comes to us with an accretion of ideas that are foreign to Boccaccio.

[8] Lydgate, *op. cit.*, p. 163.

Consequently, he is inflexible with Julian the Apostate for trafficking with the Foul Fiend, and with Mahomet, whom he regards merely as another sorcerer.

About the year 1500, the Scottish poet Robert Henryson continued Chaucer's tale of Troilus and Cressida in his *Testament of Cressida*. His version takes up the woeful story of "worthy Chaucer,"

> when Diomed had all his appetite
> and more fulfilled of this fair lady
> Upon another he set his haill delyte.

The poem is in reality Cressida's complaint, reproaching the false gods, Venus and Cupid. Angered, the gods in a council pass judgment upon her and condemn her to become a leper. After she is reduced to beggary and rendered loathsome by her disease, she encounters Troilus outside the palace gates. He passes by her without a sign, yet vaguely aware that he has seen her face somewhere. Soon after making her testament she dies.[9]

It was perhaps appropriate that one of the first predecessors of the later historical *mirrors* should have been written by the great humanist, Sir Thomas More, at the beginning of the sixteenth century. When the mother of Henry VIII died in 1503, the young courtier joined in the mourning with *A Ruefull Lamentation (Writen by Master Thomas More in His Youth) of the Dethe of Quene Elizabeth, Mother to King*

. . . . .

[9] This notion of the just retribution of Cressida's falseness appealed to the sixteenth century and we find it gaining popularity. Turberville, for example, in *Epitaphs and Sonnets* says of his love:

> I pray the Gods to plague thee
> As they did the dame of Troy.
> I mean that Cresid coy
> That linkt her with a Greek.

Henryson's poem remained popular, and we find a new edition being printed in Edinburgh by H. Charteris in 1593. For a treatment of the subject see Hyder Rollins, "The Troilus and Cressida Legend," *PMLA*, XXXII (1917), 383ff.

Henry the Eighth, Wife to King Henry Seventh, & Eldest Daughter to King Edward the Fourth, Which Quene Elizabeth Died in Childbed in February in the Yere of our Lord 1503 and in the 18 Yere of the Raigne of King Henry the Seventh. Although it does not follow the pattern set by the later *mirrors,* in being a biographical soliloquy spoken after death, yet it represents the farewell of the dying lady to her children. It follows the type insofar as it sounds a contempt for the world and the *ubi sunt* note:

> Where are our castles, now where are our Towers?
> Goodly Richmonde sone thou art gone from me,
> At Westminster that costly worke of yours,
> Myne owne dear lorde now shall I never see.
> Almighty god vouchesafe to graunt that ye,
> For you and your children well may edefy,
> My palace bylded is and lo now here I ly.[10]

And after commending herself to God's mercy, she takes farewell of her children, her sister, and all her servants.

More made use of another element of the *mirror* by presenting the medieval view of Fortune, which is such a pronounced note of the genre. To his treatise on Fortune he prefixed verses on that wayward lady, solemnly warning his readers to shun her, for:

> Thus fell Julius from mighty Power,
> Thus fell Darius the worthy kyng of Perse,
> Thus fell Alexander the great conquerour,
> Thus many mo then I may well reherse.
> Thus double fortune when she lyst reverse
> Her slipper favour fro them that in her trust
> She fleeth her wey and leyeth them in the dust.[11]

In addition, More turned the minds of his contemporaries more firmly towards history. The authorship of *The History*

. . . .

[10] Thomas More, *The English Works,* ed. W. E. Campbell (London, 1931), I, 335ff.
[11] *Ibid.,* I, 341ff.

of Richard III has caused more than one controversy, but since it is popularly ascribed to More, we may give him credit for assembling much of the material that was to prove fruitful to later *mirror* writers. A history in prose covering the period from the death of Edward IV to the accession of Richard, it was written about 1513, but was not published until 1543, when it was incorporated in the *Chronicles of John Hardyng* as prose continuation of this work. Hardyng's chronicle [12] was but one of the many contemporary manifestations of the growing importance of history in the eyes of England. The age was seething with unrest, change, downright revolt. The struggle for power of ambitious nobles during the minority of the King, as well as the great controversies which had arisen over the religious question, offered countless opportunities for ambitious men to rise. Northumberland, Somerset, Warwick, the wily Cecil, all were stalking on the stage, ready for plunder, arraying the country into bitter factions. Proscriptions, reminiscent of the days of Marius and Sulla, caused an unbelievably bitter feeling between the partisans, who through propaganda, often exalted common malefactors to the pinnacles of martyrdom. Burnings for heresy were frequent, and both sides fought bitterly out in the open or in the even more savage silent struggles.

To prepare the young for the part they must play in these controversies, to implant the right seed in the minds of students, history became a paramount necessity in Tudor times. Sir Thomas Elyot avers that the boy must be taught geography and other rudiments of education:

> but first to set hym in a fervent courage, the master in the most pleasant and elegant wise expressing what incomparable delectation, utilitie and commoditee shall happen to Emperours, Kings, princes and all other gentylmen by redyng of histories. [13]

. . . . .

[12] See below p. 13.
[13] Sir Thomas Elyot, *The Boke Called the Governour*, ed. H. H. S. Croft (London, 1883), p. 81.

Abandoned was the humanistic conception of history as a subject to delight man *per se*. It became the prized knowledge, the very foundation of the Tudor state in its struggle against the Papacy and towards world recognition. Lily B. Campbell, in her *Tudor Conception of History and Tragedy*, says:

History was perhaps the most prized learning in Tudor England because it seemed the most immediately useful. In the thinking of the time, history dealt primarily with the rise and fall of nations. The growing national consciousness progressively developing under the Tudors to the final triumph of patriotism of Elizabeth's reign, impelled the English to seek in History the way to immortality through fame, the immortality for which the men of the Renaissance never ceased to yearn. To rescue their country from oblivion became a patriotic duty.

Less disinterestedly, the Tudor sovereigns found an imperative need for history to authenticate the claims of Henry VII and his heirs to the English throne. On the one hand Henry VII was hailed by his supporters as the successor of the ancient British kings, his advent the fulfillment of the prophecies of Cadwallader, the last of the line. On the other hand, his marriage with Elizabeth the daughter of Edward IV was celebrated as marking the end of the disastrous wars between the houses of York and Lancaster and inaugurating the rule of a newly united kingdom.

Thus a good many of the literary productions of the century deal with national themes from Spenser's *Faerie Queene* to the historical plays of Shakespeare. History not only served to unite men in the national feeling, but also served to point out the fate allotted to men by the Divine Will. Thus the chronicles became important as disseminators of historical information, as means of showing that History repeats itself and that kings and statesmen could learn from the bitter lessons of their predecessors.[14]

To satisfy this demand for historical compilations, there appeared from the shop of Richard Grafton in 1543, *The Chronicles of John Hardyng in Metre, From the First Begynninge*

. . . . .

[14] Lily B. Campbell, *Tudor Conception of History and Tragedy in the Mirror for Magistrates* (Berkeley: 1936), p. 2.

of England, Unto the Reigne of Edward the Fourth, Where he Made an End of His Chronicle and From That Tyme is Added With a Continuacion of the Storie in Prose to This Our Tyme. After explaining chronicles and their function as history books, Grafton states that he is printing this English chronicle for the benefit of men who cannot understand Latin and will cast it in "balade." Hardyng extols the right of the king to the titles of England, Wales, and Scotland, adding that,

> By papal Bull ye have the right to Irelande
> Gascow, Paitowe and Normandye,
> Pountyf, Bebuile, Saunxie and Sauntignye.[15]

Boldly he states Edward's claims not only to the French lands, to Caour and the countries beyond the Charente, but also to Jerusalem.

Like all the other chroniclers, Hardyng begins with legendary times, speaking of "the xxx susters that first inhabited this land and named it Albion, that now is England, Wales and Scotland." He takes us through all the familiar scenes of English history, both mythical and historical, not omitting the traditional accounts of Aeneas, Dido and Brutus. The famous legend of Lear and Cordelia is baldly told, remaining an ungerminated seed ready for the fructifying pen of Shakespeare, while the Arthurian material, as befits the purpose of the chronicle, is given a good deal of attention. Significant also is Hardyng's use of the *lamentacion* inasmuch as it may have some bearing on the *Mirror for Magistrates*, compiled a few years later. Though Hardyng's *Chronicle* has little poetic merit, we can trace in it for the first time many of the conventions found in the more famous *Mirror for Magistrates*.

The general interest in history was supplemented by another direct ancestor of the *mirrors* compiled by David Lyndsay, a

. . . . .

15 John Hardyng, *The Chronicles*, ed. Henry Ellis (London, 1812), p. 21.

courtier of James V of Scotland. A bitter enemy of Cardinal Beaton, soon after the violent death of that prelate in 1546, he composed *The Tragedie of Cardinal Beaton*, which appeared in an English edition in 1548. The author represents himself as sitting in his study perusing Boccaccio, when Cardinal Beaton appears to him, dripping with blood, lamenting that were Boccaccio alive, he would include Beaton's tragedy in *De Casibus*. He proceeds with the tale of his rise to power, until he had the governance of all Scotland, the rule of all temporal and secular affairs; had he been Pope he could have risen no higher. Yet his downfall was as swift as his rise; soon he was plunged into a dungeon, losing in a half hour all the worldly goods which he had labored a lifetime to accumulate. So the Cardinal ends his complaint with a strong exhortation to prelates and princes to take heed and profit from his sinful example.

The work itself is distinguished neither in conception nor in execution, but some critics, such as Trench, have seen in it the prototype of the *Tragedy of the Mirror for Magistrates*.[16] Although Trench goes perhaps too far in calling Lyndsay's poem the father of the *Mirror for Magistrates*, there is no denying that many of the *Mirror's* characteristics are incorporated in it. There is the autobiographical note, the lament of the subject of the tragedy, his request to be allowed to tell the story, the meteoric rise and sudden fall, as well as the moral and didactic tone of the narrative. Whatever its ultimate importance may be, Lyndsay's *Tragedie* comes in a period when, as Courthope puts it,

> The philosopher, the moralist and the statesman were alive to the conflict of tragic forces in the life about them and strove, however imperfectly, to represent them in verse. Hence in much of the poetry conceived in England and Scotland during the latter part of the reign of Henry VIII and in the reigns of Edward VI
> . . . . .

[16] W. F. Trench, *A Mirror for Magistrates: Its Origin and Influence* (Edinburgh, 1898), p. 93.

and Mary an increased prominence was given to the idea of the State.[17]

It must have been with such a purpose in mind that a small group of Protestant writers met to prepare a work whose influence was to extend throughout the century and touch all the great works of the age, from the obscure penny ballad to the most sublime tragedies of English literature.

. . . . .

[17] W. J. Courthope, *History of English Poetry* (New York, 1895), II, p. 102.

I I

The *Mirror for Magistrates,*
Baldwin's Edition

THE POPULARITY OF HISTORICAL WORKS DUR-
ing Mary's reign was such that it was thought advisable to
issue a new edition of Lydgate's *Fall of Princes,* which had
already been issued in 1494 and 1527. Although the problem
is not yet finally settled, from the available facts it appears
that the printer John Wayland had secured the privilege of
printing the *Primer.* Finding his presses idle, however, he had
intended to occupy the available time by reprinting Lydgate,
appending to this work a new compilation, "concernynge the
chefe Prynces of thys Iland, penned by the best clearkes in
such kind of matters that be thys day lyuing", which would
bring the work up to date insofar as England was concerned.

He seems to have secured the services of William Baldwin,
who had been associated with his former master, Edward
Wayland *ca.* 1550. The relationship had continued between
Baldwin and John Wayland after the latter took over the
business in 1553, for we have records of his publishing Baldwin's *Treatise of Morall Philosophie* in 1547. This energetic

16

figure, a typical forerunner of the literary hacks that were to become so numerous at the end of the century, seems to have had his finger on the literary pulse of the time, for, beginning as a printer's assistant, we find him becoming in succession a proofreader, preacher, poet, moralist. In 1566-67, he presented a comedy *Live and Let Live* before the Queen. In 1554, however, Baldwin hardly felt equal to the task of remedying Boccaccio's omissions. The story is best told in his own words:

When the printer had purposed with himselfe to printe Lidgate's translation of Bochas of the Fall of Princes, and had made Pryvye thereto many both honourable and worshipfull, he was counsayled by dyvers of them, to procure to have the story contynewed from whereas Bochas left, unto this present time; chiefly of such as Fortune had dalyed with here in this ylande which might be as a mirour for men of all estates and degrees as well nobles as others, to beholde the slipery deceiptes of the wavering lady, and the due rewarde of all kinde of vices. Which advyse lyked him so well, that he requyred me to take paines therin. But because it was a matter passyng my wit and skyll, and more thankles than gaineful to meddle in, I refused utterly to undertake it, except I might have the help of suche, as in wit were apte, in learnyng allowed, and in judgement and estymacyon able to wielde and furnysh so weighty an enterprys, thinkyng even so to shift my handes. But he, earnest and diligent in his affayres, procured Atlas to set under his shoulder. For shortly after, divers learned men (whose manye giftes nede fewe prayses) consented to take upon them parte of the travayle. And when certaine of them, to the numbre of seven, were through a general assent at an appoynted tyme and place gathered together to devyse thereupon, I resorted unto them, bearing with me the booke of Bochas as translated by Dan Lidgate, for the better observation of his order. Which although we liked wel, yet would it not conveniently serve, seeing that both Bochas and Lidgate were dead; neither were there any alive that meddled with like argument, to whom the Unfortunate might make their mone. To make therefore a state ment for the matter, they all agreed that I should usurpe Bochas' rowme, and the wretched Princes complayne unto me: and take upon themselves, every man for his parte to be sundry personages, and in their behalfes to bewaile unto ME their greevous chances, heavye destinies, and wofull misfortunes. This done, we opened such bookes of Cronicles as we had there present. And maister Ferrers, after he had found where Bochas left, which was about the ende of Kinge Edward the Thirdes raigne, to begin the matter sayde thus.

"I marvayle what Bochas meaneth, to forget among his miserable Princes such as wer of our nacion, whose numbre is as great, as their adventures wunderfull. For to let passe all, both Britons, Danes, and Saxons, and to come to the last Conquest, what a sorte are they, and some even in his (Boccace's) owne time, or not much before! As for example, king Richard the Fyrst, slayne with a quarle in his chyefe prosperitie. Also king John his brother, as sum saye, poysoned. Are not their histories rufull, and of rare example? But as it should appeare, he being an Italian, minded most the Roman and Italike story, or els perhaps he wanted our countrey Cronicles. It were therefore a goodly and a notable matter, to search and discourse our whole story from the first beginning of the inhabiting of the yle. But seeing the printer's minde is, to have us folowe where Lidgate left, we will leave that great laboure to other that may intend it, and (as blinde Bayard is alway boldest) I will begyn at the time of Richard the Second, a time as unfortunate as the ruler therein. And forasmuch, frend Baldwyne, as it shal be your charge to note and pen orderlye the whole proces, I will, so far as my memorie and judgemente serveth, sumwhat further you in the truth of the storye. And therefore omittinge the ruffle of Jacke Strawe and his meyney, and the murther of manye notable men which thereby happened, for Jacke, as ye knowe, was but a poore prynce; I will begin with a notable example which within a while after ensued. And although he be no Great Prynce, yet sithens he had a princely office, I will take upon me the miserable person of syr Robert Tresilian chyefe justyce of England, and of other which suffered with him. Therby to warne all of his authoritye and profession, to take hede of wrong judgements, misconstruynge of lawes, or wresting the same to serve the princes turnes, which ryghtfully brought theym to a miserable ende, which they may justly lament in manner ensuing." [1]

The compilation was planned and some trial title pages were run off on the presses, but the printing was interrupted by the priority given to the *Primer*. It was not until June 4, 1555, that work on the edition of Lydgate seems to have been resumed, and this time new title pages were printed. Misfortune dogged it; the proclamation of June 13, 1555, suppressing all undesirable works, chiefly those of the leaders of the Reformation, again halted its printing. Under this general prohibition came especially Halle's *Chronicles*. Hence, a work based on this banned chronicle must also have come under the edict.

Baldwin himself in his "Dedication to the Nobilitie" says:

> The wurke was begun and parte of it prynted in Queene Maries tyme, but hyndred by the Lord Chancellour that then was, nevertheless through the meanes of my lord Stafford, the fyrst parte was licenced the fyrst year of the raigne of this our most noble and vertuous queene. [2]

Thus the works of Lydgate were printed, but the *Mirror* had to await the accession of Elizabeth. Even then, certain *tragedies* were omitted and were only added in 1563. It was not until 1578 that the *Mirror for Magistrates* included all the material that had originally been planned in 1554.

The reason for the ban placed upon the *Mirror* has been ascribed to various causes. Baldwin himself is silent, but Miss Evelyn Feasey suggests that the cause lay in three of the poems, "Humfrey, Duke of Glocester," "Elinor Cobham," and "Edward Duke of Somerset." These three *tragedies* had been included in the original plan as may be gathered from the prose interpolations of the *Mirror*, but, according to Miss Feasey, "weightier reasons" than a mere printer's error must

. . . . .

[1] *Mirror for Magistrates*, ed. Lily B. Campbell (Cambridge, 1938), p. 68ff.
[2] Campbell, *Mirror for Magistrates*, p. 66.

have been the cause of their omission. The reason for their banishment must be sought in their relationship to political events and in their applicability to powerful political figures.[3]

The first two must have been excluded well in advance, for there is no break in the foliation at the point where they appear in later editions, "Edward Duke of Somerset," however, must have been withdrawn only at the last minute because space was provided for it, and nothing inserted in its place.

Miss Feasey has assumed that the nature of these poems was such that it could be applied to the troubled days of Queen Mary. She holds the view that George Ferrers, who was supposedly a sympathizer of Edward Seymour, having served in the wars with him, had written a *mirror* too clearly applicable to contemporary events in Beaufort's scheming efforts to overthrow the former duke of Somerset. Bishop Gardiner, who like Beaufort was both Chancellor and Bishop of Winchester, could undoubtedly see his own reflection in the subtle practices of his predecessor. In order to revenge himself upon Seymour for excluding him from the Chancellorship of Cambridge and committing him to the Fleet at the death of Henry VIII, he, too, had conspired towards the overthrow of Seymour.

Consequently, according to Miss Feasey, it was not until 1559 when Gardiner was dead and another ruler on the throne that permission to print was obtained through Stafford. Because of his official influence, the latter was able to obtain a license, provided the three objectionable *tragedies* were deleted. Stafford, it is held, had a direct interest in the suppression of the Glocester *tragedy* because he had been one of the persons who had signed the decree of execution in Seymour's case and any praise of him would have placed Stafford in the category of those "who," as the title put it, "had brought him to confusion."

. . . . .

[3] Evelyn Feasey, "The Licensing of *The Mirror for Magistrates*," *The Library*, Series 4, III (1923), p. 177ff.

Although this explanation is neat, it is simpler to believe that the *Mirror for Magistrates* came under the general ban with *Halles Chronicles,* which according to the *Mirror* was "feeling the whip for having added the causes which Fabian had let slip." [4]

We might also point out that since the *Mirror* was primarily a Protestant enterprise this would be sufficient reason to cause its suppression, but, unfortunately, in those days of confused party lines, it was difficult to distinguish Protestants from Catholics. Thus among the contributors to the *Mirror for Magistrates,* we find Dr. Thomas Phaer, who dedicated his translation of the first seven books of the *Aeneid* to Queen Mary, remaining a nominal Catholic. George Ferrers was also quite active under Mary, acting as Lord of Misrule and later supposedly providing the Council with information concerning the actions of the Princess Elizabeth and Dr. John Dee, the astrologer. He is also thought to have provided information to Catholics during his stay in Parliament and to have been otherwise active on behalf of Mary Queen of Scots.[5] Sir Thomas Chaloner apparently was a trusted officer during Mary's reign, for he was sent on a confidential mission to Scotland in 1555-56. On the other hand, Baldwin was definitely a Protestant, having taken orders probably *circa* 1559.

The little group of writers, which comprised some of the most noted and influential authors of the time, as, for example, Thomas Sackville, set about reproducing the various histories in a sort of literary symposium. They were armed with the chronicles of Fabian and Halle, with other miscellaneous accounts of the time, and perhaps More's *History of Richard III.* But the work was to be no mere versification of historical material, for from the very beginning, the collaborators gave indi-

. . . . .

[4] L. B. Campbell, "The Suppressed Edition of *The Mirror for Magistrates,*" *Huntington Library Bulletin,* No. 6 (1934), p. 1.
[5] *Ibid.,* p. 14ff.

cation of the higher purpose of the compilation.[6] We cannot tell whether or not the group of authors actually met, for the assemblies reported in the prose links may have been a mere literary device designed to add dramatic effectiveness. However, there might have been an actual symposium such as we hear of in later years in connection with Spenser, Drant, and the oft-discussed metrical reforms. In his Introduction to *A Discourse of Civil Life*, Lodowick Bryskett, Spenser's friend, describes another such literary gathering held at his cottage outside Dublin in which Spenser is supposed to have participated.[7] In the case of *The Mirror for Magistrates* each of the authors was supposed to impersonate an historical character and tell his story to Baldwin, who had agreed to act the role of Boccaccio.

The Mirror for Magistrates, as it appeared in 1559, contained nineteen *tragedies* contributed by the various authors, with Baldwin, like the Host in the *Canterbury Tales*, acting as the guiding spirit. It treated the historical events from Richard II through Richard III (1377-1485), beginning, as they had stated, at the date where Boccaccio had left off, but including the *tragedies* that he had neglected to write.

To George Ferrers fell the honor of inditing the first *tragedy*, "The Fall of Robert Tresilian Chief Justice of England and Other of His Fellows for Misconstruing the Lawes and Ex-

. . . . .

[6] Lily Campbell, in *Tudor Conception of History and Tragedy*, p. 18, sees in this production the attempt to "apply to history the Tudor teaching of theocracy. They saw in the rise and fall of nations and in the life and death of men the providence of God. Inevitably they saw in the tragedies which they wrote out of English history the actions of a God who cried 'Vengeance is mine!' They did not fail to recognize that in this life the just are sometimes made to suffer; they did not fail to recognize that evil harms other than its author, but they did bring a new conception to tragedy in making their tragedies reveal how inevitable were the ends of irreligious action. In other words they foreshadowed the ideal of the tragic hero as he has become familiar to us in the plays of Shakespeare."

[7] Leicester Bradner, *Edmund Spenser and the Faerie Queene* (University of Chicago Press, 1948), p. 32.

pounding Them to Serve the Princes Affections." Here we
have a straightforward tale of the magistrates who, becoming
Richard's tools, executed all his infamous desires, until the
people rose and finally put an end to their wicked dealings.

It is followed by the *tragedy,* "How the Two Rogers Sur-
named Mortimers, for Their Sundry Vices Ended Their Lives
Unfortunately, the One Anno 1329, the Other 1387." This
piece is perhaps most interesting for the contemporary view
which it affords us of the Irish "savages" by whom Mortimer
was slain when he became contemptuous of their valour.

> They know no lawe of armes, nor none will learne,
> They make not warre (as others do) a play,
> The Lord, the boy, the gallowglas, the kerne,
> Yeelde or not yeelde whom so they take, they slay.
> They save no prisoners for ransome nor for pay;
> Theyr chiefest boote they count theyr bodoh's head
> Their end of warre to see theyr enemy deade.[8]

Cavil, who is generally accepted as the author of this poem,
seems to have followed Fabyan as his authority. There is some
dispute as to his authorship, for although the poem is signed
"Ca." in 1571 and repeated in all editions but one, in that of
1578 there appears "T. Ch.," supposedly Thomas Chaloner.
These initials might also represent Thomas Churchyard, but
it hardly seems likely that the latter could be the author because from what we know of him, he would undoubtedly have
included this *tragedy* in the list of his works which he so
scrupulously published.

Thomas Phaer contributed the *mirror* of Owen Glendower,
destroyed through the relentless pursuit of Henry IV. The
narrative follows the chronicles closely in the description of
the hunt for the Welsh prince in the mountains and the account of his ultimate starvation. Quite typically it exhorts the
people to respect royal authority and not to presume to climb
above their destined stations.

. . . . .

[8] Campbell, *Mirror for Magistrates,* p. 88.

To the editor-in-chief, Baldwin, are ascribed several *tragedies,* dealing with the conspiracies of the nobles during the reigns of Henry IV and Henry V. Among these are: "Henry Percy, Earl of Northumberland, who, for his trayterous attempts, was put to death at Yorke, A.D. 1407"; "Richard Plantagenet, Earl of Cambridge," beheaded for plotting against Henry V; "Thomas Montague, Earle of Salisbury," slain at Orleans by a piece of ordnance; "King James I," who "for breaking othes was murdered by his own subjects." All these figures, made familiar by later and more famous accounts in Elizabethan plays, parade before us in a fashion not very much changed from that of Halle's *Chronicles,* which appear to be the chief source of this section.

It seems fitting to speak at this point of George Ferrers' banned *tragedies* dealing with Dame Elinor Cobham, Duchess of Glocester, banished for practising sorcery, and her spouse, Humphrey, Duke of Glocester. The two stories are almost complementary, in that they deal with the same events, one from the point of view of the husband and the other from the point of view of the wife. Miss Feasey has pointed out that they seem to foreshadow the treatment of material in *The Ring and the Book.* Lady Elinor's fate was a popular subject and her practise of sorcery was recorded in a good many of the ballads of the period. Her rivalry with Henry VI's queen, Margaret, although not historically true,[9] has become classic through Shakespeare's adoption of it in *Henry VI.* The account found in the *Mirror* was so dramatic that Shakespeare retained it in his play. At any rate, there is apparent in this *tragedy* a tenderness in mood, a feeling of forgiveness on the part of Elinor for her husband's temporary lapses from conjugal vows:

> His wife was I and he my true husband,
> Though for a while hee had the company
>
> . . . . .

[9] Queen Margaret did not come to England until four years after Elinor had been sent into exile.

> Of Lady Iaquet (the) Dutchesse of Holland
> Being an heyre of ample patrymony
> But that fell out to be no matrimony.[10]

Humphrey, on his part, makes a full confession of his behavior and repays her with sympathetic forbearance for her sorcery, at that time the gravest of crimes:

> Elinor my wife, my duchess only deare,
> I know not how, but as the nature is,
> Of women all, aye curious to enquire
> Of things to come, (though I confess in this
> Her fault not small . . . . :[11]

The history of this great nobleman, patron of scholars and founder of a renowned library unfolds, as in Halle, down to his murder while he lay in his bed.

The *tragedy* of "Tiptoft, Earl of Worcester" offers unusual interest in view of the fact that it exhibits the writer's view of the function of history. Tiptoft challenges Baldwin to find fault with his behavior, since his only crime lay in obeying his "Prince's butcherly commandments" and since he acted through "a desire of honor blinde." He berates historians,

> This doth appear (I dare say) by my story,
> Which divers writers diversly declare;
> But story writers ought for neither glory,
> Feare nor favor truth of things to spare,
> But still it fares as always it did fare,
> Affections, feare or doubts that dayly brue
> Do cause that stories never can be true.
>
> Unfruitfull Fabyan followed the face
> Of tyme and dedes, but let the causes slip;
> Which Hall hath added, but with double grace,
> For feare, I thinke, lest trouble might him trip:
> "For this or that" sayeth he "felt the whip:"

> . . . . .

[10] Campbell, *Mirror for Magistrates*, p. 433.
[11] *Ibid.*, p. 453.

Thus story writers leave the causes out
Or so rehearse them as they were in dout.

But seeing causes are the chiefest things
That should be noted of the story writers,
That men may learne what endes all causes bringes
To be unworthy the name of chroniclers
That leave them cleane out of theyr registers,
Or doubtfully report them: for the fruite
Of reading stories standeth in the suite.

And therefore, Baldwin, eyther speake upright
Of our affyres or touch them not at all.[12]

Here then we have the philosophy of history of our authors,
that causes, their explanation and honest narration are the
proper and true subject of history.

This first part of the *Mirror* ends with John Skelton's "King
Edward IV," who, through surfeiting and intemperate life,
came to a sudden end in 1483. It is a typically Skeltonian piece,
with a characteristic medieval refrain *"et ecce nunc in pulvere
dormio,"* quite in the mood of the *tragedies,* and, with it, the
authors thought it fit to end the compilation.

With the issue of the *Mirror for Magistrates* in 1559, the
vogue was definitely launched, and we observe a number of
mirrors of all varieties. It will be better, however, to withhold
a discussion of these for the present and to treat first of the
remaining editions, the amplifications of the *Mirror for Magistrates* itself.

. . . . .

[12] *Ibid.,* p. 198.

III

The Subsequent Editions of
the *Mirror for Magistrates*

IN 1563 THE COLLABORATORS MET ONCE MORE,
with Baldwin still at the helm, only Ferrers being absent. In
the prologue to this edition, he is pictured as making a dramatic entrance, apologizing for his lateness, explaining that
he had picked up a rich booty; his own tragedy of "Somerset,"
Churchyard's "Jane Shore," Dolman's "Hastings," Sackville's
"Buckingham," Segar's "Richard III," and Cavil's "Black-
smith." In all, there are eight new *tragedies* in the 1563
version. The high point of the entire *Mirror* is reached in
Sackville's contribution, the "Induction," and "The Complaint
of Henry, Duke of Buckingham," for this great nobleman was
doubtless the ablest contributor to the compilation. The prefatory matter to this *tragedy* reveals that Sackville, upon hearing
that the Council had placed a ban on the *Mirror*, had planned
to secure all the *tragedies* before "The Complaint of Henry,
Duke of Buckingham" and to preserve them in one volume.
He had entertained serious intentions of going back by himself as far as William the Conqueror, just as Lydgate had done.
It was thus that he came to devise the "Induction." This am-

bitious plan never was executed, for in the 1563 edition only the "Complaint of the Duke of Buckingham" was included; it is believed that by this time he had been attracted by the subject matter of *Gorboduc* and was devoting his time to the composition of this play.[1]

The "Induction" presents a very woeful picture; it is a bleak winter's day and all Nature is wrapped in a mantle of gloom.

> Hawthorne had lost his motleie liverie,
> The naked twigs were shivering all for colde:
> And dropping doune the teares abundantlie.[2]

In this grisly setting, Sorrow appears to the poet, clad in black, a "pitous wight that woe had all forwast." This creature proposes to lead him to Hell. Following this guide through a terrifying wood, resounding with the howling of dogs, the poet comes to the entrance of the dreadful place,

> An hidous hole, al vast, withouten shape,
> Of endles depths, orewhelmed with ragged stone,
> With ouglie mouths, and grislie iawes doth gape,
> And to our sight confoundes it selfe in one:
> Here entered we, and, yeading furth anon
> A horrible lothlie lake we might discerne,
> As black as pitche that cleped is Auerne.[3]

Here are to be seen the various inhabitants of this place of woe, Remorse of Conscience "all besprent with teares," Revenge gnashing her teeth, Pale Maladie, Old Age, Famine, and lastly Warre, grim, black and with naked sword on whose targe are depicted all the great slaughters of antiquity. Poet and mystagogue are ferried across Acheron by Charon and conveyed to the kingdom of Pluto. Here, supposedly, the various unfortunates whom Sackville had proposed to record are to pass by in review. The first is Henry, Duke of Buckingham,

· · · · ·

[1] Thomas Sackville, *The Complaint of Henry Duke of Buckingham*, ed. Marguerite Hearsey (New Haven, 1936), Intro. pp. 26-7.
[2] Campbell, *Mirror for Magistrates*, p. 298.   [3] *Ibid.*, p. 305.

somberly clad, wringing his hands as he rails against Fortune and complains so piteously that his heart seems likely to burst at each sigh.

Thrise he began to tell his dolefull tale,
And thrise the sighes dyd swalowe up his voyce.[4]

And he recounts the details of his compact with the unspeakable Richard III, especially the subtle dealings that secured the crown for the latter. He seeks to disavow his responsibility in the death of Richard's two innocent nephews, for he claims,

Me selfe not bente so moche for to aspire
As to fulfill that gredie dukes desire.[5]

Thus, through his allegiance to the tyrant, he is led from crime to crime, until the suspicious king, fearing his power which had become too great, begins to seek means to undo him. Once fickle Fortune turns her wheel the Duke's downfall is swift. A trusted friend betrays him for the sake of the reward on his head; Buckingham is taken to Richard, and put to death. Curiously enough, the Duke indulges in little self-recrimination; he ascribes his downfall more to Fortune, which changes for no good reason, than to a just retribution for his crimes, committed in conjunction with Richard. Nor does Sackville seem to hold a different view of a *casus* which a stricter moralist would have exploited to the fullest extent.

The poem is by far the best of the *Mirror for Magistrates*, as may be judged from the scattered passages quoted. Its verse has a smoothness and variety that compare favorably with some of Surrey's, and one can easily understand why Sackville was erroneously credited with having conceived the plan of the *Mirror*. Lavish praise has been heaped upon the poem by Warton, who compares it favorably with the *Divine Comedy*, to which it bears some resemblance.[6] The strength of Sack-

. . . . .

[4] *Ibid.*, p. 317. [5] *Ibid.*, p. 320.
[6] Thomas Warton, *History of English Poetry* (London, 1840), III, 181ff.

ville's verse, his ability to conjure up a vivid picture of the nether world and its inhabitants certainly recompense the reader for the poet's numerous disgressions into classical history and the overabundance of examples from the world of antiquity. But at the same time, the definitely partisan assembly does not spare its criticism of Sackville, for at the end of "Buckingham" they question his descriptions, saying,

But whereas he fayneth to talke with the Princes in hell, that I am sure will be mislyked, for some of their souls be in heaven, and although hee heerin doe follow allowed poets, in their description of hell, yet it savoureth so much of Purgatory which the Papists have digged thereout that the ignorant may be deceived.[7]

The argument is broken up, however, by someone who pointedly remarks that this is poetry and not divinity!

Worthy of mention in this section is also "The Tragedy of Jane Shore," a piece to which Thomas Churchyard very punctiliously laid claim, by repeatedly including it in the list of his works. Later, he amplified and again made use of this poem in his volume, *Churchyards Challenge* (1593). Jane Shore, the mistress of Edward IV, who survived her downfall until 1527, was a very popular character. Despite her frailty she had captured the fancy of Tudor readers. Even a strict moralist like More has extended in his *History of Richard III* a very chivalrous treatment to this notorious woman. The accounts point to her as an early counterpart of Nell Gwynne, a merry, beautiful young commoner who, having been forced into an early marriage with a tradesman she did not love, forsook him for the alluring position of king's mistress. Her charm and gay mien, her ready wit endeared her to the people, even in her downfall. More has left us a complete and sympathetic picture of her.[8]

In 1574 a new edition, brought forth by John Higgins, extended even further back into antiquity the scope of the

. . . . .

[7] Campbell, *Mirror for Magistrates*, p. 346.
[8] A further treatment of this character will be found on p. 60ff.

Mirror. It was called *The Firste Parte of the Mirrour for Magistrates, Containing the Falles of the First Infortunate Princes of this Lande: from the Coming of Brute to the Incarnation of our Saviour and Redeemer Jesus Christ.* Here was the very stuff for which Englishmen were clamoring, the foundation of the Tudor hold upon the imagination of the people and the answer to the English yearning for a national history. It would not be long before this desire would be completely satisfied through Spenser's glorification of Elizabeth in the *Faerie Queene.* The English were compiling their pedigree!

This section begins with the "complaint of Albanact," youngest son of Brutus and first king of Albany, "who was slayne by King Humber and his Hunnes the yeere before Christ 1085." Following the mythical accounts of the chroniclers, principally the *Chronicle of St. Albans,* this version relates the coming of Brutus into England, the founding of Troynovant and his bequest of the three principal parts of Britain to his three sons.

"The Legend of Locrinus, the eldest sonne of Brutus who lived vitiously and was slaine in battaile by his wife Queene Guendoline" and its complementary piece, the "Legend of Queene Elstrid," relate the tale of the king who was bewitched by the beauty of Elstrid. Already bound to Guendoline by a previous agreement, he, nevertheless, contrived to keep his new love by concealing her in his palace and meeting her by means of a secret vault, the fruit of this illicit union being Sabrina.

Here we also have an account of "How Queene Cordile in Dispaire Slew Herselfe the Year Before Christ 800." The bare facts of the legend are set down, but not of course as in Shakespeare's *King Lear,* where the details are altered appreciably. For example, in this version, Cordelia helps her father regain his kingdom by means of her husband's troops. Subsequently, however, through the vengeance of the sons of Goneril and Regan, she is plunged into the utmost misery. Her lot is made even more wretched by the appearance of the Ghost of

Despayre, who shows Cordelia the instruments of death beneath her garments. Dido's blade appeals to her and she commits suicide. This tale enjoyed widespread favor. To mention only a few of the versions, it was treated by Hardyng in his Chronicle; appeared again in the *Mirror for Magistrates* of 1587; and was used also by Spenser in a minor episode of *The Faerie Queene*.[9]

Among the new *mirrors* is the tale of Morindus, an usurper who, after achieving his nefarious ends, is overcome by pride and self-confidence. A monster has been ravaging the coast and the usurper engages him in combat, only to find himself powerless before the dragon who devours him. In a version strikingly similar to the account in Geoffrey of Monmouth's *Chronicle*, we also encounter the *mirror* of Duke Nennius. He protests that his deeds have been neglected by most of the chroniclers, Fabian, Lanquet, Rastell, Stowe and the writer of the *Polychronicon*:

> I may by right some later writers blame,
> Of stories olde as rude or negligent
> Or else I may them well unlearned name
> Or heedless in those things about they went
> Some time on me as well they might have spent
> As on such traytours, tyrants, harlots, those
> Which to their countreyes were the deadliest foes.[10]

After the account of his struggle against Caesar, wounded to death by the famed sword, Crocea Mores, he views the fleeing Romans and in an exulting outburst of nationalism cries out, "They flie, they flie!" We are face to face with intense patriotic fervor, the mood of England facing the Armada.

In 1578 Thomas Blenerhasset undertook to add to the incomplete *Mirror*, which he regarded much as "the unperformed image of Venus by Apelles." He thus composed *The*

. . . . .

[9] *Faerie Queene*, II, 10.
[10] *Mirror for Magistrates*, ed. Campbell, *Parts Added to The Mirror for Magistrates* (Cambridge, 1946), p. 191.

Mirror for Magistrates Contayning the Falles of Princes of this Lande from the Conquest of Caesar unto the Comynge of Duke William the Conqueror. Blenerhasset confessed in the "Epistle to his Friends" that "not having Bochas' pen," he was rather appalled by the task; therefore, he asked the reader to forget the high standard of excellence set by Sackville, Churchyard and others:

> And if you chaunce to see the meter or matter, not so well polished, as beseemeth, then remember that they whose falles, I have here penned, were not of late tyme but such as lyved presently after the incarnation of Christ; and I have not thought it decent that the men of the old world shoulde speak with so garnished a style as they of the latter tyme.[11]

With this humble explanation Blenerhasset manages to clear himself of any future charges of incompetence. He begs the forgiveness of his readers, reminding them that he is but a soldier. Furthermore, he explains that he is destitute of books, having with him only the incomplete works of Titus Livius, Boswell's *Concord of Armorie*, "Monsignor de Lange, that notable warrior," and the imperfect *Mirror for Magistrates.* He had not at his disposal Grafton, Polydore Virgil and Cooper, nor was he surrounded by learned men of Italy, Spain or France, but wrought his version in Garnzie Castle, "a rock in the sea."

Blenerhasset emphasizes that he has consciously tried to be plain, "so that he who doth reade them shall not need to be an Oedipus, for every playne Dauus reading them shall easily understand the author's drift." As an interlocutor he has used plain Inquisition, "who can find out al things while Memorie who knoweth al thinges" becomes the arbiter of his matter. He proudly asserts that he is not like Higgins "who used (I know not what) Morpheus, the God of dreames, but I dreamt not. The others had Baldwin for their hearer."[12]

. . . . .

[11] *Ibid.,* p. 381.   [12] *Ibid.,* p. 321.

In the "Induction," Inquisition is told by Memorie to look "in the bottomless pyt of blind Oblivion" where there remain many examples of famous men ignored by the *Mirror for Magistrates*. And here we have among others, the *mirrors* of Lady Hellina, Constantine's wife, who is offered almost as an atonement for "that other Helen." Also prominent are: "The Complaint of Uther Pendragon, Enamoured of the Wife of the Duke of Garelus Lost his Kingdom by Lawless Love" and that of Harold, who despite his valor finally succumbed to the rightful heir, William, Duke of Normandy.

Still another edition of the *Mirror* was brought out in 1587, by John Higgins, who added several stories, including one of Churchyard's, "The Tragedy of Wolsey." It is generally considered to be the finest of all the editions of the *Mirror*, as it contains the *mirror* of Cordelia and a good many new stories.

Finally in 1610, Richard Niccols compiled a new, inclusive gathering of all the *tragedies*, under the title, *A Winter Night's Vision*. He reverts to an old device: Memorie comes to him, since many kings had been overlooked, bidding him "this night her penman be." As a consequence, he adds ten pieces dealing with untreated characters, including Drayton's *tragedy* of Lord Cromwell. At the end of his edition, Niccols sings a great paean to the Queen, "England's Eliza." This reminds us of Spenser's projected gathering of all the characters at the end of the *Faerie Queene*, but it makes us wish that someone else had undertaken the task. Here is great praise for Elizabeth and all her counsellors, Grey, Warwick, Drake and others. However, it is nothing more than a chronicle of the principal events of the reign, recording such notable happenings as the Armada and Babington's plot, with indiscriminate praise lavished upon all the participants.

In all, the *Mirror* went through nine editions from 1554 to 1610 (1554, 1559, 1563, 1571, 1574, 1575, 1578, 1587, 1610), an eloquent testimony to the amazing vitality of the chronicle and its unmistakable appeal to the English people.

During the fifty years that intervened between the conception of the *Mirror* and the 1610 edition countless imitations issued from English presses. It is well-nigh impossible to estimate their number, for a good many have disappeared with the passing of the centuries and exist only as entries in the records of the Stationers' Company. However, they bear ample witness to the popularity of the genre and to the general avidity for new versions of both legendary and historical materials. Nevertheless *mirrors* did not supplant the popular chronicles; we find, instead, that they set a fashion, causing chronicles which were originally conceived in prose to be recast in verse form. This practice lasted down to the very end of the century, as may be seen in Warner's *Albion's England*. Worthless or sublime, the material has but a single aim, the diffusion of popular knowledge concerning history and the past; it aids in creating that consciousness and pride in a growing England which eventually brought about national unity and promoted the growth of a great empire.

Despite this interest in history, the moral intent of the *mirrors* remains paramount. We have seen passing before us the train of the wicked magistrates, the cruel and the unjust, the wrathful and the bloodthirsty, the rebels against kingly authority, the licentious and dissolute, the lavish and the proud, their fate a constant reminder that sin inevitably incurs retribution. Always before the reader is the lesson that God, through his profound justice, will visit his wrath upon the transgressors of the Law. But the admonishment is not solely for rebels against divinely conferred authority. At the same time, the *mirrors* convey a warning to those in authority: let the magistrates refrain from becoming tyrants, for the wheel of Fortune spins swiftly and tyranny generates rebellion and civil war. The lesson is unmistakable: obedience on the part of the people, but justice and rectitude from the magistrates.

I V

The Progeny of the *Mirror for*
Magistrates: Collections of *Mirrors*

THE PUBLICATION AND THE POPULARITY OF
the *Mirror for Magistrates* brought forth a tremendous number of *mirrors* from the pens of Englishmen, who employed
the type for the most varied purposes. Collections of *mirrors*
modelled directly upon Baldwin's efforts, others dealing with
Biblical material, obituary *mirrors*, purely satirical *mirrors*,
literally rolled off the presses during the forty-odd years of
Elizabeth's reign. As has been shown, the type had not been
infrequent before the publication of Baldwin's *Mirror*, for we
have the notable examples of More, Lyndsay, and Skelton, yet
it would almost appear that the period of quarantine imposed
upon the *Mirror* had increased its popularity.

A strict classification of the works produced during this period defies the critic, for the various types intermingle, and
often exhibit characteristics of other groups. Nevertheless,
there are three principal divisions into which these works
naturally fall. The "progeny" of the *Mirror*, as Farnham terms
it, may be divided into: 1) the various collections of *mirrors*,
written in direct imitation of their prototype; 2) the large

number of single historical or pseudo-historical *mirrors* chron-
icling some individual; and 3) fictional *mirrors* which are
largely biographical in character. The second group, the single
mirrors, may be further subdivided into classical material dealing mostly with mythological, Biblical or classical characters;
English historical material, both real and legendary; and contemporary *mirrors,* recording the deeds of some individual of
his own time whom the poet has chosen to immortalize.

The collections of *mirrors* which imitate the *Mirror for
Magistrates* give little evidence of originality or poetic worth.
In general, they confine themselves to presenting the life of
the subject; they are also burdened with the usual amount of
moralizing and admonition to the reader. The reasons for their
flaws are obvious; no one writer could muster up the time necessary for the composition of such a monumental work. Even
Baldwin had realized that in a vast undertaking of this sort,
collaboration was necessary. As a result, these collections show
signs of hasty compilation and descend to the level of mere
hack-work. Typical is "A Myrrour of the Fall of Pride," included in George Turberville's *Epitaphs, Epigrams* (1567).
This compilation consists of a medley of mythological and
classical stories which illustrate an obvious moral. The "Myrrour of the Fall of Pride" occupies itself with the revolt of the
Titans against Jove, who finally decides to hurl Vulcan's
thunderbolts at them, for:

> Such plagues had pride in former years, the gods abhorred so,
> That mortall men should dare to clime the heavens hie to
> know.[1]

Those who seek glory and high rank may take example from
Narcissus and Icarus, who braved the heavens but were
quickly reduced to misery.

Turberville's work is quite unusual because it deals with
mythological subjects, a field hardly ever touched by the

. . . . .

[1] George Turberville, *Epitaphs, Epigrams* (London, 1570), p. 86.

mirrors, since they confined themselves mostly to history or pseudo-history. All the conventions found in the *mirror* are here, however, including the metre, which is the fourteener couplet.

Richard Robinson, a retainer of the Earl of Shrewsbury, passed many of the long vigils while he guarded the Scottish Queen in composing *The Reward of Wickedness, Discoursing of the Sundrye Monstruous Abuses of Wicked and Ungodly Worldlinges.* The author dated it, "from my chamber in Sheffield Castle, the xix of Maie, 1574." In an undistinguished prologue which sets the season as winter, the narrator arrives at an inn, drinks with other "ale-knights" and goes to bed somewhat the worse for it. During the night, Morpheus takes him to Hell, where Robinson engages in conversations with several of the chief sinners neglected by Baldwin and his collaborators. Robinson brings his collection up to date by including Pope Alexander VI, who is to be found among "the shaueling, greasie, chuffhead friars." The author rubs elbows with Pope Joan and her college of Cardinals, with Midas and Helen of Troy. He listens to the tale of the two judges who slandered Susanna, and includes for good measure the *mirror* of Rosamond, a theme later handled by Daniel. However, it is hardly to be inferred that Daniel's *Rosamond* found its source here, for her tale was common history. When Robinson appears, each ghost clamors to tell his tale. The narrative is usually followed by a judgment on the speaker, with an appropriate punishment for each sin. Robinson's collection was undoubtedly planned as an imitation of the *Mirror,* with one eye on Sackville's "Induction." We find here Morpheus, used by Higgins as an interlocutor a few years later. As one may readily perceive, the account is a mixture of mythology, history and Biblical lore, colored by a strong Protestant feeling.

Robinson did not confine his efforts to this compilation, for in 1576 he published *Certain Selected Histories for Christian Recreation, Brought into English Verse with Moralizations,* another strange miscellany of Biblical and legendary material making a pitiful pretense to convey an allegorical significance. One example will suffice. In the time of Caesar Augustus, a knight witnesses a toad and a serpent fighting, with the latter being visibly worsted. The knight rescues the serpent, but is wounded by the toad in the process. As he lies at the point of death from the poisonous wound, the knight perceives the serpent at his gate. He allows him to enter and the serpent in gratitude sucks the poison from the wound. The toad is then destroyed. Robinson identifies the knight with Jesus Christ and the toad with Satan, while the serpent represents Man. The story implies the constant struggle of man against the devil and his poison, Sin. Even the didactic value of this piece is destroyed by the wretchedness of the verse and the immaturity of the conception.

Undaunted, in 1589 Robinson brought forth *The Golden Mirror,* a mixture of allegorical praise for certain noblemen and puritan scorn for the wiles of the world. Once more he falls asleep, this time in Marfeld Forest while hunting, and "in this slumbering sleep the richest Dreame I had." He dreams that he sees Elizabeth, "a virgin in rich attire clad," who receives the homage of all the denizens of the forest. Among them we find "a valiant hound as white as silver," an allusion to George Talbot, Earl of Shrewsbury in whose service Robinson was. After panegyrics in praise of Shrewsbury and Lord Derby, there follows a long account of the Spanish danger. But the elements and the gods combine to defend the noble lady,

> Then said Eolus with a blustering blast,
> I for my part shal make their course but short;
> I will brak Anker, Cable and also mast
> So that destruction shall acquite their sport.[2]

Drake's part in the destruction is emphasized; at the height of the carnage, Morpheus awakens the poet bidding him write

. . . . .

[2] R. Robinson, *The Golden Mirror,* ed. Thomas Corser (Manchester, 1857), p. 7.

the exploit. The poem is apparently an attempt to curry favor with the praised noblemen and to win public interest through the description of contemporary events, such as the Babington plot and the recent Spanish disaster.

In the last "dreame," Robinson perceives in a "glass of skill" the true characters of some persons in whom he had set too much trust. Here, he centers his condemnation especially on women who abuse the name of gentlewomen,

> Stay yet, said lambe, behold more of this glasse,
> See where one bounseth in a players gowne:
> Furde like a foole as nice as ere she was,
> The bravest tipling tib, that is within the towne:
> While she at tick tacke tryes to prove her chaunce,
> Her husband is content a hornpipe for to daunce.

> Five hundreth Asses milke she daily had the bathe,
> For to increase her vice, and bewtie to preserve:
> As at these days our countrey women crave,
> Out of a little hyde, a thong too large they crave,
> For every poor mans daughter now is prankt in silke,
> Which doth Sabinas bath incounter made of milke.[3]

Despite the extremely fawning character of the verse, Robinson's *Golden Mirror* is not devoid of a certain amount of skill in the handling of his lines. He essays various meters from lubberly fourteener couplets to graceful stanzas, but unfortunately the latter are infrequent. Furthermore, as narrative poetry, they are negligible, inasmuch as they are quite frankly eulogistic in their conception.

Basing his work upon Hall's *Chronicles*, Ulpian Fulwell brought forth *The Flower of Fame, Containing the Bright Renown and Most Fortunate Reign of Henry VIII* (1575), a medley of prose and poetry in which the most spectacular events of that monarch's reign were chronicled. In imitation of the *Mirror for Magistrates*, Fulwell reached back into history

. . . . .

[3] *Ibid.*, p. 54.

as far as the broils of Lancaster and York. He introduced James IV of Scotland who, believing Henry's forces to be occupied in his struggles with France, attacked him from the rear. But the Queen and the Earl of Surrey defeated him at Brampton. James utters his complaint "in forme of the *Mirror for Magistrates*," bemoaning his hasty deed and his well-deserved fate as "gwerdon meete for breach of sacred vow." A second *complaint* from James' son voices his regret at having broken faith with his uncle, although he explains that he was constrained to do so by the prelates upon whose heads he calls down vengeance. The younger James wishes he had been born to "pen the sheep in their folde," but now the "grave is his course, the shrouding sheet his robe." Throughout the narrative, Fulwell takes pains to explain that he does not go into fuller details "lest he seeme to rob Grafton or Halle of their labours." Fulwell also included a commemoration of some of Henry's queens, notably Katherine Parr and Anne Boleyn. In fact, he says, "lest I may seeme parciall by omitting Henry's other wives, I must confess I have in my handes a treatise of all their lives which I await your kindly favor to publish," a work which does not seem to have reached the press.

In his explanation of how he came to write this book, Fulwell tells us that when Fame rang out her larum bell to secure a poet to sing Henry's praises, his Muse sought him out and though he demurred, for

> Shall Coridon take harp in hande
> Where Orpheus is in place?

she brought him to Hermon Hill and

> There where heavenly dewe doth dwell
> I wrote as she mee taught,
> God grant it be Full well! [4]

. . . . .

[4] Ulpian Fulwell, *The Flower of Fame*, reprinted in *Harleian Miscellany*, IX, p. 375.

Anthony Munday, another gentleman of fortune who devoted a great deal of his time to writing, tried to capitalize on the popularity of the *Mirror* by devising his *Mirror of Mutabilitie, or Principall Parts of the Mirror for Magistrates. Describing the Fall of Divers Famous Princes, and Other Memorable Personages. Selected out of the Sacred Scriptures* (1579). It follows in the footsteps of its predecessors, the chief difference lying in Munday's selection of material from the Bible rather than from history. There is very little new in Munday's attempt. He has no Induction, nor do the characters tell where the action takes place. He adopts the framework of the Seven Deadly Sins, using a familiar example from the Scriptures to exemplify each sin. Nabuchodonozor begins:

> On highest tip of lofty name,
> I sometime did in Princely pomp remayne:
> Both farre and neer I bore the golden fame,
> And who but I in cheefe estate did reigne?
> Till suddainly, in all my peacocks plumes,
> I was throwen down for all my freating fumes.[5]

Thus we have Pride typified by Nabuchodonozor, Envye by Herod, Wrath by Pharao, and the remainder of the sins by suitable Biblical characters. Each of these figures tells his tale in the traditional *mirror* fashion, with copious sighs and laments. The second book abandons this procedure, and sinks to a mere prose account of various sinners. Munday holds up to the reader the fate of Absalom and Jezabel, reduced from fortune through their excesses. Sin will incur God's wrath. But instead of the punishment falling on the sinners through irrational Fortune, God Himself now assumes the task by dealing out His infinite justice. The new doctrines are being injected into the *mirrors*. Munday seems to have experimented, too, with various types of meter, consciously avoiding the regu-

. . . . .

[5] Anthony Munday, *The Mirror of Mutabilitie,* reprinted in J. P. Collier, *A Bibliographical Account of the Rarest Books in the English Language* (New York, 1866), II, 341.

lar seven-line stanza characteristic of this genre. For example, "King David," the *mirror* of Lechery, is in ballad form:

> O Bersaba! forgiveness I doo crave,
> For that I, wretch, thy body did defile,
> Unlawfully desiring thee to have,
> To spot thy name by such an unkinde guyle.
>
> And thou, Urias, through my deede was slayne;
> O, where remaind the bounds of princely sway,
> That for my lust should so desire thy payne,
> And to thy foes unjustly thee betray? [6]

Interesting, too, is Munday's use of blank verse in the "Complaint of Dives," which places this author among the earliest writers of blank verse, ahead of Aske, Vallans, and Sabie. The third part of the *Mirror of Mutabilitie*, which Munday had promised, seems never to have been written.

George Whetstone also was very active in making use of this genre, for, besides writing many single *complaints,* he is recorded as producing in 1584 *The Myrour for Magistrates of Cyties,* a prose work directed against dicing houses, taverns and other such haunts. Fortified with examples from the classics, he showed how the disorders surrounding him in England could be unfavorably contrasted to the order that existed in ancient Rome. The piece was not popular, however, and R. Jones, the printer, was forced, two years later, to change the title and republish the work as *The Enemie of Unthryftiness, Discouering the Unsufferable Abuses Reigning in our Happie English Commonwealth.*

Whetstone's *Englysh Mirror,* 1586, also in prose, is in reality a historical miscellany, designed to demonstrate that the evils which befall commonwealths really derive from Envy. The Wars of the Roses, the Ghibelline broils, the troubles of the Medici are all laid to this cause. An account of Tambur-

. . . . .

[6] *Ibid.,* p. 341.

laine and his phenomenal rise is even included, along with a report of the plotting of Edmund Campion.

At about this time, we have also Thomas Proctor's *Triumph of Truth,* written *circa* 1585, which contains several condensed histories of classical origin, written in worthless verse. The stories of Caesar, the triumph of the Greeks and the desert of Dives are some of the short accounts found in this compilation by the author of *The Gorgeous Gallery.*

Richard Johnson's *Nine Worthies of London* (1592) is an interesting example of the general trend during the closing years of the sixteenth century to glorify the middle class, in the same manner in which Deloney had done in prose. Planned in imitation of the *Mirror,* but shorn of the latter's moral implications, this piece is typical of the contemporary distortion of the *Mirror's* didacticism. It was obviously intended to glorify the merchant class. A flowery prologue introduces Johnson, journeying with Clio to the "Elizian shades" in a chariot provided by Fame. Here they encounter a group of personages, all members of the trading classes of London, who recount their tales. The first is Sir William Walworth, fishmonger, sometime Mayor of London, who ill conceals his pride in his achievements beneath an apparent scorn for earthly fame,

> For when the pomp of earthly pleasure's gon,
> Our goasts lie buried underneath a stone.

Finding himself in the midst of the rebellion of the men of Essex and Kent, led by Wat Tyler, he is shocked by their treacherous behaviour and arrogant demands upon the king, their burning and sacking; therefore:

> Yet with a loyal guard of bills and bowes,
> Collected of our tallest men of trade,
> I did protect his person from his foes.[7]

. . . . .

[7] Richard Johnson, *Nine Worthies of London,* reprinted in *Harleian Miscellany,* VIII, 442.

The king desires a parley with Tyler and his rebels. During the negotiations at Smithfield, the men refusing to heed the king's exhortations to lay down their arms, grow bolder and defiant, instead. Walworth, an uncompromising individualist, no respecter of safe-conducts, becomes indignant, and in his own words he:

> did arest Wat Tyler on the pate.
> The stroke was given with so good a will,
> I made the rebell coutcht unto the earth!
> His fellows that beheld ('tis strange) were still
> It mared the maner of their former mirth.
> I left him not but ere I did depart,
> I stabbed my dagger to his damned heart.[8]

As a reward he is dubbed a knight, thus initiating a long career of fame and honor. Upon their leaving him, Fame promises to erect him a statue.

Of similar character are the stories of Sir Henry Pritchard, vintner, also Mayor of London, who had the honor of dining with his King (Edward III); of Sir William Sevenoake, grocer, who followed Bellona in Henry V's time, famous for his administering the Dolphin a great blow when the latter accused him of laziness. Among the others are Sir Christopher Croker, a simple vintner's clerk, who loved his master's daughter Moll. Eager to distinguish himself, he joined the war and was the first to enter Bordeaux's gate. Created a knight for this exploit, he returned to England, eventually winning Moll as his wife. Sir John Hawkwood, merchant tailor, joined the Prince of Wales in France and conducted himself with such great fame that he was knighted. After journeying into Italy, to relieve the Duke of Milan, he won great renown with his band of fifteen hundred Englishmen and secured a wealth of castles and towers. Finally, he humbled even the pride of the Pope, and ended his days in a castle in Padua, for,

. . . . .

[8] *Ibid.*, p. 443.

All wars you see do ende as well as peace
And then remaineth but a tumble of dust.[9]

At the end, Fame bids everyone to keep in mind that citizens
have ever flourished in the world, Caesar in Rome, Themi-
stocles in Athens and Hannibal in Carthage.

The collection has little significance as a literary work, for
it is told with little skill; the verse is fustian, with a great deal
of straining after a rhyme in its six-line stanzas. As a narrative
biographical work, however, it illustrates admirably the attempt to win the favor of the powerful merchant class, which
at this time was rising to prominence, by adapting one of the
most popular genres of the day to its glorification.

. . . . .

[9] *Ibid.*, p. 457.

V

Single *Mirrors*: Classical and Biblical Material

LEAVING THE COLLECTIONS OF "MIRRORS," WE proceed to the great body of *complaints* dealing with single individuals, produced during the remainder of the Tudor reign.[1] As the genre gains in popularity, the tendency to concentrate upon a single individual becomes increasingly evident. In the preceding pages we have seen that even though classical material was not generally popular, a certain amount of it was used in the collections of *mirrors,* particularly those by Turberville, Proctor and Munday. One notable exception were the *mirrors* based on the Lucrece story, and among these was Shakespeare's *Rape of Lucrece.*

. . . . .

[1] The *mirror's* popularity during the last quarter of the century increased so much that the title was used for all purposes. We have recorded: *A Mirror of Madness* (1576); Mancinus' *Mirrour of Good Manners;* B. M., *A Triall of True Friendship or Parfit Mirror* (1569); Laurence Saunders, *A True Mirrour or Glasse* (1556); Thomas Salter, *A Mirrour of Modesty* (prose) (1579); Robert Greene, *Mirrour of Modesty* (1584); *The Mirrour of Man's Miserie* (1584?); Thomas Turwell, *A Mirrour for Martinists* (1589); *The Mirrour of Mirrours* (1598); *The Mirrour of Magnanimitie* (1599); *The Mirrour of Policie* (1599); the list is too long to draw out.

47

In the Dedication to *Venus and Adonis* (1593), Shakespeare had vowed to the Earl of Southampton "to take advantage of all idle hours till I have honoured you with some graver labor." And the following year appeared *The Rape of Lucrece,* from the shop of Richard Field. With this poem, Shakespeare joined the growing band of *mirror* writers. Like its predecessor, *Venus and Adonis,* it is written by a poet flushed with youth, revelling in the wealth of his own imagery; it possesses the virtues and the sins of the decade. It is written by a man who has not yet acquired the trenchant manner of expression, the sobriety of phrase of his later years. Yet, at the same time, there are unmistakable indications of the powers that were to single him out as the great poet and dramatist.

Shakespeare plunges at once into the heart of the story, showing "lust-breathed Tarquin" as he leaves the Roman host, besieging Ardea. At the same time, he reveals the background of the story, Collatine's boast before a gathering of Roman generals that his wife is the most virtuous among Roman ladies. Instead of developing the story in the step-by-step fashion typical of the *mirrors,* however, Shakespeare concentrates on a few dramatic incidents. The brief meeting at Collatium reveals to us Lucrece's ingenuous pleasure at Tarquin's praise of her lord; this is followed by the piteous scene where the chaste Lucrece vainly pleads with the lust-maddened tyrant. By thus focussing the action upon two or three dramatic episodes, the poet has eliminated the interminable chronicle-like effect so characteristic of the type. Wise also is Shakespeare's presentation of the action in the dramatic present and not as in the *mirrors,* from the retrospect of the ghost telling the tale.[2] Yet for all this dramatic handling, the poem is burdened by a good deal of extraneous material, an overabundance of decoration and the elaboration of incidents to be expected from works of the time. The first seven hundred lines of the poem

. . . . .

[2] This is hardly an innovation on the part of Shakespeare, however, as Ovid's and Chaucer's accounts are both told from this point of view.

analyze Tarquin's lust and his motives, the conflict within him, as he attempts to resist his evil intent, while the remaining eleven hundred lines are given over to Lucrece's complaint of the abominable action of her ravisher. Still, one might justify the inclusion of the long wavering, the hesitation on Tarquin's part, as aids in building suspense and preparing the reader for the imminent catastrophe.[3]

The same may hardly be said, however, for the long apostrophes which Lucrece addresses to Opportunity, after Tarquin has crept away like a thievish cur. It would also be difficult to justify the necessity of the description of the paintings of the siege of Troy in the development of the story. They need not be defended, beyond pointing out that they are there from the very nature of Elizabethan poetry, its love of color and decoration. The long address to Opportunity is but one of many such reflections found in the poem. It is directly in the tradition of the gnomic element to be found not only in the *mirrors,* but also in the amoristic poetry such as *Venus and Adonis* and *Hero and Leander.* The reader has only to look at Daniel's lengthy address to Beauty as the cause of all Rosamond's woes or Drayton's address to Chastity in *Matilda* to find parallels for such sententiousness. Despite the inclusion of extraneous and decorative elements, the poem moves with characteristic swiftness when Shakespeare chooses. The favorite medium is dialogue. Lucrece speaks to her maid after the fateful night,

> But tell me girl, when went (and there she stay'd
> Till after a deep groan) Tarquin from hence?
> Madam ere I was up replied the maid,
> The more to blame my sluggard negligence:
> Yet with the fault I thus far can dispence;
>
> . . . . .

---

[3] This hesitation and wavering is typical of the later *mirrors;* it is to be found profusely in Rosamond's inability to resist the king, in the long persuasive arguments which the king brings forward in seducing Matilda.

> Myself was stirring ere the break of day,
> And ere I rose was Tarquin gone away.[4]

Again the narrative moves swiftly, poignantly, after the kinsmen have arrived. Briefly she tells her tale; vainly they try to console her. Her knife is unerring. Aghast, her kinsmen vow their vengeance. The poem ends as suddenly as it began.

But Shakespeare, the young poet, is hardly concerned with the speed with which the poem is advancing. To him the creation of conceits, redolent with color, is far more important. Like most of his contemporaries, he is weaving a rich tapestry. As a result, the Euphuistic element is heavy; abundant are the antitheses, the apostrophes, the quibbles, all the rhetorical apparatus of the time.[5] But Shakespeare cannot be submerged by Petrarchism or Euphuism. He always remains the poet, and even the rant and muddled conceits cannot dim the beauty of lines such as: "Threat'ning cloud-kissing Ilion with annoy."

The story of Lucrece could have been suggested to Shakespeare by a good many accounts.[6] It is to be found in Ovid's *Fasti*, lines 781-852. Livy gives his version of this outrage; Chaucer took Lucrece as an example of virtue for his *Legend of Good Women;* and the theme was also treated by Gower in *Confessio Amantis.* A few years before Shakespeare, William Painter included the story in *The Palace of Pleasure* (1566-67). Shakespeare introduces some new material and does not seem to have followed any one source, for it is most likely that he knew several versions and incorporated into his own whatever he deemed useful.[7] The poet seems to have been influ-

. . . . .

[4] Shakespeare, *The Rape of Lucrece,* ed. C. Knox Pooler (Arden ed., 1927), lines 1275ff.
[5] For a further study of this question see Wilhelm Ewig, "Lucrece, Eine Litterar Historische Untersuchung," *Anglia,* XXII (1899), 1-32, 343-363, 393-455, where the poem is minutely analyzed from the standpoint of structure, style, sources, etc.
[6] For a full treatment of the sources see *Rape of Lucrece, ed. cit.,* Introd., p. liiiff.
[7] The question is argued by Dr. Ewig, *op. cit.,* 393ff.

enced also by *The Complaint of Rosamond,* many verbal echoes of it appearing in *Lucrece.*

After Shakespeare's treatment of Lucrece, its obvious continuation, *The Ghost of Lucrece* by Thomas Middleton (1600) comes rather as an anticlimax. True, the author of the continuation tried to emulate or at least follow his model, but the attempt is totally unsuccessful. However, the poet's youth must be taken into account, for the poem appears to be one of his earliest literary efforts.[8] Even here, Middleton shows a predilection for dramatic structure which he was to essay for many years as he attempts to fashion a sort of dramatic sequence by employing a prologue and an epilogue. Middleton summons the ghost of Lucrece from Hades, after the trumpet has thrice sounded a "surge," the characteristic blast, heralding the opening of a play; he bids all the

> sad spirits, soft hearts, sick thoughts, souls sod in tears
> Well-humour'd eyes, quick ears, tear-wounded faces,
> Enrolled vestals, Dian's hemispheres,
> Rape-slaughtered Lucreces, all martyr'd Graces,
> Be ye the audience; take your tragic places![9]

while the

> Black spirits, heard hearts, thick thoughts, souls boiled in lust,
> Dry fiery eyes, dull ears, high bloody looks,
> Made of hot earth, moulded in fire and dust,
> Desire's tru graduates, read in Tarquin's books,
> Be ye our stage's actors.[10]

After Lucrece has played her part, relating her woeful story she brings the drama to an end:

. . . . .

[8] J. Q. Adams who reprinted the poem, *The Ghost of Lucrece,* (1600) facsimile (N. Y., 1937), deduces that the poem was composed *ca.* 1597, not only from its amateurishness but also from a statement in the Dedication where Middleton alludes to his poem as "the young ground of unskillfulness." The point is developed fully in the Introduction, pp. xviff.

[9] Middleton, *The Ghost of Lucrece,* Prologue, lines 8ff.

[10] *Ibid.,* lines 15ff.

And now Melpomene hales my spirit in.
The stage is down and Philomela's choir
Is hushed from prick-song: [11]

Despite the attempt to give the story some dramatic coher-
ence, the poem resolves itself into a series of long, frigid apostrophes and ranting attacks upon Tarquin. No doubt, the fact
that Shakespeare had already set his stamp upon the tale
placed Middleton under a handicap, yet other authors had
solved a similar difficulty, as for example, Chute with the story
of Jane Shore. Middleton presents the *complaint* of Lucrece,
but, though he gives evidence that he is acquainted with some
of the best pieces of his time, he draws but little from them.[12]
Most of the poem is taken up with playing upon Tarquin's
name in extravagant conceits of which the following is typical:

Tarquin the Night-owl: Chastity beware!
Thou are beset with millions of deceits;
Thy eyes have leaden lids, they take no care;
Thy senses rock'd asleep, and the conceits
Temp'red with silence, fear nor snares nor baits.
Tarquin the Night-owl: in whose flaming eyes
Lust and Desire bandied their balls of blood,
Chasing my spirit with fiery mysteries
Unto the hazard where Destruction stood
Ready to strike my soul into a cloud,
So, when the sun had seen my vapour rise,
Then with his beams to dash me from the skies.[13]
· · · · ·

[11] *Ibid.*, lines 534ff.
[12] There are of course numerous verbal echoes from the *Rape of
Lucrece*; cf. *Ghost of Lucrece*, lines 359ff., to *Rape of Lucrece*, lines
785ff.; *Ghost of Lucrece*, lines 514ff., to *Rape of Lucrece*, lines 439ff.
He knows Drayton's *Piers Gaveston*, for lines 4-5 of that poem:

Prepare the stage, I mean to act my parte,
Singing the scenes from my tormented hart,

suggest the beginning of *The Ghost of Lucrece* with its theatrical
setting.
[13] Middleton, *op. cit.*, lines 148ff.

Very few of the details of the story are brought out, one of the few exceptions being a reference to the contest of the Roman lords as to whose wife was the most virtuous. Otherwise the poem is developed by means of apostrophes to Chastity, to Iniquity, to Lust. As Professor Adams has pointed out, Middleton does not follow the usual *mirror* or *complaint*.[14] Rather, he prefers to combine the *mirror* with the heroical epistle which Drayton in imitation of the *Heroides* of Ovid had popularized in his *Heroical Epistles*.

Lucrece says:

> Bleed no more lines, my heart! This knife (my pen),
> This blood (my ink), hath writ enough to Lust.
> Tarquin, to thee (thou very devil of men)
> I send these lines: thou art my fiend of trust;
> To thee I dedicate my tomb of dust;
> To thee I consecrate this little-most,
> Writ by the bloody fingers of my Ghost.[15]

All in all, even though the *Ghost of Lucrece* appeared at a date when the *mirror* had achieved its full development, Middleton availed himself but little of the noteworthy examples which had preceded him, and this work remains a feeble example of the genre.

It may readily be perceived how avidly Elizabethan authors seized upon even "hethnick" materials to draw their moral lessons. There was no subject which could not be used to drive home the lessons of chastity and virtue, no situation which could not point out how abhorrent were lust and concupiscence. But, if examples could be drafted from classical history, Biblical accounts served even more admirably the purpose of edifying the reader, for many of the Scriptural characters were ideal as models to hold up for Englishmen to imitate. Doubtless out of reverence for the source, the poets who used this material took few liberties with it, preferring to follow the

. . . . .

14 Adams, *op. cit.*, Introd., xxiiff.
15 Middleton, *op. cit.*, lines 505ff.

Scriptures slavishly. Consequently, many of these ponderous works are no more than mere versifications of the Bible, far below the literary standard set later by the King James version. As a result of the great esteem in which the subject matter was held by the middle classes during the last half of the sixteenth century, these Biblical accounts became very numerous. Though they contain a good deal of narrative verse, they are best regarded as examples of devotional or religious poetry, and as such, are outside the scope of this work.[16]

Besides these versifications of the Psalms and other Old Testament legends, there exist a good many single pieces which are of a definitely narrative character. *The History of Joseph the Chaiste*, 1569, is typical. This poem, begun in 1545, was written at various intervals by William Forrest, a priest, who in 1558 had already published a defense of Queen Catherine in his *Hystory of Grisild the Second*.[17] The poem is divided into two parts, dealing with Joseph's "adversity" and his "felicity." Although one might expect some improvement in poetic technique, there is no sign whatsoever that twenty-four years of versifying improved Forrest's verse. The author follows the Old Testament very faithfully, but introduces a jolly, homely conversation between a baker and a fellow-prisoner, after Joseph's interpretation of the dream. It has a flavor of the rogue pamphlets common at the end of the century; and the prisoners are merry fellows who live high and who, if "they be take, their neck-verse they can."[18]

Of the numerous examples of Biblical material, typical specimens are William Hunnis' *A Hyvefull of Hunny, Contayning the First Book of Moses* (1578), and John Marbeck's *The*

. . . . .

[16] One has only to glance at John Marbeck's or William Hunnis' works for typical specimens of such poetry. For a discussion, see Warton, *op. cit.*, III, 167ff.

[17] For a discussion, see below p. 59ff.

[18] Another interesting example of the story of Joseph is *The History of Jacob and His XII Sonnes*, originally printed in the days of Edward VI, but reprinted in 1569 by John Allde.

Holie Historie of King David (1579). Although the latter is thoroughly faithful to his source, he cannot refrain from instilling into the Biblical characters some of the characteristics of his age. Consequently, David appears as a doughty Elizabethan gentleman, while Goliath becomes a giant, striding out of one of the prose romances,

> Into the bottom of the vale, a strong and mightie clowne:
> His name it hight Goly of Gath, so bigge and huge a man,
> As was in length from top to toe six cubits and a span;
> An helmet on his head he had of hard and massy brasse
> A coat of male upon his backe of passing weight it was,
> A shield and bootes of brasse, likewise, which he was wont to weare
> And scarcely could a weavers beame well counterpeise his speare.[19]

Needless to say, the story of the passion and crucifixion of Christ was a great favorite. A typical example is found in Abraham Fraunce's *The Countesse of Pembroke's Emanuell* (1591), told in rhyming hexameters and substituting wherever possible classical for Biblical names. Robert Holland's versified *Holie Historie of Our Lord and Savior, Jesus Christ* follows the Scriptures in conventional fashion in his attempt to bring their message to the attention of English readers.[20]

Hunnies Recreations, compiled by William Hunnis in 1595, contains "four godly discourses" namely, "Adam's Banishment," "Christ his Crib," "The Lost Sheep," "The Complaint of Old Age," besides other pieces, among which is a history of Joseph. Hunnis may be credited with a certain skill in verse, even when he is merely presenting theological arguments. His portrayal of Adam in an ungallant mood, as the latter tries to shift upon Eve the blame for the Fall, is amusing.

. . . . .

[19] William Hunnis, *A Hyvefull of Hunnye,* Sig. A4r.
[20] Other specimens might be included such as Samuel Rowlands, *The Betraying of Christ* (1598); Gervase Markham, *The Teares of the Beloved* (1600).

Biblical in character but much nearer to the spirit and the conventions of the *mirrors* is Francis Sabie's *Adams Complaint* (1596), in which we witness his rueful lament at the lost Paradise:

> Rowse up thyselfe (my Muse) a tale to tell,
> A dolefull tale in sad and plaintive verse:
> How man in blisse from happiness once fell.[21]

Adam regards his fallen estate, reviewing all the preceding events, the Serpent's temptation, his own inability to withstand it. He reflects upon all this, venturing the thought that had not God forbidden him the fruit, he might have withstood temptation much more easily. And now Pride and Strife have assailed the ruman race; princes seek to be kings; Greed, the cause of all human misery, is rampant:

> The small shall subject be of greater,
> Nobility through strength shall make his entrie,
> The welthyer shall thynke himself the better,
> For covetousnesse will spring, the root of Gentry.[22]

The poem degenerates into a sermon on covetousness and pride, an invective against Eve, the wretched mother condemned to suffer and conceive in pain.

Despite the heavy layer of sententiousness, the poem has a good deal of color and realism. Sabie has a good eye for natural description,

> Ye winged birds send out your woful quips,
> In leafless trees, once glutting you with berries;
> Cold winter now your tender bodies nips,
> Depriving earth of herbs and trees of cherries.[23]

There are numerous references to Nature, for Sabie is never tired of preaching by pointing to the worthy examples of the

. . . . .

[21] F. Sabie, *Adams Complaint*, Sig. A2r.
[22] *Ibid.*, Sig. B4v.
[23] *Ibid.*, Sig. B4r.

ant and the bee. Perhaps it is for this tendency that the poem merits some notice, because it indicates the change in the genre from the moralization of the early period to the didacticism of the seventeenth century.

In general, these single *mirrors*, originating in Biblical legend, exhibit the usual characteristics of this type of poetry. They show a definite adherence to the source with little desire to alter facts or interpolate new material, although one notes the usual dressing of Hebrew figures in Renaissance costumes. And ever present is the intent to teach and to draw a moral lesson, whether it be from Eve's frailty or from the avarice of Judas.

VI

Single *Mirrors*: English History, Real and Legendary

BY FAR THE LARGEST NUMBER OF SINGLE *mirrors* deal with English history, real and legendary. This is hardly surprising, in view of the fact that the prime purpose of the genre was not only to instruct, but also to disseminate a knowledge of English history.[1] We have already seen how some of the pieces in the *Mirror for Magistrates* made use of past events to draw attention to contemporary political conditions. Many other *mirrors* were composed, airing both sides of the bitter controversy between Catholics and the Reformed Church.

If the Protestants appeared to be hard at work propagandizing for their cause, the Catholics were not far behind, as is apparent from the work of William Forrest, the priest, who has left a voluminous record of his activities. On the 25th of June,

. . . . .

[1] Even as early as 1510, Francis Dingley had penned his *Tragedy of Flodden Field*, while in 1567 there was reprinted the *Testament and Tragedie of King Henrie Stewart*, a poem based on Lydgate, in the usual Troilus meter, which gives every indication of having been written early in the sixteenth century.

58

1558, he finished *The Hystory of Grisild the Second*, which extolled the virtues of Queen Catherine, likening her to Grisild, the patient, and drawing the unmistakable comparison between Walter and Henry VIII. In reality, the poem is a recapitulation of historical events, presented so as to exalt the qualities of the Queen. Thus, by implication, it heaps scorn upon the enemies who could treat so basely this paragon of wifely virtues and Christian resignation, a resignation lost only momentarily at the death of her child:

> She wepte, she sobbed, she sighed, ofte witheall,
> She wrounge her handys of motherly pytee,
> She wolde not holde state undre clothe of pall,
> She whoale forgot her high regalytee
> She took his death as most calamytee
> For that it was her fyrst begoten childe,
> For whom all joyes she utterlye exilde.[2]

Abetted by Wolsey, who was fearful of the soothsayers' predictions that his downfall would be a woman, the sowers of discord eagerly labored to obtain a divorce, so that Henry might remarry the sister of the King of France. The part played by Anne Boleyn in the story of the divorce is followed by lengthy discussions of Henry's seizing the religious supremacy in England and by an account of Catherine's banishment to Cowelmolton, where she finally dies a most exemplary death, singing a litany.

The surprising aspect of the poem, whose author bluntly states that he regarded truth higher than accuracy of metre, is its frankness, its outspoken statements concerning Henry's cupidity and cruel behavior towards this blameless Queen. After all, Forrest was attacking Mary's father. However, he does not seem to have been deterred by this consideration, although he is inclined to excuse Henry as being misled by evil counsellors. But still he censures this ruler, since he did not

. . . . .

[2] William Forrest, *The History of Grisild the Second*, ed. W. D. Macray (Roxburghe Club, 1875), p. 40.

have even Walter's excuse of being wedded to a basely born wife. The ecclesiastical tone is plain in Forrest's heavy moralization, in Catherine's complete acceptance of God's will. This life is a period of preparation for the next world. Thus, Forrest's attitude is medieval and totally in keeping with the sentiments of the *mirrors*.

Mention has already been made of Churchyard's "Jane Shore," which had appeared in the 1563 edition of the *Mirror for Magistrates*. Evidently, this soldier-poet felt that his authorship of the piece was not quite evident to the reading public, because he felt the need to reiterate his claim to it from time to time.[3] In 1593, he issued an amplified version of this *tragedy*, increased chiefly by the inclusion of twenty-one stanzas on the evanescence of glory and the insecurity of earthly fame.

Although Churchyard was the first to realize that Jane Shore was a fit subject for a *mirror*, she had been living long in the popular imagination. As we have seen, she had appeared in Sir Thomas More's *History of Richard III*, where her undeniably adulterous conduct had been glossed over by the charitable More. With the passing of the years, the charm and wit of this daughter of the people, her modest mien during her hour of triumph and her patient submissiveness while she was imprisoned in the Tower and forced to do public penance, had

. . . . .

[3] Churchyard presents an interesting example of the literary hack quite common during the last quarter of the century. His productivity is amazing, his works comprising innumerable gratulatory verses, funereal remembrances, descriptions of campaigns, versified accounts of battles and a wealth of occasional verse. He figures largely in the progresses of Elizabeth, where he seems to have found steady employment writing eulogistic verses. Yet, all this activity does not seem to have provided security for him; he is forever complaining of the ingratitude of princes and the heartlessness of the court. He pictures himself as old and forgotten; he draws a few compassionate words from Spenser in *Colin Clouts Come Home Again*, lines 396ff.

And there's old Palemon free from spight,
Whose careful pipe may make the hearers rew
Yet, he, himself, may rewed be more right
Who sung so long until quite hoarse he grew.

endeared her to the populace until she had achieved the stature of a heroine. Daniel reflects the contemporary opinion of her,

> Shore's wife is graced and passes for a saint;
> Her legend justifies her foule attaint.[4]

Churchyard preserved More's condoning attitude. He holds that after all she was but a frail woman, married to a man unworthy of her wit and beauty, wedded to a lout through the greed of her relatives long before she had any conception of love and its power. Yet her resignation to fate was exemplary; let the reader make a mirror of her life![5]

Despite the sympathy he accords to Jane, Churchyard cannot refrain from pressing home a moral to his readers. This is Churchyard's "croaking voice" to which Spenser had so commiseratingly alluded. We are treated to a series of platitudes:

> The setled mind is free from Fortunes power,
> They neede not feare, who look not up aloft:
> But they that clime are careful every hower,
> For when they fall: they light not very soft;
> Examples hath, the wisest warned oft
> That where the trees, the smalest branches beare
> The stormes doe bloe and have most rigoure there.[6]

Besides his "Tragedy of Jane Shore," Churchyard had included in *Churchyard's Challenge* (1575) another *mirror*, "Sir Simon Burleis Tragedie Who Lived in the XI Yeare of Richard the Second." Burley demands a hearing:

> Am I of blood or yet of birth so base,
> O Baldwin now, that thou forgetst my name?

And he berates the editor of the *Mirror* soundly for not having included him in the collection, adding that were Lydgate or

. . . . .

[4] Samuel Daniel, *Complaint of Rosamond*, lines 25-6.
[5] The story was also used as the theme for one of Deloney's ballads, *The History of the Life and Death of Master Shore and Jane Shore His Wife* (1599). Drayton included her in his *Heroicall Epistles* (1598).
[6] Campbell, *Mirror for Magistrates*, p. 381.

Boccaccio alive there might be some hope for him to be eternized. With "weeping blubbring eyne," he narrates to Churchyard the tale of his rising to high station and then being brought to misery through the envy of his foes. Envy, instead of Fortune, acts as the motivating force of the *tragedy*. Burley had led a blameless life; he had quelled riots, acted honorably, but Envy,

> a mighty monster great,
> That swims like Whale amongst the little fry
> Whose gaping mouth would soone confuse and eate
> The Gogious small that in small corners lye
> His thirsty throate would drink all places dry
> And sucks up all, and so of all leaves nought.[7]

After being accused of treason, he is beheaded. Despite the outrageous verse, it is pleasant to note here less of the moralizing tone and more of the plain historical narration that later *mirrors* were to adopt.

Another historical *mirror* is "The Earl of Murton's Tragedie, Once Regent of Scotland and Alwayes of Great Birth, Brought to Lose his Head on a Skaffold in Edenbrough, the Second of Iune, 1381." This is again the story of a man placed upon the pinnacle of fame as high as a king. When fickle Fortune decides to spin her wheel, his secret foes plot his downfall. There follows the usual story of accusations, disgrace, failure in the attempt to rescue him and the inevitable scaffold. Nowhere is Churchyard as pedantic and long-winded as in this *tragedy*. He moralizes interminably in the best manner of an ascetic monk:

> Death is the end of all that beareth life,
> Not one shall scape, this world is but a dreame,
> The seedes of sinne brings forth but flowers of strife
> In painted robes lies many a rotted seame,
> It is but grief to guide and rule a realme:
>   . . . . .

[7] Thomas Churchyard, *Churchyard's Challenge*, Sig. F1r.

Great charge and care, a great accompt must make
And when I frown, the whole round world I shake.[8]

Despite the fact that in some of his work he displays remarkable ability, here Churchyard's attempts at realism proved ludicrous:

In deadly dreame my tongue callde on that man
(As headless folke, may fumble out a worde)
You must beleeve the tongue a tale beganne.[9]

In the works of this poet, we find several other pieces cast in the form of a *mirror*. *Churchyards Choice* contains "A Pitefull Complaint in Maner of a Tragedie of Seignor Anthonio Dell Donaldoes Wife," supposedly translated out of the Italian, a piece which appeared later in the *Challenge* as "The Tragicall Discourse of the Dolorous Gentlewoman." As we have already seen, this device of duplicating his material or merely revising older matter for new publications was one of Churchyard's favorite practices.

Perhaps, Anthony Chute's *Beawtie Dishonored* (1593) may have prompted Churchyard to reassert his authorship of Jane Shore. Chute's work was entered in the Stationers' Registers the 16th of January, 1593, while Churchyard's *Challenge* was entered the 9th of April, 1593. Since the printer for both was John Wolfe, it is not unreasonable to assume that Chute's work, entered almost three months before, would have been published first. Despite many handicaps and a lack of skill, Chute really succeeds in presenting to us a masterful little study of a woman ill-matched and her gradual downfall at the hands of forces which she was unable to ward off. He narrates the ruin of this unfortunate woman by presenting her in *mirror* fashion as she laments her fate.

She records her humble but happy youth. Well-versed in women's ways, Chute tells us of "madding" thoughts, of her

· · · · ·

[8] Churchyard, *Chippes*, Sig. C4ᵛ.
[9] *Ibid.*, Sig. D3ʳ.

girlish discontent. Yet, despite her inward tumult, Jane is still maidenly and pure, fearful of the hastily-contrived marriage to Shore, the London tradesman:

> My fathers house obscure and I not knowne,
> But cloistered up to secresie and sadnesse,
> My friends misdoubting that as I was growne,
> Tempting desire might win my will to badnesse,
> Wise-indiscreete perforce they me constrained
> To wed myself to one that I disdained.[10]

She feels that her life will be wasted and that her husband will be worthless. And she becomes the eternal type, the beautiful woman, married to a brutish husband, silently grieving, pining for happiness. She envies others who are happily married and eloquently blames the greed of her parents for her woe. Soon, her despair becomes unbearable; she fears that she will betray her scorn for her husband, for she feels that everyone must guess her aversion. And this has an effect on her beauty; her figure droops; she loses her freshness:

> Who sees the secret of that widow thought,
> The silent musings and the discontent
> Moving impatience in her mind hath wrought
> Whose beawtie's subject to inforst content
> Or how may we thincke she her passion brookes.
> That dare not speake but plead her greefe in lookes.[11]

Before long, the suitors who have been covetously eying her perceive this change and, moved by pity for her, begin to plot against her husband. Fascinated by them, Jane seeks to justify her conduct by asking herself if there lives a woman who can resist compliments and blandishments. If old women could not do it, how can she who is youthful? She is more importuned than Ulysses' wife; still, Penelope's example of constancy does not stiffen her resistance. Her protestations to her

. . . . .

[10] Anthony Chute, *Beawtie Dishonored*, stanza 35.
[11] *Ibid.*, stanza 74.

suitors are of no avail. They pursue her relentlessly, until she falls prey to their suggestions. She broods on her unfortunate plight. Why should she remain chained to an old dotard?

Chute gives us a lively description of Master Shore's antics, his calling "Kate, who must come and kiss him." He is jealous, to boot; yet he does not realize that jealousy will only secure him infidelity in a wife. Inevitably, the unfeigned admiration and the determined intrigues of the admirers about her, her growing scorn for the loathsome Shore subtly transform her, and the chaste, beautiful woman becomes a wanton.

> My speeche from humble, decent, pure and true,
> That hid no secrecie in a plainly meaning
> To courtlike, wanton, pleasant did insue: [12]

And now, with virtue gone, her fame spreads throughout London until the king hears of her and bids her appear before him. Having learned her lessons well, Jane holds him off. When she finally capitulates, she gains complete sway over Edward, eventually becoming the uncrowned queen of the land. But this triumph merely foreshadows her fall, for remorse sets in, and, with it, all the haunting of self-recrimination. Yet, this is only the beginning of her woes. After the King's death, she must beg her bread from door to door, pursued by Richard Gloster's hatred. There follows banishment, accompanied by the threat of death to any who will help her.

The poem has many faults, not the least of which is the verse in which it is told; such wretched verse, at times, that not even the extenuating fact that this was Chute's infant muse, as he states in his dedicatory letter to Sir Edward Winckfield, can excuse it. There is far too much alliteration; the verse is crabbed, while the diction is outrageous. Chute often forgets that Jane is telling the story and lapses into the third person. Nothing is said of the husband's reactions, nor of her hours of triumph as the king's mistress. Structurally, also, the

· · · · ·

[12] *Ibid.*, stanza 39.

poem is bad, since it leaves too many loose ends; yet, it does not deserve the censure heaped upon it, because it still remains a good study of a woman's gradual lapse from virtue. Chute portrays for us a sensitive wife, matched to a brutish dotard. She is a far cry from the trulls like Meg-of-Westminster or the wives who sported in the London inns, carving horns for their husbands. This is the picture of the love-starved wife who listens to the siren song of her flattering admirers and who is unable to resist. Taken in this light, it cannot be condemned too categorically.

If the career of Jane Shore demonstrated convincingly that wantonness could not thrive, the rise and fall of Cardinal Wolsey offered alike to moralist-poets and to dramatists a superb chance to fashion their *tragedies*. The great Cardinal's pride, unchecked ambition, and lofty aspirations had been mirrored early in the sixteenth century by John Skelton. Incensed by the great prelate's contempt, this satirist had turned about like a hornet and stung him, only to find his sting removed by Wolsey's effective henchmen, who had forced him to repent of his actions with the proper show of contriteness.

A few years later, George Cavendish, a member of Wolsey's own household, seized upon his master's career as an eminent subject for one of the poems in his *Metrical Visions*, a collection of short poetical biographies dealing with the notables of the years between the fall of Wolsey and the death of Mary in 1558. Wolsey led the procession:

> O ffortune quod he shold I on thee complayn
> Or of my necgligence that I sustain this smart
> Thy double visage hath led me to this trayn
> Ffor at my begynning thow dydest ay take my part
> Untyll ambysion had puffed up my hart
> With vaynglory, honor and usurped dignyte
> Fforgetting cleane my naturall mendycitie.[13]

. . . . .

[13] George Cavendish, *The Life of Cardinal Wolsey*, ed. S. W. Singer (London, 1825), Vol. II, p. 9.

Although Cavendish seems to have held his former master in high regard, his account is entirely unprejudiced. Perceiving clearly Wolsey's faults, he does not try to gloss over his pride, his love of opulence, his subtle dealings. He gives Wolsey credit where he deserves it, especially when alluding to the Cardinal's munificence to his retainers. He is also inflexible with Henry and his dealings with the church, and here, perhaps, may lie the reason why these over-frank poems, together with Cavendish's well-known prose biography, remained unpublished until our own time. Such frankness was perhaps best left unexpressed in the days of Elizabeth.

With his customary knack for treating popular subjects, Churchyard also turned his hand to Wolsey and contributed "The Tragedy of Cardinal Wolsey" to the *Mirror for Magistrates* of 1587. It is a typical *mirror*, told in the conventional manner of the *complaint*, tracing the familiar events of the rise of Wolsey from an unknown priest to the highest position in the land. Then just as suddenly as he ascended comes his downfall. Churchyard grasps the opportunity to put into Wolsey's mouth a sermon on Pride, the sin most abhorrent to God, since it was the cause of Lucifer's fall. Earthly pomp is but transitory and

> He needs must fall that looks not where he goes
> And on the stars walks staring gosling like.[14]

He comes to the conclusion that the prime aim of man should be consideration for others, and that he who showed no thought for anyone else is now returned to dust. But with scarcely concealed pride, he adds,

> I made as great a crack
> As doth an oak or mighty tottering wall
> That whirling wind doth bring to ruin and wrack.[15]

. . . . .

[14] Campbell, *Mirror for Magistrates*, p. 507.
[15] *Ibid.*, p. 511.

Although he does not miss the fine opportunity to attack the popish toys that made Wolsey fall and to have a fling at the Roman idols that are responsible for his disgrace, the usual vein of moralization so frequent in Churchyard is subdued in this *tragedy*. The reader is sometimes allowed to peer beneath Wolsey's none-too-well subjugated pride in his own achievements. The Cardinal makes excuses for himself: he gave money to his subordinates; he took care that his servants should serve him well. A good casuist, Wolsey tries to point out that his luxury was merely a lack of niggardliness in his character. We do not come away convinced that he is wholly sorry that he stared at the stars. And after all, Fortune's rise and fall is as inevitable as the tides of the sea.

The theme was once more taken up in 1599 by Thomas Storer, a student of Christ Church, who developed it in a somewhat dramatic fashion into *The Life and Death of Thomas Wolsey, Cardinal, Divided into Three Parts, His Aspiring, Triumph and Death*. The piece makes use of the usual seven-line stanza, with the subject uttering the complaint. There is no alteration of the basic facts of Wolsey's life. In the first part, "Wolseius Aspirans," Storer traces the Cardinal's rapid rise after he realizes that in this world one must be a courtier and thus becomes "a saint in sight, a machiavel in mind."

In "Wolseius Triumphans," Wolsey has already reached the dizzy heights—only one honor is out of reach,

> They chose me cardinal and sent a hat
> What choice? What hat, where was the triple crowne?
> A Monmouth-man can do as much as that.
> O had his holiness bin in a sowne,
> Or surfeited or tooke some potion downe;
> St. Peter's Church, St. Angel's famous towre
> The seven-hills-citty, had bin in my powre.[16]

. . . . .

---

[16] Storer, *Life and Death of Wolsey*, lines 43ff.

When he becomes High Chancellor, he goes on his proud, haughty way, in progresses as stately as his King's. Swollen with pride, he holds the people in contempt. But soon the wheel of Fortune spins dizzily, and he is brought to earth, back to the abjectness whence he sprang. Then he decides,

> My mother earth mine onely wife shall be:
> And yet no incest sithens onely she
> Beares all her sonnes and daughters in one wombe,
> She Europes Amerikas Affricke's and Asiae's tomb! [17]

And with this last conceit he awaits his doom calmly and with dignity.

Storer's *Wolsey* avoids all mention of the religious troubles; in fact, his eulogy of Henry VIII is in strong contrast to the outspoken sallies of some of the preceding poets, such as Cavendish. He introduces the inevitable moralization, emphasizing Wolsey's unchecked ambition which in the end brought on his ruin. Strangely enough, there is not the slightest hint that Wolsey is conscious of the great forces warring within him; he crashes because the wheel of Fortune spins,

> But see, even when my joyes did most abound,
> My crowned pillar most untimely fell. [18]

He apparently accepts his fate with complete resignation:

> Oh hidden doome of that eternall spirit
> That sentence gives, the righteous man shall die! [19]

Although Storer attempts to introduce dramatic divisions in his *tragedy*, it remains a piece of straightforward narrative, cast in the usual alliterative verse, employing the current rhetorical devices, and overloaded with a good deal of unnecessary verbiage.

Sharing the popular favor with eminent warriors and statesmen as subjects of *mirrors* was the female historical figure. Ever since Churchyard had first exploited Jane Shore in the

. . . . .

[17] *Ibid.*, lines 284ff.   [18] *Ibid.*, lines 316-17.   [19] *Ibid.*, lines 337-38.

Mirror for Magistrates of 1563, women had been favorite subjects of historical narratives. One of the most prominent was appended to Samuel Daniel's collection of sonnets, *Delia* (1592), under the title, *The Complaint of Rosamond*. The link between the narrative poem and the sonnet sequence is very tenuous, for Rosamond appears to the poet in the familiar ghost convention, as a poor afflicted spirit whose sin is so enormous that she is never allowed to sleep.

> And which is worse, my soule is now denied,
> Her transport to the sweet Elisian rest,
> The joyfull blisse for Ghosts repurified,
> The ever-springing Gardens of the blest:
> Caron denies me waftage with the rest.
> And saies my soule can never passe the River,
> Till Lovers sighs on earth shall it deliver.[20]

She hopes that

> Delia may hap to deigne to reade our story,
> And offer up her sighs among the rest.[21]

Slight though the connection may be, at least Daniel made some attempt to tie the long poem to his sonnets. Later writers who seem to have adopted the practice did not even trouble to establish a link between their love lyrics and the long poem which was usually added to such sonnet sequences. Whether this was considered fashionable, or done merely to add bulk to the little volume is undetermined. That it became widespread among poets is confirmed by the long list which may be compiled.[22] A notable exception is Richard Lynche's *Diella*

. . . . .

[20] Daniel, *Complaint of Rosamond*, lines 8ff.
[21] *Ibid.*, lines 43-44.
[22] In the group, we may list Lodge's *Phyllis* to which is attached *The Complaint of Elstred* (1593), Fletcher's *Licia,* accompanied by *Richard III* (1593) [?]; Lynche's *Diella* with the poem of *Dom Diego and Ginevra* (1595); R. Barnfield's *Cynthia,* with *The Legend of Cassandra* (1595); H. L., *Of Loves Complaint with the Legend of Orpheus and Eurydice* (1597).

in which the poet provides a definite link between the sonnets and the poem.[23] In most cases, however, the connection is impossible to find, and, perhaps, Spenser's otherwise incomprehensible addition of his *Epithalamion* to the *Amoretti* may be explained by this practice.

Rosamond's tale is the familiar one of the young girl whose lapse from virtue ends in shame and death. Rosamond, the daughter of a good family, is drawn from the calm of her native shire by the gayety of the Court. Her beauty is at once her friend and her foe; soon she learns that it may bring her the highest honors, serve to fulfill all her desires. Courtiers and even King Henry, fresh from his conquests in France, are all her willing subjects. But she goes on serenely,

> And safe mine honor stood, till that in truth
> One of my sexe, of place and nature bad,
> Was set in ambush to intrap my youth.[24]

The old familiar arguments are produced by the feminine Pandar; youth is fleeting, the cup of pleasure must be sipped at the right moment; the tempter dangles all the enticements, wealth, the king's favor, all the lures designed to reduce a none-too-impregnable rock. It is obvious that these blandishments have undermined her resistance; before long she finds herself wavering and virtue is doomed. She allows the king to shower her with gifts, flattering to her womanly vanity. From a lowly grange she is removed by Henry II to more splendid quarters,

> A stately pallace he fortwith did build,
> Whose intricate innumerable wayes
> With such confused errors so beguilde
> Th' unguided Entrers, with uncertaine strayes,
> And Doubtfull turnings kept them in delayes;
> With booteless labor leading them about,
> Able to finde no way, nor in, nor out.[25]

. . . . .

---

[23] See p. 118.
[25] *Ibid.*, lines 470ff.

[24] Daniel, *op. cit.*, lines 218ff.

Here in a garden at the very center of this labyrinth, attended by a few trusted maids, she lives, frequently visited by the King. But it is not long before the vengeance of the jealous Queen is upon her. Having discovered the affair, she seizes an occasion when the King is absent and, aided by the thread that guided the King in the maze, the enraged wife comes upon Rosamond and forces her to swallow a deadly poison.

Over this framework, Daniel weaves the story of youthful wavering and a tragic downfall. Rosamond is always the young girl who tries to avoid ruin, but is too feminine, too weak, too sorely tempted to resist. Immediately after yielding, she is seized by remorse; only then is impressed upon her the full import of her guilt. But it is too late, and her inclination to follow the easiest path leads her to her tragic end. Tortured to the full by her conscience, during the brief moment between her swallowing of the drug and death, she is made to realize fully her shame and guilt. Even the bed upon which she has flung herself is an added reminder of her unchastity. All Rosamond's brief career of shame rises to accuse her before the shadows fall upon her to shroud her forever.

Foregoing the customary conceit of Fortune's spinning wheel, Daniel chooses to draw a character who has within her the seeds of her own tragedy. Consequently Rosamond emerges a far more tragic character, in that her own weakness, her own failure to adhere to the rigid standards of chastity, her own venality bring about her downfall. Sin generates its own retribution; the culpable Rosamond expiates her crime before uttering her last moan.

The tale is well told. Its few incidents reveal a discerning selection; only the most essential are retained, and those are well elaborated. The persuasive arguments of the seducing "matron" and the wrath of the enraged Queen as she forces Rosamond to swallow the poison are wisely introduced. But the attempt to create suspense, to show the lapse of time between the swallowing of the draught and death, by means of Rosamond's self-recrimination, is not convincing. Fundamentally, Daniel lacks dramatic power. He is above all the sonneteer, the Renaissance poet, always ready to sacrifice incisiveness of phrase to the honeyed conceits of the Petrarchist. We encounter the customary use of figures, from the quatorzains:

> Looke how a Comet at the first appearing,
> Drawes all mens eyes with wonder to behold it;
> Or as the saddest tale at sudden hearing,
> Makes silent listning unto him that told it,
> So did my speech when Rubies did unfold it;
> So did the blazing of my blush appeare,
> T' amaze the world, that holdes such sights so deere.[26]

A similar *mirror* dealing with English legendary history issued from the pen of Thomas Lodge in 1593, *The Tragicall Complaint of Elstred*, appended to his collection of sonnets, *Phyllis*. The tale of Elstrid had already been told by Higgins in *The Mirror for Magistrates*, but it contained little of the elaboration supplied by Lodge. For one thing, although he provided all the essential facts of the story, Higgins had made no attempt to create a setting. Lodge remedied this deficiency, retaining at the same time most of the details, especially Guendoline's invective against Elstrid when she discovers that the latter has won her husband's love.

Lodge pictures his encounter with the doleful Elstrid as taking place on the banks of the Severn. Both mother and daughter shed many tears as they recount to the poet their tale of woe:

> Within that Region where proud-byllowed Rhine,
> Doth animate the babes of fruitfull earth:
> And baines the bosom of the swelling vine:
> From thence my of-spring came, and thence my birth.
> In swathing clowtes, for happy Princesse heried,
> In shrowding sheets, a haplesse Princesse buried.[27]

. . . . .

[26] *Ibid.*, lines 120ff.
[27] Thomas Lodge, *Phyllis*, *The Complete Works of Thomas Lodge* (Hunterian Club, 1883), p. 60.

Having thus stated the theme, Lodge proceeds with the tale. Prince Humber, accompanied by Elstrid, seeking shelter on the Albanian coast (Scotland) is forbidden by its ruler, Albanact, to land. In the subsequent battle, Humber slays his foe and gains the kingdom, only to be, in turn, slain by the victim's brother Locrinus. Elstrid's fears are dissipated during all this turmoil, when the new King falls in love with her,

> For where I lost my love, my friends my hope,
> There found I hope, there faithful friends, there love.[28]

But her happiness is cut short when Locrinus is forced to marry Guendoline for political reasons. Realizing that he cannot part from Elstrid, Locrinus convinces her that she is still "soveraigne of his soule" and builds for her "a second Cretan wonder," a sort of labyrinth where he may visit her in secrecy. After Sabrina is born to them, the King, overjoyed, even wishes to dismiss Guendoline and her son. Elstrid is installed as virtual mistress of the court.

Enraged at this, Guendoline's father raises an army and pitches his field for the decisive battle near the "azure-mantled streame, where we now rewe." The unfortunate Elstrid plunges into a bitter arraignment of Fortune:

> Ah Fortune, nurse of fooles, poyson of hope,
> Fuell of vaine desires, deserts destruction,
> Impugner of preventions, errors scope
> Supposed soveraigne through our vaine construction,
> Princes of Paganisme, root of impietie,
> Devill on earth masked in deitie.
>
> Scorne of the learned, Follies eldest sister,
> Bastard of tyme, begot by vaine opinion
> Against thy power, O peevish proud resister,
> Mother of lyes, and mistresse of illusion
> Vampe of vaine glory, doble faced shroe,
> Whose smyles at first successfull end in woe.[29]

. . . . .

[28] Ibid., p. 66.   [29] Ibid., p. 74ff.

And well she may lament, for the king is slain and she is left with her little daughter at the mercy of Guendoline. The Queen's revenge is not long in coming:

> So gan she to evacuate by her tongue,
> The Hydraes of revenge she had intended.[30]

Useless are the tears of Elstrid, the plaints of Sabrina; they are bound and cast in the waters. As soon as their lament is ended, the two figures "both seek their Tomb with the Waves," while the author

> gotte home and weepingly thus pend it,
> Carelesse of those that scorne and cannot mend it.[31]

It is true that here we have a *complaint* containing all the customary elements and conventions, but as we have seen in Daniel's case, the mood is changed. We have the spirit of the Renaissance sonneteer and not the conventional moralizing of the *mirror*.

Lodge employs all the verbal nimbleness and phraseology of the sonnet sequence; the plaint of the lover for his lady replaces the lament of evil doers pursued by Fortune:

> So from their humbled closure lightned fast
> My lovely lampes, which earst made intercession
> And by one looke, of all harts took possession.[32]

Again, Lodge is very fond of Euphuistic references and comparisons to natural history:

> Or as the royalle monarche of the Ants,
> Arranging of his little-labouring traine,
> (In summer tyme foreseeing Winter's wants)
> By theyr indevors stores his nest with graine,
> Where each industrious elf for common good,
> Doth gather, seeke, regather happy foode.[33]

The inflexible Guendoline is likened to the "Fatheroake," a strenuous fight is compared to the goading of bulls. Occasion-

. . . . .

[30] *Ibid.*, p. 78.   [31] *Ibid.*, p. 80.   [32] *Ibid.*, p. 67.   [33] *Ibid.*, p. 63.

ally, the poet borrows from the sonnets the neo-platonic conceit:

> Behold in me the Tragedy of Fate,
> The true IDEA of this worldly woe: [34]

Structurally the poem presents little of note. The events are told chronologically, move quite swiftly, but there is little attempt to dramatize the important incidents. Yet the poem runs fairly smoothly and marks an advance upon the earlier *mirrors*. For example, there are none of the grisly ghosts of the earlier poems; Elstrid tells her tale with composure. Striking progress is also shown by the lack of moralization, for Lodge makes no attempt to judge right and wrong. Elstrid is pictured as a poor unfortunate, the victim of love, one who could not resist the king. "What is the wren to wrestle with the gripe?" she says in her own defence to Guendoline:

> It was not I, it was thy husbands youth
> That made him love and traind him to the lure
> What should poor captives doo? Or what should I?
> Twere better love and live, than loath and die.[35]

Fortune is no longer a divine agent bringing retribution for sin; she is merely blind, "the nurse of fooles." Once again the moralist has been superseded by the Renaissance word-painter.

To the mounting group of historical *mirrors*, Giles Fletcher added *The Rising to the Crowne of Richard the Third*, (1593)[?], which was appended to *Licia*, his collection of sonnets. As in the case of many other such sequences, there is no apparent relation between the love poem and the *tragedy*; Fletcher is merely following the convention.

Richard speaks the prologue:

> The stage is set for stately matter fitte,
> Three partes are past which Prince-like acted were
> To play the fourth, requires a kingly witte
>
> . . . . .

[34] *Ibid.*, p. 68. [35] *Ibid.*, p. 79.

Else shall my muse their muses not come nere
Sorrow sit down and helpe my muse to sing,
For weepe he may not, that was cald a King.[36]

It has been suggested that this refers to the characters from
the three popular *mirrors* of the day. Shore's wife, he says, had
little cause to lament, for she was of mean birth; Rosamond
was fair, but a mere woman. Although he pities Elstrid, for
she was a queen and her fall great, Richard III is the fittest of
all as a subject for tragedy. Fortune and he played tennis.
Though he won the first match,

> We played againe and then I caught my fall,
> England, the Court, and Richard was the ball.

> Nor weepe I nowe as children that have lost,
> But smyle to see the poets of this age:
> Like silly boates in shallow rivers lost,
> Loosing their paynes and lacking still their wage
> To write of women and of women falles
> Who are too light, for to be fortunes balles.[37]

Richard might well be an English counterpart of Caesar
Borgia judging by the tenacity which he shows in pursuing
his objective, in his utter disregard of any obstacle that stands
between himself and the throne. He alludes to his brother
George, remarking quite blithely, "men say that he was slain
by me." Without the least sign of repentance he continues:

> Henry the Sixt deprived of his crowne,
> Fame doth report I put him to the death,
> Thus Fortune smiled though after she did frowne
> A dagger's stab, men say did stop his breath
> I careless was both how and who were slaine,
> So that thereby a kingdom I could gaine.[38]
>
> . . . . .

---

[36] Giles Fletcher, *The Rising to the Crowne of Richard the Third*, reprinted in Grosart's *Miscellany of Fuller's Worthies*, III, 586.
[37] *Ibid.*, III, 587.   [38] *Ibid.*, III, 589.

Everyone is swept from his path, his two little nephews, their guardians, Grey and Rivers. Buckingham and Hastings are disposed of, one by "heading," the other through a judicious marriage and the bestowal of the Earldom of Herford. Richard finally achieves his crown, but all his crimes evoke not one trace of remorse in him:

> Blood and revenge did hammer in my head,
> Unquiet thoughts did gallop in my braine:
> I had no rest till all my friends were dead,
> Whose helpe I usde the kingdom to obtaine.
>
> Nor speake I now as I did repent
> Unless for this a crown I bought so cheaply
> For meaner things men wittes and lives have spent,
> Which blood have sown and crowns could never reap.[39]

In its colorless presentation, the poem presents a striking contrast to the later dramatic treatment of the material by Shakespeare in *Henry VI* and *Richard III*. Even the simplicity of Holinshed, from whose pages this *mirror* is largely drawn, disappears, and the narrative becomes flat, with neither the color nor the artifice found in Lodge or Drayton. Fletcher's poem seems to be a mere poetical exercise, written to take advantage of the popularity of the historical subject matter. The poet offers an apology for this by having Richard remark:

> My verse is harsh, yet (reader) do not frowne,
> I wore no garland but a golden crowne.[40]

Although in purpose, Michael Drayton's *Legend of Peirs Gaveston, Earle of Cornwall, his Life, Death and Fortune*, (1594)[?] resembles the *mirrors*, it illustrates admirably the change which the genre underwent during the thirty-odd years that had intervened since Baldwin's publication. What confronts us still is the lament of a man who is expiating his

. . . . .

[39] *Ibid.*, III, 587.　　　　[40] *Ibid.*, III, 599.

life and misdeeds, but the mood is now changed.[41] There is no more moralizing, no exhortation to the reader to view Piers' life as one to be sedulously avoided, but rather a plain narrative of his sad fate, used merely as a framework upon which to hang a series of exuberant descriptions. We are confronted with one of the numerous examples of the change in mood which took place towards the end of the century, when the Puritan movement gave way momentarily to an outburst of paganism. This change will be apparent again and again, not only in *mirrors*, but in the verse romances and in mythological poetry.

The story of *Piers Gaveston* is the one rendered familiar to all readers by Marlowe in *Edward II*. Gaveston, young, dashing, was endowed with a beauty that was fatal:

> My lookes perswading orators of Love,
> My speech divine infusing harmonie,
> And every worde so well could passion move,
> So were my gestures graced with modestie,
> As where my thoughts intended to surprise,
> I easly made a conquest with mine eyes.[42]

He immediately becomes the darling of the King, and the two go about engrossed in each other like Jove and Ganymede. But soon the courtiers, envious of Gaveston's fame and good fortune, begin their infamous work, and his reputation,

> the verie image of perfection,
> With the black pensill of defame is blotted,[43]

causing his ultimate exile into France. When events change, he is recalled, and once again his fortunes climb still dizzier heights. Not content with showering gold upon him, the young king even assigns to him Wallingford, Queen Eleanor's

. . . . .

[41] Drayton had already contributed "The Legend of Thomas Cromwell" to the 1587 *Mirror for Magistrates*.
[42] Drayton, *Legend of Piers Gaveston*, lines 133ff.
[43] *Ibid.*, lines 288-90.

stately dower. Later, the king's niece, a daughter of the famous house of Gloucester, is given him as wife. He is made Lord Protector of the realm. But eventually pride conquers him:

> Loe thus ambition creepes into my breast,
> Pleasing my thoughts with this emperious humor,
> And with this divell being once possest,
> Mine eares are filled with such a buzzing rumor,
> As onely pride my glorie doth awaite,
> My senses soothed with everie self-conceite.[44]

Forced to flee to Ireland when the barons demand his death, Gaveston soon returns to bewitch the King anew. But this time, the nobles force the issue to a head; with the help of the Queen, they accuse him of various crimes, among them that of being "King Edwards Ganemed." Though the King storms and rages, the favorite is banished. Eventually, having been captured by Beauchamp during an attempt to return to England, he loses his head on a scaffold at Blacklow.

The poem brims over with the luxuriance of the Renaissance and only occasionally are we aware that we are reading a *mirror*. In a few instances, Drayton feels duty bound to drag in Fortune in order to show her power. But it is no medieval Fortune; she is a siren who beckons to Gaveston with her alluring call, at the same time relentlessly plotting his downfall. Gaveston emphasizes her fickleness, her lack of purpose or reason, for he calls her

> O frayle and slyding state of earthly things,
> Blind Fortune, chance, worlds mutability,
> Advauncing peasants and debasing Kings,
> Od hap, good luck, or star-bred destinie:
> Which still doest fawne and flatter me so oft,
> Now casts me downe, then sett'st me up aloft.[45]
>
> . . . . .

[44] *Ibid.*, lines 709ff.
[45] *Ibid.*, lines 123ff.

No longer is Fortune the instrument for the punishment of sin; she is now blind and purposeless as quicksand.

Though the ghost tells the story in *mirror* fashion, we might be reading one of the mythological poems. Indeed, the color, the luxuriant descriptions so characteristic of Drayton are all here. All his exuberant love of display is woven into the rich tableaux. Piers incurs the ire of the barons through his extravagance, much as Wolsey did.

> In ritchest purple rode I all alone,
> With diamonds imbroidered and bedight,
> Which like the stars in Gallixia shone,
> Whose luster still reflecting with the light,
> Presented heaven to all that ever gazed;
> Of force to make a world of eyes amazed.
> Upon a stately jennet forth I rode,
> Caparisoned with Pearle-enchased plumes,
> Trotting as though the Measures he had trode,
> Breathing Arabian Civit-sweet perfumes: [46]

Again Drayton recurs to the familiar comparisons and conceits drawn from mythology and natural history. The king's roar is as the roar of the Leviathan; the two of them are always together like Leda's twins. Such allusions to mythology are much more frequent than is usual in the *mirrors*. In fact, the scholar often dominates the poet as is shown by his frequent references to contemporary literature. Venus and Adonis, Hero and Leander, are constantly on his lips; he portrays the furious king who is,

> Lyke as the furious paladine of Fraunce,
> Forsaken of Angelica, the fayre.

This is a reference to Ariosto's *Orlando Furioso* which was extremely popular at the time. The poem inevitably suffers from this surfeit of conceits. Though this may be excused as a common sin, indulged in by the greatest poets of the time, still

. . . . .

[46] *Ibid.*, lines 817ff.

Drayton carries the failing to excess. In the final analysis, he merely embroiders phrases and rich verbal tapestries on the framework of fact. He lacks the dramatist's skill to select three or four significant scenes, advancing his action by means of them, as Shakespeare does in the *Rape of Lucrece*. As a result, the poem is too drawn out; it suffers from a repetition of identical situations; and we are ready for Gaveston's execution long before it actually takes place.

Well-chosen, however, is Drayton's motivation of the catastrophe, which he pictures as arising out of Gaveston's great pride and the jealousy of the barons for the favorite's high position. Throughout the poem, the unfortunate Piers strenuously denies the carnal sin of which he is accused, even though frankly admitting that he and the King are lovers. To Drayton's Renaissance mind, this was perfectly possible, of course, no taint being attached to it.

One is led to speculate whether Marlowe's *Edward II* had any influence upon Drayton's poem, for the play, entered in the Stationers' Register on July 6, 1593, must have been acted during 1593, while *Piers Gaveston* was entered on December 3 of the same year. It is obvious, however, that Drayton has not made much use of the playwright's skill in selecting incidents, as for example, in condensing Pier's two banishments into one, which Drayton fails to do. Nor does Drayton catch the spirit of Marlowe's Gaveston, insolent and utterly contemptuous of the barons, for Drayton's Piers almost repents of his actions, his great pride and worldliness. The guilty love of Gaveston and the king is also portrayed differently by the two poets. What in Marlowe is the unnatural passion of a weak king, pitiful in his misery, made even more wretched by his plaintive, "my Gaveston," Drayton represents as the attachment between two young men frankly, but not reprehensibly, in love. It is merely the complete friendship of two Renaissance young men.

Among the host of poems and ballads dealing with historical subjects may be noted *The First and Second Books of the*

Preservation of King Henry VII When he Was but Earl of Richmond, Compyled in English Rythmical Hexameters by R. B. (1599). Like many of his predecessors, the poet gathered his material from Grafton, merely turning it into rhymed couplets. However, he never got beyond the first two of the five projected books. The author seems to have been especially concerned with metrical experiments, declaring that he hopes to wean the public "from the jingle of rhyming mother wits." Quite often he alludes to Stanyhurst, Golding and Fraunce and their experiments with classic meters. He is rather bumptious in quoting from his own works, frequently stating in his *Epistle Dedicatorie,* "as I have elsewhere written." The piece contains the usual overabundance of Biblical and classical allusions and is undistinguished in its mediocrity.

Quite in the same vein, the broils between Henry Beaufort, Cardinal of Winchester, and Humphrey of Gloucester, treated by Shakespeare in *Henry VI,* served once more as the basis of an historical narrative poem. Obviously based upon the *tragedies* in the *Mirror for Magistrates,* Christopher Middleton's *The Legend of Humphrey Duke of Glocester* (1600) is a production distinguished neither by its conception nor by its poetical merit and serves merely as an additional specimen of the great output of historical material during this decade.

Middleton's Humphrey is an old man, rendered philosophical by adversity, fighting a gallant but unequal struggle with his enemies. He is presented to us vainly trying to act as a stabilizing force in a kingdom racked by the greed and the luxury of princes and prelates, during the minority of Henry VI. But,

> The Bishope, like the proude insulting winde,
> Disturbes the quiet streams where Gloster runnes,[47]

and continues his overbearing conduct despite the apreals of Humphrey and the King's inability to check this turbulence.

. . . . .

[47] *Harleian Miscellany,* X, 171.

Anxious to bring about his downfall, Gloucester's enemies attack him through his wife, who has been accused of witchcraft. In addition, the new Queen repays Gloucester's kindness with malice and ingratitude; thus he is divested of his honours and of the Protectorship and finally is brutally murdered.

The story does not differ in its essentials from Holinshed. In many cases, it is a verse expansion of the facts found in that mine of English history. Middleton even includes a mention, found in Holinshed, of the apparent curse which lay on the nobles who bore the title of Duke of Gloucester, *viz.*, Thomas of Woodstock, Hugh Spenser and, after Humphrey, Richard III. The author excludes some of the details found in George Ferrers's *mirror*,[48] especially those dealing with his conjugal infidelity, although he alludes to the tender regard which Humphrey has for Eleanor. Nor is Middleton's Humphrey like Shakespeare's vigorous old man who bids his men draw against Winchester's henchmen, saying:

> Priest beware your beard;
> I mean to tug it, and to cuff you soundly;
> Under my feet I'll stamp thy cardinal's hat;
> In spite of pope or dignities of church,
> Here by the cheeks I'll drag thee up and down.[49]

Middleton did not try to imitate the *Mirror* tradition by having the ghost recite his own woes; in this poem Humphrey's *tragedy* is told in the third person. The author is recording it because he wishes to raise Humphrey's name from oblivion. Moreover, he is loath to sink

> in those muddy streames
> Where now swims many wits whose worth affoords
> Sinfull foule subjects, detestable theame,
> Set foorth in worse and more detested words,
> . . . . .

48 See above, p. 24.
49 Shakespeare, *1 Henry VI*, I, 3, lines 47ff.

Whose sound even sinfull men refuse to heare
As objects farre unfit for any eare.[50]

Once more we hear a voice of protest raised against the licentious spirit which was invading English poetry.

Generally speaking, the single historical *mirrors* exhibit the best efforts achieved in the genre. We notice a great deal of improvement in technique and the absence of the glaring ·faults that are so obvious in earlier specimens. It is not surprising to see this improvement, in view of the fact that skilled poets like Daniel, Lodge and Drayton all tried their hand at such pieces. A further reason for the superiority of the single *mirror* is that authors wisely realized that by limiting the scope of the subject matter, the theme could be expanded to its natural proportions, thus assuring an organic whole.

Yet, in a sense, the sins of their ancestors are visited even upon these single *mirrors*. They suffer principally from a lack of dramatic structure. Since they adhere too closely to their chronicle sources, their action is usually too episodic and strictly chronological. Only occasionally, when there appears a great dramatist like Shakespeare, do we observe real dramatic development; only then we may see the *mirror* approach true tragedy. Then the human flaws within the subject himself generate the circumstances that bring about his downfall. Only in such cases is Fortune, though recognized as mighty, relegated to a secondary role. Of far-reaching consequence too, is the unusual interest paid to feminine characters. Jane Shore, Matilda, Rosamond are but the forerunners of the hundreds of women who are to play important roles in later English poetry and drama.

Most striking of all, however, is the gradual but unmistakable change in attitude which becomes apparent in this type of *mirror*. Morality gives way to a new interest in artistic development. Towards the end of the century, the didactic ele-

· · · · ·

[50] *Harleian Miscellany*, X, 166.

ments yield ground to the word-pictures of the sonneteer, who is more interested in music than in moralizing. Again and again, we have proof that the temper of the latter years of Elizabeth's reign is totally different from the mood of godliness of the 50's and 60's. As we shall observe in subsequent pages, there were definite reasons for the new attitude. Mighty forces were at work bringing about the change, striving towards an ultimate goal.

Single *Mirrors*: Contemporary,
Necrological and Fictional

A NUMBER OF "MIRRORS" DEALING WITH CON-
temporary subjects either exalting the virtues of some recently
deceased nobleman or celebrating some recent valiant exploit,
also exist. Since they were usually written by hacks with an
eye upon immediate sale, they suffer from haste of composition
as well as from the mediocrity of the authors themselves.

We have already seen George Whetstone employing the
mirror as a medium for venting his spleen upon his contemporaries. Indeed, Whetstone seems to have adopted the genre as
his special literary vehicle. He used it a number of times in
extolling the merits of various deceased noblemen, a practice
in which he specialized. Perhaps the most important of these
"funereal *mirrors*" is *A Remembraunce of the Well Imployed
Life and Godly Ende of George Gaskoygne* (1578)[?]. In the
poem, Gascoigne is depicted as imploring his friend, Whetstone, to help him tell his tale, entreating him "to defend when
I am dead my life and godly end." Gascoigne recounts the familiar tale of his adventures among the Dutch, his imprison-
ment, his disappointments, and his work as a literary hack.
Throughout the piece, he complains bitterly of the ingratitude

of a cruel world. Like many of his fictional works, it becomes a medieval sermon on the futility of human pursuits:

> What is the world, a net to snare the soule . . .
> What is the world, a cankerworm of care.

Thus Whetstone pictures his friend, bidding a last farewell to England, touchingly bequeathing his heart to the Queen—but also his family.

Many similar accounts poured forth from Whetstone's pen. He joined in the flood of laudatory verses written upon the death of Sir Philip Sidney; he wrote *A Remembrance of the Vertues of Sir James Dier* (1583). His *Mirror of Treue Honnour and Christian Nobilitie, Exposing the Life and Death and Devine Vertues of Francis Earl of Bedford* (1585) is really typical of the short laudatory biography which reviewed the nobleman's achievements and must have served as a sort of funeral sermon. Such pieces are the reverse of the *mirrors*, in that they record the virtues rather than the sins of the subject. However, this is vague, generalized poetry, lacking in details or concrete evidence, even in the case of Gascoigne. It raises suspicion concerning its value as biography, and makes one wonder just how close the personal relationship between Whetstone and Gascoigne really was.

Whetstone was not alone in the production of this type of verse, for at about the same time John Phillips was composing *A Commemoration of Margaret Douglas,* (1578) in seven-line stanzas, in obvious imitation of the *Mirror*. He uses "her godly life, her constancy and perfit patience" as an example for the reader to follow. This John Phillips must also have been the author of one of the many effusions on Sidney, *The Life and Death of Sir Philip Sidney* (1587). A few years later he composed *A Commemoration of Sir Christopher Hatton* (1591) in six-line stanzas, which rehearsed the life and deeds of that statesman. All this, however, is colorless work, lacking inspiration as well as finish.

The daring of England's mariners furnished constant ma-

terial for the professional hacks who served up the news of
their exploits to a nation-conscious and news-hungry citizenry.
We have already seen how Drake's fame had been sung in
Richard Robinson's *Golden Mirror*. Literally hundreds of
broadsides and laudatory poems were written about his heroic
deeds.

For another variant of the *mirror*, *The Most Honorable
Tragedie of Sir Richard Grinvile Knight* (1595), the volumi-
nous Gervase Markham seized upon the well-known exploit of
Sir Richard Grenville, commander of the *Revenge*.

Finding himself face to face with the majestic San Felipe,
fifteen hundred tons, Grenville grappled with her, though his
ship was many times smaller. During the fray, he was fatally
wounded. To the patriotic Markham, this is a proud occasion,
and he proceeds to dress it up befittingly, so as to provide his
countrymen with an account of the glory of England's sons.
Thus he calls upon all the Muses and all the mythological
saints to aid him in portraying the fame of the great captain.
Grenville has cast anchor in the Azores in order to give his
"shyppe's citizens" a chance to recover from scurvy and to re-
pair his ship from the ravages of a sea journey. A messenger
comes to warn him of the danger from the Spanish fleet. To
Markham, this is the tidings of a deadly fray, begun in Heaven,
the age-old fight between Fortune and Ill-fortune, daughters
of Jove and Saturn. Upon being worsted, the latter has cast in
her lot with Spain and has sworn to be revenged upon Grenville. The Spanish fleet, strong in artillery and with fifty-three
sails, approaches, but Grenville refuses to flee, even in the face
of such danger. Therefore, he awaits almost certain annihila-
tion, while he summons his men back to the ship. The remainder is well-known history. At first, Grenville beats off the
attackers, but overwhelmed by the great odds, he is wounded
and wishes to split the keel in two. Upon being offered safe-
conduct, however, he yields, and his "mangled carkasse but
unmaimed minde" is brought to the Spanish, where a few days
later the hero dies in the Admiral's ship.

The poem is far too long-winded, being filled with clumsy, bombastic verse. At every turn, the author attempts to display his classical erudition, in consonance with the new attitude towards the *mirror*, which formerly in most cases had scrupulously avoided mingling historical and mythological elements. Interesting, however, are the allusions to "Renaldo." Grenville is held up as braver than Rinaldo and Roland, the heroes of Ariosto's *Orlando Furioso* which Harington had recently translated.

The *Complaynte of Anthonye Babington, Sometyme of Lincolnes Inne, Esquire, Whoe with Others Weare Executed for High Treason* (1586) also is typical of the historical ballad occasioned by subjects of popular contemporary interest. This is cast in the familiar seven-line stanza of the *mirror* with an induction in quatrains. It contains all the usual trappings, the recriminations of the traitor, tearfully complaining that had he been trained otherwise, he might have turned out to be a loyal subject and a good member of the commonwealth, whereas "now hee becomes a reproche and a scandal to the same." The poem recounts the salient facts of the conspirator's career until "his misdeameanors lead hym to skorn and to the gallows."

Of great contemporary interest must also have been Thomas Greepe's *The True and Perfecte Newes of the Woorthy and Vauliant Exploytes, Performed and Doone by that Valiant Knight, Syr Frauncis Drake* (1587). This purported to record the deeds performed by Drake and Frobisher in the Canaries, following them on their odyssey until their final triumphal entry into Portsmouth Harbor.

More pretentious is Charles Fitzgeoffrey's *Sir Francis Drake, his Honorable Life and his Tragical Death's Lamentation* (1596) in which the deeds of the valiant mariner are set down at great length. The author calls upon all the gods of Olympus to witness his work and reviews the achievements of all the great heroes in English history from Richard the Lion Hearted to Cabot, "mirror of Britains Magnanimity." Drake belongs with this valiant troop because of his dauntless scorn of Spanish frigates and his courage against all hazards. Despite this ambitious aim, the piece is hopelessly ponderous, overloaded with repetitions and mythological allusions. It makes use of all the stylistic tricks known to the age and more often than not resolves itself into mere bombast.[1] But it displays the intense nationalism and the undisguised pride of the English in their heroes. It is a worthy prototype of all this kind of verse produced at the time.

Before bringing this discussion of the *mirrors* to a close, it may be well to call the reader's attention to a few scattered pieces which illustrate still another of the uses to which the genre was put during its evolution. The general change from a didactic to a purely narrative purpose is perhaps best illustrated by some pieces in George Whetstone's *Rocke of Regard* (1576), a miscellany composed of prose and verse, with themes taken from Italian novelists, mythological history and other popular sources of material. Although Whetstone still intends to impress upon the reader the disadvantages of an evil life with its inevitable retribution, we need only to peruse a few pages to realize that beneath this avowed purpose there is also the desire to tell the story for its own sake. The characters begin to be subjects of an interesting tale rather than sinful historical figures.

Thus, the "Life of Bianca Maria, Countess of Celaunt," whose protagonist rues a life replete with murder, poisoning and intrigue, is in reality a *mirror*, but the tale is told in the same mood as Webster's *Duchess of Malfi*. Despite numerous

. . . . .

[1] A stanza of this poem will furnish an adequate example:

> Tomb? ah, no tomb, but Neptune's frothing waves!
> Waves? ah, no waves, but billow-rolling seas!
> Seas? ah, no seas, but Honours hallowed graves:
> Graves? ah, no graves but bones eternal ease:
> Ease? ah, no ease, but rest born to displease:
> Whate'er it be where worthy Drake doth lie;
> That sacred shrine entombs a Deity.

Charles Fitzgeoffrey, *Sir Francis Drake*, stanza 13.

moralizing stanzas on pride, Whetstone's prime interest is fictional. He seems to have kept an eye on Bandello's collection of tales, for several of his pieces may be traced to the Italian.

The ever popular theme of Cressida holds up another *mirror* to young maidens and a warning of the perils of wantonness and of coquetry from one who tells them that

> Though now I am anoynted with annoy,
> My hyde bepatcht with scabs of sundry hewe,
> I sometimes was the star of stately Troy: [2]

Whetstone included several other *complaints* of ladies or lovers forsaken, one of them being that of Medea, abandoned by Jason.

The same tendency may also be observed in several of Churchyard's pieces, especially *A Heavye Matter of an English Gentleman and a Gentlewoman in Maner of a Tragedie; A Pirates Tragedie Beyng a Gentleman of a Verie Good House; and A Piteful Complaint in Maner of a Tragedie of Seignior Anthonio Dell Donaldoes Wife,* all of them found in the second part of *Churchyards Chippes* (1579). These poems have many of the characteristics of the *complaint,* varying only in their metrical form, the four-line tetrameter stanza. However, they tend to accent the fictional mood, rather than the historical or the didactic.[3]

Glancing back upon the enormous body of material to be found in this genre, one realizes the definite changes brought about during the sixteenth century. Beginning as a purely devotional or religious work, the *mirror* passed through various stages until it became the vehicle for all sorts of literary purposes from the satirical to the fictional. Perhaps the most significant use of the *mirror* in England was its employment to spread historical knowledge and political doctrines. Seizing

· · · · ·

[2] George Whetstone, *The Rocke of Regard,* reprinted in J. P. Collier, *An English Poetical Miscellany* (London, 1867), p. 36.

[3] A discussion of these poems will be found in the section dealing with verse romances, p. 169ff.

upon the examples offered by Boccaccio and Lydgate, dipping at the same time into the material of the chronicles, the *Mirror for Magistrates* by its uniform excellence set the theme for all later works in this genre. Edition after edition of this popular work dug deeply into the mine of English history and brought before intensely patriotic Englishmen the chief figures of the realm, characters who a few years later would crowd the stages of Shakespeare, Marlowe and Greene.

Spurred by the example of *The Mirror for Magistrates*, many other collections of *mirrors* sprang up, but in general they proved too arduous an undertaking for a single author. As a result, they achieved little merit, either through their literary quality or through their influence upon later works. On the other hand, the single *mirrors*, which include material gathered from the most varied sources, may boast of far greater success. Of the *mirrors* of a classical nature, Shakespeare's *Rape of Lucrece* stands out as the most noteworthy, despite the fact that it is an early work of the great poet. By far the largest number of *mirrors* dealt with single individuals drawn from English history. It was in this field that the genre achieved its greatest development. We may mention among the foremost, Churchyard's "Tragedy of Jane Shore," Lodge's *Complaint of Elstred*, Daniel's *Complaint of Rosamond* which exploited the interest in the feminine historical personage. The growing concern with history at the expense of didacticism is well illustrated by Storer's *Wolsey* and by Drayton's *Peirs Gaveston*. A large number of necrological *mirrors*, written chiefly to praise some dead nobleman, put in an appearance also. At the same time there existed several *mirrors* with definite fictional characteristics, exemplified best by Whetstone's and Churchyard's work. At the height of its development the *mirror* is no longer a purely devotional or historical poem, seeking to point the way to salvation by holding up the sins of its subject to the reader. It tries, instead, to entertain him; edification has given way to amusement; utilitarianism, to art.

The
Verse
Romances

V I I I

The Medieval Background

THE GAP WHICH LIES BETWEEN THE NARRATIVE
art of Chaucer and that of Marlowe is a wide one and, to all
appearances, one that is unbridged. Consequently, literary
critics are mostly content with dismissing the phenomenon, by
conceding that the art was lost during the fifteenth century
and was not rediscovered until fairly late in the following century with the advent of Spenser and the other "new poets."
Actually, however, when we examine the poetry of the intervening period, we perceive that interest in narrative poems
continued unabated, even though the quality may not have
been as high or the production as great as it had been in former
times.

In England the fifteenth century represents the transition
from the Middle Ages to the Renaissance; it is only natural,
therefore, that in such a period of readjustment, literary production should suffer and that in examining it, critics should
pass over it hurriedly in order to devote all their attention to
the great works of the Age of Elizabeth. Nevertheless, we may
observe in these obscure transitional works the evidence of significant social changes, as for example, the rise in importance

97

of the great trading middle class. We may witness a gradual shift from an easygoing attitude towards morality to an uncompromising rigorousness of living, such as was demanded by the Puritans, and again its gradual change into the Renaissance luxuriousness exhibited by Drayton and Marlowe.

With the death of Chaucer, narrative poetry seemed to settle back into the comfortable mediocrity from which he had momentarily lifted it. When we compare the wealth of characterization and the narrative art of the *Canterbury Tales* with contemporary pieces, we are more and more struck by Chaucer's evident genius. We are impressed by the superiority of Chaucer's skilled verse over the harsh, bewildered rhythms of a Lydgate or the dull prolixity of a Gower. Nevertheless, although beset by linguistic and metrical problems, the writers of this transitional period continued to bring forth their stories in prose and in verse. There were tales and poems to suit the court and the tradesman's shop; there were mysteries and romances, satirical poems and stirring ballads.

Much of the popular narrative poetry of the fifteenth century finds expression in the ballad. Throughout the years between Chaucer and Shakespeare, these compositions are sung in great numbers, delighting their hearers with tales of martial deeds or triumphant love. Unadorned, yet forceful as a result of their very artlessness, they dramatically present events and popular figures in past or contemporary history. Now and then, great characters like Robin Hood are created and are given the individuality that has immortalized them. Occasionally, the simplicity and the charm of the subject matter, in pieces like *The Nut Browne Maid*, commend them strongly to our notice. In common with all other genres, however, they suffer from too much familiarity and they are eventually debased or given a coating of indecency. Thus Robin Hood becomes a poltroon, even as did Arthur and Charlemagne before him. But many of the characteristics of these poems are retained in works of the Elizabethan period. The metre of the ballads and their loose, episodic construction are reflected in the later verse tales. One may readily perceive, for example, that the alternating tetrameter and trimeter lines, rhyming *abcb*, of the ballad fuse and become in effect the fourteener couplet of the verse romances.[1] Nor must we think that with the advent of the new literature, with the triumphal sweep of lyric poetry and drama, the ballad was obliterated. In the last decade of the sixteenth century, we still find Thomas Deloney publishing numerous collections of ballads, singing of every conceivable historical personage from the Arthurian heroes to Rosamond and Shore's wife.

Throughout the fifteenth and early sixteenth centuries the *fabliaux,* imitating or actually corrupting Chaucerian material, were also very popular. They consist mostly of vulgar anecdotes, coarse jests or witty escapades. Very frequently, the butt of the jests is a corrupt clergyman or a scoundrelly friar, whose unclerical behavior is satirized with great relish. In these popular tales, the exploits of the tippling wife are welcomed and enjoyed side by side with the pious conduct of the saint. One of these stories, mentioned in *Robert Laneham's Letter* (1575), is entitled *A Merry Jest of a Shrewd and Curst Wife Wrapped in Morrel's Skin* (n.d.). It recounts the ruse employed by a young man in reducing his bride to wifely submission. Its theme resembles that of *The Taming of a Shrew.* Despite all the warnings of his friends, a young man marries a wealthy but irascible young woman. Following the wedding, he takes her to his estate, where she immediately proceeds to

· · · · ·

[1] Compare:

> In somer when the shawes be shewn
> And leves be large and long,
> Hit is full mery in feyre forests
> To here the foulys song.

Robin Hood and the Monk, lines 1-4.
with:

> The oldest named Lurcanio that speare and sheld desired,
> The other eke Ariodant that more to love aspired.

Peter Beverley, *Ariodante and Jenevra,* Sig. A4ᵛ.

fly into a tantrum. After soundly beating his shrewish bride, the husband causes an ass to be slain and wraps her up in its salted hide. Through a repetition of this treatment, she is quickly tamed.

The Tale of the Basyn is another typical *fabliau*, narrating the device by means of which a priest traps his brother's wife and her merry lover, an over-lusty friar, through the use of an enchanted basin. Many other such pieces were popular. Among them might be included, *The Milner of Abington*, a variant of Chaucer's *Reeve's Tale*; *The Churl and the Bird*, a popular beast fable; *The Merry Devill of Edmonton*; *Fabyll's Ghost*; etc.

The Knight of Courtesy and the Lady of Faguell (n.d.), a narrative resembling an Italian *novella*, also had a wide vogue during the fifteenth century. Somewhat like Boccaccio's often imitated *Guiscardo e Sigismonda*,[2] this tale and Boccaccio's may, in fact, have been drawn from some common source. Though the Knight of Courtesy has fallen in love with the Lady of Faguell, he respects her position as a married woman. Some time later, upon being wounded in battle, the faithful lover leaves instructions that his heart be sent to his mistress. Enraged at their mutual devotion, the villainous Lord of Faguell causes the heart to be cooked and served to his wife. When she is informed of the gruesome deed, the Lady resolves never again to touch food and soon dies.

With the coming of the Tudors, the minstrel moved from the castle to the public square and to the burgher's home. Although the new patrons of the arts, the wealthy tradesmen, were known for their hard-headed business proclivities, they found great delight in the marvellous, and a good many of their favorite tales still abounded in magic and supernatural events. There were innumerable saints' lives, replete with miraculous escapes and wonderful rescues. Readers eagerly welcomed stories of Merlin and other sorcerers, to be found in

. . . . .

[2] See p. 143 for a discussion of Boccaccio's tale.

poems such as *The Treatise of the Birth of Merlin* (1510), or *The Lyfe of Petronylla* (1493). The latter records the patient endurance and other Christian virtues of a counterpart of Griselda, in incidents which might well have come out of the *Legenda Aurea*.

Despite the favor enjoyed by this type of material, a more sophisticated, satirical strain was also popular. There remain scores of works recording contemporary witticisms and Latin *facetiae*. At the same time, there exist numerous *testaments*, analogues of the famous poems by François Villon. *Colyn Blowbol's Testament* (n.d.) is typical of these. The last will of this confirmed drunkard is quite in keeping with his life, whose end has been hastened by "drinking a tanke of Teynt and Alycaunt wine 'til he was as drunk as any swine." Colyn requests that his body shall be buried in the Temple of Bacchus. After making appropriate bequests to the bawds of the town, to his secretary and to his confessor, and ordering that a hundred marks shall be spent on wine and other beverages to comfort those who attend his funeral, he exhorts all his well-wishers to carry on their useless lives:

> And me remember with your devocion,
> Heartely with all your mention,
> With some good prayers when ye upon me thinke,
> Which hath been ever a lover of good drynke.[3]

Even these few lines will be sufficient to show that despite all his zest for life and love of carousing, the unknown author is hardly a rival of the great French poet. The same may be said for all the other extant *testaments*, which include *The Testament of Andro Kennedy, Wil Bucke, His Testament, Jyl of Brentford's Testament*, and, as late as 1575, George Gascoigne's *Last Will and Testament of Dan Bartholomew of Bath*.

John Skelton's lively *Tunnyng of Elynor Rummynge* and

. . . . .

[3] *Colyn Blowbol's Testament*, lines 395ff. in W. Hazlitt's *Remains of the Early Popular Poetry of England* (London, 1866), Vol. IV.

the lesser known *Twelve Merry Jests of the Wydow Edith* by William Smith follow this same vein of scurrility. The adventures of the Widow Edith, a medieval Moll Flanders, are quite spirited, as one moment she is compelled to listen to a clerk lecture her on covetousness and the next, she is dallying with pilgrims and yeomen. The poem shows verve and narrative power. The *Boke of Mayd Emlyn* (1525) also deserves mention. Its chief character is a lusty young woman, strongly reminiscent of Chaucer's Wyfe of Bath in her love of life and her penchant for marriages. It is not long after her first marriage that her husband finds her passing her days in taverns with her paramours. When he remonstrates, she retorts:

> It is a pity that a knave
> A prety wife should have; [4]

and she excuses her behavior by claiming that Sir Sym is her cousin and that she only sings ballads with him. This treatment has its inevitable effect upon the unfortunate husband.

> She cherisshed her husband with bred and chese,
> That his life he did lese,
> Than made she mornynge
> And drank devoutly for his soul. [5]

She observes her period of mourning by limiting herself to a friar as a lover, but soon replaces him with a lustier youth. Husbands follow each other in quick succession, until she ends her life quite appropriately—in the stews. Although she shows plenty of vigor and zest, Emlyn can hardly be compared with her more illustrious predecessor in subtlety of characterization or in humor. We have here, in the main, the portrait of a wanton, lacking all moral sense and feeling.

The satiric nature of the foregoing pieces appealed strongly to the powerful burgher class which had risen to prominence

. . . . .

[4] *The Boke of Mayd Emlyn*, lines 25-26, in Hazlitt, *op. cit.*, Vol. IV.
[5] *Ibid.*, lines 83ff, in Hazlitt, *op. cit.*, Vol. IV.

with the advent of the Tudor dynasty. Their cynical quality, the absence in them of elevated sentiments must have suited the tastes of the middle class, who found in them a change from the works of piety to be encountered at every turn. The chivalric romances were also favorite reading during the Tudor period. They, too, served to relieve the humdrum of the daily existence of the middle classes. In reading these, the shopkeeper and his apprentice abandoned, for the moment, all preoccupation with salvation, in order to battle giants with Guy of Warwick or to rescue ladies with King Arthur's knights. Though filled with impossible escapes and miraculous rescues, these accounts provided the broad fare which today is supplied by our pulp magazines and film stories to the same class of people. The very characteristics of improbability, which gradually alienated the favor of the more sophisticated readers, retained for these romances the approval of the lower classes. Works such as *Huon of Bordeaux, The Four Sons of Aymon,* continued to be popular throughout the sixteenth century. The influx of the Portuguese and Spanish romances into England about 1580 even provided fresh material.[6] The fame achieved by Anthony Munday through his versions of these tales from the Amadis cycle will suffice to indicate their favor with the public. The diminishing cost of popular editions and the practice of issuing the tales in parts also contributed to their popularity. Through such devices, this type of fiction was made available to the masses. We need only glance at Captain Cox's collections, described in Robert Laneham's Letter, a collection representative of Elizabethan middle class taste, to realize how important a place the romances occupied in the burgher's reading.[7]

. . . . .

[6] For a detailed discussion of this topic see L. B. Wright, *op. cit.,* Chapter XI. See also R. S. Crane, *The Vogue of Medieval Chivalric Romances During the English Renaissance* (Menasha, Wisconsin, 1919).
[7] *Robert Laneham's Letter,* ed. F. J. Furnivall (London: Chatto and Windus, 1917), p. xii.

The vicarious thrills obtained by tradesmen from the adventures of knights errant were not sufficient, however. Their consciences forbade them to dally with works that offered no moral profit; consequently printers and authors labored valiantly to point out the ethical value of their publications. As will be seen later, every preface claims that the author is presenting his story for the edification of the reader. Even tales which were definitely bawdy were thus justified; they pointed out a moral or exposed the evil practices of papists. Thomas Twyne did exactly this with some stories from Boccaccio, and Arthur Brooke purported to tell the tale of Romeus and Juliet in order to reveal the dire results arising from "auricular confession." With the passing of the years, as the puritan spirit waxed, this didacticism became more and more marked.[8] It made use of the verse romances as a typical bourgeois medium in order to convey certain moral lessons, at the same time that it narrated a popular tale.

During its evolution, the sixteenth-century verse romance adapted itself to the changing times, but retained many of the characteristics of the older versions. It forsook the older themes for newer ones, either imitating them from the Italian *novelle* or inventing them from native materials. Like its prototype, it was still encumbered by a profuseness of episodes, but the incidents became more realistic, closer to everyday life, even though they constantly jarred the reader with their implausibility. But always, the verse romances of an Elviden or a Garter declared their didactic intent, even though it might be only to serve as aids in learning a foreign language. Frequently they pointed out the evils of marrying in haste and without the consent of one's parents. At every turn they seized the opportunity to depict love as a treacherous sentiment to be strictly watched and governed at all times.

. . . . .

[8] Further evidence of this may be seen in the moralization of pieces like *The Nut Browne Maid*, which became *The New Nutbroune Mayde Upon the Passion of Christ*.

This attitude lasted throughout the Elizabethan period, being abandoned momentarily only towards the close of the sixteenth century. Undoubtedly, one important factor in this change was the increasing influence which Italian culture came to exercise upon England. Ever since the middle of the century, scholars, travellers, and statesmen had brought back with increasing frequency from the Italian centers of art new ideas and new forms. English narrative poetry began to look for fresh inspiration in these new models. Equally important, however, as has already been pointed out in previous chapters, was the fact that as she consolidated her hold on England, Elizabeth's policy towards the Puritans gradually hardened. Their views and program in disfavor, all the propaganda of the Puritans was further nullified by the new spirit of paganism which swept over England. Scores of sonnet-sequences, proclaiming a new attitude towards art and morality, simply brushed aside the older, cruder works, and we shall find that after 1590 the popular verse romances never again manifest the same militant didacticism.

The Italian Background

IT WAS ABOUT THE YEAR 1560 THAT, ALONG
with the general revival of letters in England, a new interest
was shown in the *novelle*, which for a long time had formed
part of the popular literature of Italy. The gradual increase in
reading among the masses, perhaps the revived interest in
Chaucer and Lydgate, spurred the curiosity. At any rate, we
find that England begins to translate and imitate Boccaccio
and Bandello, the premier *novellieri* of the Italian Renaissance.
Although these authors were not unknown in England during
the first half of the sixteenth century, it was not until 1620
that a complete English translation of the *Decameron* was
made. In view of the reputation enjoyed by Boccaccio during
the Renaissance, this is very surprising. Yet there are factors
which tend to explain this anomaly. It is interesting to examine
the evidence for this apparent neglect of Boccaccio's major
work.

Willard Farnham, who has investigated the question at
length, has demonstrated fairly conclusively that knowledge of
Boccaccio in England was by no means as widespread as has

been supposed.[1] He minimizes to a large extent the reputed influence of Boccaccio on Chaucer and shows that the salaciousness of the *Decameron* and Boccaccio's own repudiation of this work during his later life would militate against its obtaining a widespread recognition. To this may be added Petrarch's conviction of its insignificance as a lasting work of art because it was written in the vernacular. Such factors, Farnham holds, would hinder a young traveller like Chaucer from hearing about the *Decameron* during his visit to Italy. He is inclined to think that Chaucer actually "missed" the book. In this manner, he explains Chaucer's seemingly incomprehensible failure to mention the work. The first known mention of the *Decameron* in England is in the catalogue of the library of Humphrey, Duke of Glocester who owned, not the Italian original, but a copy of the French translation by Laurent de Premierfait, made in 1414. Farnham points out that Boccaccio's work was evidently unknown even to Lydgate, who was busy translating other works of Boccaccio.[2] Not until late in the sixteenth century was the *Decameron* translated, and even then only in part.

However, certain individual tales were well-known. Even Petrarch retold the tale of Griselda. Its authorship was popularly ascribed to him and it circulated throughout Europe in scores of versions. Other stories were also current, one of the favorites, "Titus and Gesippus," having been translated into Latin as well as English. The tale of Guiscardo and Sismonda,[3] latinized by Leonardo Bruni and Filippo Beroaldo, was also

. . . . .

[1] Willard Farnham, "England's Discovery of the *Decameron*," *PMLA*, XXXIX, (1924), 123ff.

[2] Farnham holds that the misconceptions concerning the importance of Boccaccio to Chaucer and English literature may have arisen from a statement by Sacchetti in his "Proemio" to the *Trecento Novelle*, where he states, in speaking of the *Decameron*, "*che insino in Francia e in Inghilterra l'hanno ridotto alla loro lingua*," a claim which Farnham is inclined to call mere hearsay.

[3] *Decameron*, IV, I.

extremely popular. It became known in England through versions by Gilbert Banester, Master of the Children in the King's Chapel during the last half of the fifteenth century, and through a redaction by William Walter in 1532. But, in spite of these occasional translations of individual *novelle,* Boccaccio was not extensively translated until 1566, when Painter included a good many of the stories from the *Decameron* in his *Palace of Pleasure.* This work was followed the next year by Geoffrey Fenton's *Tragicall Discourses* which tapped a new and rich vein of stories, the collection by Bandello. Hence, it is at this time that Boccaccio and Bandello begin to capture the interest of the Elizabethan translators.

The reasons for this gain in popularity are evident. It must be noted, first of all, that the *novella* as a type did not become popular in England until the sixteenth century, that is to say, until political conditions became settled and the great middle class began its rise. Thus in England, as in Italy almost two centuries before, the *novella,* a typically bourgeois genre, became the favorite of the middle class, beginning for the first time to feel its power and its importance. Another great factor was the tremendous interest in man as a personality, which was perhaps the fundamental belief of the entire Renaissance. Antiquity, of course, was a prized subject; the deeds of the past, the glories of the classical world were eagerly scanned, but along with it went a healthy interest in all human activities and especially in the pursuit of the humanistic "virtù." All Renaissance education was focussed upon training man in this essential quality. Every courtesy book stressed it as the basis of the perfect gentleman. It was the manifestations of this "virtù" which the *novellieri* explored, projecting every angle, investigating every possibility. Thus they appealed to the most varied tastes. And it was this universal appeal of the *novelle* which brought about their tremendous popularity and caused Ascham to record with regret that of these "ungratious bookes many have been set into print within these few months and are now to be found in every shop in London."[4]

Mingled with the powerful interest in man, however, was the English inheritance from the Reformation, the feeling that in man's life there ought to be a discipline, a moral code designed to make him seek writings that would be conducive to honest living and thus shun works which condoned debauchery and licentiousness. William Painter makes this clear when, in the Epistle to the Reader prefixed to his *Palace of Pleasure*, he discusses his choice of stories:

All of which (I truste) be both profitable and plasaunt, and wil be liked of the indifferent reader. Profitable they be, in that they disclose what glorie, honour and preferment eche man attaineth by good desert, what felicitie by honest attempts, what good successe, laudable enterprises do bring to the couragious, what happy joy and quiet state godly love doth affect the imbracers of the same. Profitable, I say, in that they do reveale the miseries of rapes and fleshlie actions, the overthrow of noble men and Princes by disordered government, the tragical ends of them that unhappely do attempt practices vicious and horrible. Wilt thou learn how to behave thyselfe with modestie after thou hast atchieved any victorious conquest and not to forget thy prosperous fortune amyd thy glorious triumphs by committing a facte unworthy of thy valiance: reade the first novel of the fortunate Romane Horatius? Wilt thou understande what dishonour and infamie, desire of libidinous lust doth bring, read the rape of Lucrece. Wilt thou know an unkinde part it is unnaturally to abuse the state of thyne own countrie, read Martius Coriolanus? Wilt thou learn what fruit is reaped of wicked lust to dispoyle virgins and maidens of their greatest virtue, see the historye of Appius Claudius and Sir Didaco, the Spanish knight? Desirest thou to knowe how closely thou oughtest to keepe the secretes of honorable marriage, peruse the hystorie of Candaules? . . . . Is not the merchaunt already contented with his goodes already

. . . . .

[4] Roger Ascham, *The Scholemaster* (London: 1570), Arber's Reprint, I, 78.

gotten, but will needes go seeke some other trade, let him note and consider the daungers wherein the Adventurer Landolpho was . . . . If the poore maiden of base birth be advanced (by fortune's grace) to high estate: let her fixe in mynde the lady of Thurin. Finally for all states and degrees, in these Novelles be sette forthe singular documents and examples, right commodious and profitable to them that will vouchsafe to read them.[5]

Preface after preface offers the same views. In his Epistle Dedicatory to the *Tragicall Tales*, Fenton exhorts his readers to lead righteous lives by following the examples set by the worthies of antiquity. He counsels them to eschew the practices of wicked men. In this wise, through their careful culling of the Italian collections and their weeding out of the more bawdy tales, the translators acted as guardians of the public morality. An examination of Painter's and Fenton's collections, as well as of other *novelle* translated piecemeal at later dates, will show that by far the greater number of them deal with incidents which praise friendship, place love on a lofty plane, exalt womanhood, or deal with acts of pure violence inspired by love. It is striking to observe that these tales scrupulously avoid all mention of love intrigues and vulgar escapades. They have none of the satirical flavor which we associate with Bandello and Boccaccio and which is the essence of their charm for us today. Since most of the Italian tales glorify the wit of women who trick surly, jealous husbands and condone adultery, if conducted discreetly, to conscientious puritans, like Fenton, the inclusion of such stories would only tend to corrupt the English public. Only in rare cases do we find tales of this nature translated or versified, and even then, only in order to illustrate moral truths.

An illustration from the *Palace of Pleasure* will perhaps corroborate these statements. Painter is speaking of his selection of tales from various sources:

. . . . .

[5] William Painter, *The Palace of Pleasure*, ed. Joseph Jacobs (London, 1890), p. 11.

Certaine have I culled out of the "Decamerone" of Giovanni Boccaccio, wherein be conteined one hundred *Novelles,* amonges whiche there be some (in my judgmente) that be worthy to be condemned to perpetual prison, but of them such as I have redeemed to the libertie of our vulgar, as may be best liked, and better suffered. Although the sixt part of the same hundreth may full well be permitted. And as I myself have already done many other of the same, yet for this present I have thought good to publish only tenne in number, the rest I have referred to them that be able with better stile to expresse the author's eloquence, or until I adjoine to this another tome, if none other in the meanetime do prevent me, which with all my heart I wish and desire: because the worke of Boccaccio for his stile, order of writing, gravitie and sententious discourse is worthy of intire promulgation.[6]

From these examples, we may gather the declared purpose of the fictional art of the day; it aims to instruct, at the same time that it delights the reader. But nothing must be included which might jeopardize the morals of the common people. Hence, the reason for avoiding topics that might be considered risqué. Here, perhaps, lies the reason for the lack of a complete translation of the *Decameron.* Morally inclined authors felt that there was in it too much reprehensible material; many of its stories were so licentious that they had better be consigned to oblivion. Consequently, a complete translation of Boccaccio was delayed for half a century, even though England appreciated his motives and his art.

Again, the delay in offering such a complete translation to the English public might have been due to the fact that this would prove to be a large and expensive undertaking. We must consider also the fact that Elizabethan authors might have been unwilling to devote their time to translating single authors. They apparently preferred to compile miscellanies which gave a broad view of the continental *novelle.* Such works were frequent; Painter's, Fenton's collections, Whet-

. . . . .

[6] *Ibid.,* p. 11.

stone's and Turberville's miscellanies were typical. Therefore, the need for a translation of the *Decameron* was met by a large number of translations and versifications of individual tales. These could be supplied quickly and at a very small cost. Since the single incident of the Italian *novella* lent itself admirably to amplification, the original tale was frequently expanded into a verse romance. Based upon situations close to reality and dealing with people from all walks of life, they appealed greatly to the burghers of England. Moreover, their heavy moralization as well as the treatment of the material found great favor with this class of readers.

These verse romances raise other interesting problems. For example, their plots are taken almost exclusively from Boccaccio's and Bandello's tales. Only occasionally is a plot based on an incident from Ariosto. The numerous other collections by Lasca, Cinzio, Sacchetti and Straparola are left untouched. Yet we know that these authors were known and appreciated. Their stories are to be found in many typical prose collections such as H. C.'s *Forrest of Fancy* (1579), H. W.'s *A Courtlie Controversie of Cupid's Cautels* (1578), Humfrey Gifford's *Posie of Gilliflowers,* Barnabe Rich's *Farewell to the Military Profession, The Cobler of Canterbury,* and *Tarlton's Newes.* Although it is possible that these minor versifiers may have known the originals, in general they preferred to draw their materials from other sources, such as Fenton's and Painter's collections or French and Latin versions which may have been more familiar or more accessible to them.

The large number of verse romances produced after 1560 may be separated into five main groups: the tales taken from Boccaccio, those adapted from Bandello, several from Ariosto, a number of tales of native composition, and a final group of pseudo-Greek and Oriental origin and other scattered sources.

x

Verse Romances Translated from Bandello

CURIOUSLY ENOUGH, THE REVIVAL OF INTEREST in the *novelle* begins not with stories from the *Decameron*, but with Arthur Brooke's *The Tragicall History of Romeus and Juliet*, translated from Bandello in 1562. Perhaps no story in literature has received as much attention as the tale of the "star-crossed" lovers. It has travelled to every land; it has been the subject of poet, novelist and playwright until it has become the very symbol of the legend of ill-fated lovers whose love could not surmount adverse circumstances. It begins as a simple account containing only the crude details of tragedy, but as a result of numerous variations, it adds on characters and details, until it emerges full-bodied as the immortal Shakespearian play.

The story of Romeo and Juliet goes back to such obscure beginnings that the passage of time has clothed it with historical fact. It has been accepted as true by reputable historians.[1] Even Dante has immortalized it in *Purgatorio*.[2] The

. . . . .

[1] Alessandro Torri, *Giulietta e Romeo* (Pisa, 1831).
[2] Dante, *Purgatorio* VI, 106ff.
> *Vieni a veder Montecchi e Cappelletti*
> *Monaldi e Filippeschi, nom senza cura!*
> *Color gia tristi, e costor con sospetti.*

113

earliest *novella* containing the important elements of our tale is to be found in Masuccio Salernitano's collection. However, he lays his action in Siena instead of Verona.[3] Matteo Bandello, whose version Arthur Brooke followed, found many of his details in an account by Luigi da Porto, another *novelliere.* Bandello himself introduced the nurse with her worldly advice and easy-going morality. Other characters such as Lorenzo, Count Paris and Pietro, Romeo's servant, appear at this time.

Despite the fact that Brooke entitled his *novella The Tragicall History of Romeus and Juliet, Written First in Italian by Bandell, and now Englished by Ar. Br.,* clearly indicating the origin of his tale, he chose to work from a French version. This was a redaction of Bandello's collection published by Pierre Boisteau in 1559, under the title *Histoires Tragiques, extraictes des Oeuvres Italiennes de Bandel.* Why Brooke chose to work from a French translation, rather than go to what he considered the ultimate source, is perhaps not difficult to guess. The greater accessibility of the French version, published only three years before his own, or possibly his greater familiarity with the French language may account for it. Boisteau saw fit to advise his readers that he had departed from Bandello's style, since he considered it meagre and ill-chosen. He expanded several suggestions found in Bandello, such as the scene at the apothecary's and the incidents at Juliet's tomb.

Brooke's verse tale can hardly lay claim to great literary distinction. However, he termed it the "eldest whelp" of his Muse and alluded diffidently to other works, "unlicked as yet," which, for the time being, he preferred to keep in obscurity. He followed Boisteau closely, adding nothing original to the action. The poem bears all the characteristics of its age. Its young lovers are stock figures of Elizabethan literature. At the beginning of the poem, Romeus is revealed as the conventional lovelorn youth, mournfully pursuing his obdurate mistress. The latter might be any one of the ladies in the Petrarchistic

. . . . .

[3] Masuccio Salernitano, *Cinquanta Novelle* (Napoli, 1476), tale 33.

sonnet sequences, for the more fervent he waxes, the colder she becomes. His friends give him sound advice:

> But if unto thy will so much in thrall thou art,
> Yet in some other place bestow thy witless, wandring heart.[4]

Accepting this advice half-heartedly, Romeus goes to the Capulet's feast, there to find his true love in Juliet.

Brooke portrays the emotions of his young lovers so minutely that he often courts tediousness. Deeply shocked by Juliet's revelation that she is a Capulet, Romeus wastes his days bemoaning his fate. Juliet, too, is plunged into despair upon learning his identity. The author describes her anguish, her wavering between love and loyalty to her family, her self-reproach for having allowed this love to overpower her. She subjects her passion to a detailed examination and, as in a modern analytical novel, she is torn by the struggle between conflicting emotions. At times, the lovesick girl suspects Romeo's declaration to be motivated only by his desire for revenge upon her and her family. She remembers Dido and all the

> Thousand stories more, to teach me to beware,
> Which in Boccace and in Ovid's book too plainly written are.[5]

Then, her heart regaining sway over her mind, she feels sure that his love for her is true and that through this love, the feud between the two families will be composed. This is sublime irony, which, however, under the inexpert hand of Brooke misses fire.

Taken by and large, Juliet and the other women in the poem are portrayed far more ably than the men. Juliet emerges as somewhat of a minx who, despite her youthfulness, knows exactly what she wants. She has a fine power of logic and none of her nurse's earthy comments are lost upon her. Child of the

. . . . .

[4] Arthur Brooke, *The Tragicall Historie of Romeus and Juliet*, ed. J. J. Munroe (New York, 1908), lines 131-32.
[5] *Ibid.*, lines 394-95.

Renaissance, she becomes a ready pupil in the art of Venus, revealing herself a lusty young woman, with none of that poetic delicacy characteristic of Shakespeare's younger heroine. Even in breathless moments of love, she finds time to lecture Romeus on his intentions:

> For if you do intend my honor to defile,
> In error shall you wander still, as you have done this while;
> But if your thought be chaste, and have on virtue ground,
> If wedlock be the end which your desire hath found,
> Obedience set aside, unto my parents due,
> That quarrel eke that long ago between our households grew,
> Both me and mine I will all whole to you betake,
> And following you whereso you go, my father's house forsake.[6]

She laughs at deceiving her mother and so as to gain time, following her lover's banishment, she wilfully leads Paris on in his suit for a number of days. Eager to share Romeus' exile, the uneasy maiden pleads to be taken with him, disguised as his man, if needs be. When he hesitates, she stings him with a sharp: "art thou counsel-less?," "canst thou shift no device?." In spite of her complete love, Juliet's hot blood flares up when she hears of Tybalt's slaying. Bitterly she reproaches Romeus for having broken the peace, for having taken the life of her beloved kinsman. If he so thirsted after the Capulets' blood, why did he spare her? Why did he not shed hers first? Then struck by repentance, she forgets that she is a medieval Italian girl, forgets her loyalty to her family and kinsmen. She becomes again the eternal woman. For, having reasserted her love for Romeus, having reassured herself of his innocence— she faints.

Both Juliet's mother and the nurse in their attitude towards the world and their practical handling of the girl also reveal themselves as creatures of flesh and blood, much more real than the male characters. The nurse, especially, shows a cynicism worthy of Pandarus. When her beloved Juliet complains

. . . . .

[6] *Ibid.*, lines 533ff.

of her prospective marriage to Paris, she suggests very cheerfully that Juliet is indeed fortunate to have as a husband Paris, who is wealthy and noble, while she can always retain Romeus as her lover.

Despite these realistic touches, there is in *Romeus and Juliet* an inherent quality of sentimentality, reminiscent of secondrate melodrama. Its characters are too suddenly swept up by their emotions from the depths of despair to the pinnacles of joy. They lack a fine balance; they lack a certain human quality which turns creations of the mind into real creatures of flesh and blood and moves us by its very kinship to our own emotions. Even more than its poetic immaturity, this deficiency detracts from the poem as an artistic creation. But writing in the year 1562, Brooke suffered from a lack of precedents; he did not have the brilliant models available to poets of later decades. As a result, his work suffers from certain faults that are characteristic of the time. Although Brooke occasionally displayed latent ability, he frequently stifled his verse with tiresome repetitions, tedious soliloquies and a profusion of details. For a certainty, he overlooked the virtue of selectivity.

In view of the quality of abandon which is inherent in the tale, the manifest moralizing approach which Brooke takes towards the theme is interesting. He may be merely seeking justification for writing the poem when he says:

Though I sawe the same argument lately set forth upon the stage with more commendation than I can look for—being there much better set forth than I have, or can do—yet the same matter penned as it is, may serve to like good effect.[7]

Still, his Address to the Reader rings with an obviously sententious note. He says:

The glorious triumph of the continent man upon the lusts of wanton flesh, encourageth men to honest restraint of wild affections; the shameful and wretched ends of such as have yielded

. . . . .

[7] *Ibid.,* lxvi.

their liberty thrall to foul desires teach men to withhold themselves from the headlong fall of loose dishonesty. So to like effect, by sundry means the good man's example biddeth men to be good, and the evil man's mischief warneth men not to be evil. To this good end serve all ill ends of ill beginnings. And to this end, good Reader, is this tragicall matter written, to describe unto thee a couple of unfortunate lovers, thralling themselves to unhonest desire; neglecting the authority and advice of parents and friends; conferring their principal counsels with drunken gossips and superstitious friars (the naturally fit instruments of unchastity) attempting all adventures of peril for th'attaining of their wished lust; using auricular confession, the key of whoredome and treason, for furtherance of their purpose; abusing the honorable name of lawful marriage to cloak the shame of stolen contracts; finally by all means of unhonest life hasting to most unhappy death.[8]

If these were Brooke's true sentiments, then he had hardly a romantic conception of one of the great love stories of the world; it was a harsh, unsympathetic view of the tragic end of a pair of "star-crossed" lovers.

This puritanical approach is evident throughout the entire poem. We meet it repeatedly in the obvious sententiousness which the author frequently spouts. It may be seen again and again, as in Juliet's careful determination of Romeus' intentions before she will accede to his desires. Nevertheless, the beliefs stated in the Preface are not difficult to explain in view of the Puritan activities during this period. It is obvious that Brooke is catering to the public taste which exacted a full measure of didacticism from all works of fiction. At the same time, he vents his enmity towards Popery, perceiving in the actions of the friar an opportunity to attack the hated Roman church. As will be evident in all the subsequent tales, the moralizing protrudes in the strangest places and at the strangest times. The heroine never loses a chance to lecture her youth. Authors are constantly wagging a finger in admonition

. . . . .

[8] *Ibid.*, lxv.

to the reader, bidding him pursue the paths of righteousness, sobriety, and thrift. Despite all this didacticism, however, the paganism of the Renaissance in England became too marked in subsequent decades to let such views color too strongly the story of Romeo and Juliet. Neither in this poem nor in the succeeding versions of it can the moralizing cloud the beauty of the tale. Certainly it did not mar Shakespeare's treatment of it, for the dramatist took from Brooke only the pure gold, leaving the dross behind, fashioning for the world a new and more spiritual conception of this unfortunate pair of lovers.

The Most Notable Historie of John, Lord of Mandosse, written by Thomas de la Peend in 1565, had no such distinguished literary connections. Although its title tells us that it was "translated" from the Spanish, it bears the closest resemblance to one of Bandello's tales.[9] Like most of the versifications of Italian novelle, it is one of the "proper" tales, designed not to shock the reading public, for the love intrigue between Don John and the Duchess of Piedmont is carried on in the most decorous fashion.

The Duchess has fallen in love with Don John upon listening to his sister's extravagant praises of his prowess. After feigning illness, the Duchess goes on a pilgrimage to St. James of Compostella, where she contrives to meet the Duke. However, their happiness is halted by the arrival of the husband who takes the lady home. Left alone by her husband during one of his campaigns, she repulses the advances of a loathsome steward. Yearning for revenge, the latter dupes his young nephew into entering the lady's chamber; then he surprises the two and runs a rapier through the youth's body. Accused of adultery, the lady faces death, until Don John comes disguised to her rescue, gives her accuser the lie, and slays him. But their troubles are not over, for he must return to rescue his besieged city. They meet again and are finally reunited in

. . . . .

[9] Bandello, II, 44. The tale is also found in Painter's Palace of Pleasure, I, 45.

England, where, upon the demise of her husband, she has returned to the court of her brother. She recognizes Don John by means of a ring which she had given him after he championed her cause.

The story follows closely Painter's version, with many interpolations and expansions. Crude attempts to introduce dialogue relieve in part the monotony of the poem, but long harangues are too frequent. The name of the Duchess's confidante is incomprehensibly changed from Giulia to Emilie. Some measure of popularity must have been gained from the introduction of the English element because the author dwells at length upon the voyages to the English court. Following the common procedure of extolling the happiness of England, in contrast to the turbulence in other European countries, Peend often lingers to praise:

> The happy Ile in Ocean wyde
> Whose sacred soyle doth bringe,
> In feilde such valiant men,
> And doth with plenty greate,
> Increase all things which may for them
> In any wise be meate.[10]

The poem is, in general, a straightforward narrative, offering little of the moralization to be found in most of the verse romances of this period. It is perhaps the only distinguishing quality of a very pedestrian piece.

Utilizing the various versions of Bandello's tale, which he found in Painter and Fenton, John God[11] brought forth in 1569 a metrical tale entitled *A Discourse of the Great Crueltie of a Widow: Towardes a Gentleman and by What Means He*

. . . . .

10 Thomas Peend, *The Most Notable Historie of John, Lord of Mandosse,* Sig. B7ᵛ

11 The author is John God and not "Gobourne" as Miss Scott claims in her *Elizabethan Translations from the Italian,* p. 232, for in the Epistle to the Reader, he signs himself in an anagram as "Ioannes Goddus."

Requited the Same. Although the author did not state where he borrowed the tale, familiar to us as the story of Filiberto and Zilia (Bandello III, 17), he made little attempt to disguise his sources. The account of the cruelty of the widow Zilia unfolds very much in the same manner as in his original:

> Within the reach of Europe land, a pleasant soyle there is,
> Which Thurin hight, a cittie fair abounding in great blisse,
> Whose pastors green Euridanus doth moysten with his Poole.[12]

Here dwells the fair widow, Zilia, who, after her husband's death, has become a miserly recluse. She scorns the honest love of Filiberto, a valiant and well-favored gentleman, heeding neither his pleas nor those of her friends in his behalf. Finally, upon condition that he will fulfill any request whatsoever from her, she yields him a kiss. The gentleman is then informed that he will have to remain silent for three years. True to his word, although stunned and disgusted by her treachery, he leaves for France, where he distinguishes himself under the banner of the king of France and for his valor is made chamberlain. So great is the love that the king bears him that he offers a large sum to anyone who will cure him of his affliction. Hearing of the great reward, Zilia's cupidity is aroused; and she journeys to France, confident that his love for her will make him speak. But Filiberto has been cured by her unreasonable cruelty; therefore, though she yields fully to his pleasure, she is unable to make him utter a word. In the end, the courteous knight saves her head by relating the strange story to the king who dispatches her back to her country, a much chastened woman.

In this version, John God altered somewhat Zilia's characterization, by painting her even blacker than she originally was. In Bandello, she is a woman bent upon conserving her estate for a small son and, for that reason, she shuns the usual

. . . . .

[12] John God, *A Discourse of the Great Crueltie of a Widow*, Sig. A5ʳ.

pastimes and becomes a recluse. Her insistence upon Filiberto's silence is in reality intended to determine whether his vows of love are as fervent as he avers. John God, on the other hand, begins in this vein but gradually turns Zilia into a fiendish creature who revels in her lover's misery and who, through sheer malice, traps him into his vow. He also heightens her cupidity.

Our author makes several attempts to improve on his models. He tries to hold interest by manipulating the various threads of the action simultaneously. He refines certain details; for example, when Filiberto first sees Zilia, he is so rapt by her beauty and so unaware of the passing of time that he is certain that the priest has hurried with the Mass. When Zilia first reads his letter, it bears a tone so sincere that for a moment she is caught off guard and almost yields to the tender sentiments which it has evoked. But she quickly regains mastery over herself, taking refuge in her insurmountable aloofness. There are other like touches, but they are offset by more serious faults.

The action of the tale is wholly motivated by the granting of the kiss and the penance demanded by the implacable Zilia. At the very beginning of his account, Bandello states that it is the custom of the country for ladies to kiss their guests when they come to visit them. John God, however, makes no mention of this important point which really heightens the triviality of the act and increases the discrepancy between the kiss and the payment demanded for it. The author spends much time on long protestations and in tedious descriptions of the woe caused to Filiberto by Zilia's harshness. The course of the story is further slowed by the numerous allusions to figures of legendary history, material which is found neither in Fenton nor in Painter. True to the convention of the day, God adds, whenever convenient, sententious allusions and generous chunks of moralization. In general, he seems to have preferred making use of Painter's version. The language and phrasing constantly remind us of this version, and in some places we

have actual word for word copying. An example is the letter
which Filiberto sends to Zilia; it begins:

> The roaring tempest huge which thou hast made me felt,
> The raging stormes whereof well neere my heart hath swelt.[13]

The entire sixty-three lines of the letter are copied word for
word from Painter's *novella*, the only changes being such as
are necessitated by metrical requirements.[14]

Although George Whetstone's *The Rocke of Regarde* (1576)
is considered to be mainly a prose work, it contains several
metrical pieces which come within our scope. These illustrate
once more the didactic and middle class nature of this genre,
already demonstrated by preceding poems. In Part I, "The
Castle of Delight," appears "The Disordered Life of Bianca
Maria, Countess of Celaunt."[15] The account, drawn from
Bandello's *novella* (I,4), is a typical tale of blood and excesses.
While the unspeakable Countess recounts her long list of
crimes, we find the author indulging in long homilies on pride,
the cause of her downfall. We follow the miserable career of
the young woman who marries the Count of Celiano merely
to attain social position. Not satisfied with this success, she
revels in the number of suitors who flock about her. Lover after
lover is jilted, the discarded paramours being conveniently
murdered by their successors. Finally, called to account for her
misdeeds, she is beheaded.[16]

. . . . .

[13] *Ibid.*, Sig. D5ʳ.
[14] Other versions of this popular tale as listed by Miss Scott in her
Elizabethan Translations, p. 232, are: *Westward for Smelts*, No. 6;
The Fishwife's Tale of Hampton; Gervase Markham's and Lewis
Machin's play, *The Dumb Knight*; and *The Queen or the Excellency
of her Sex*, Anon.
[15] This poem possesses many of the characteristics of the *mirror*. For
a discussion see *ante* p. 91.
[16] The story was a favorite one in England, having been translated by
Painter in *The Palace of Pleasure* (II, 24), by Geoffrey Fenton in
Certain Tragicall Discourses (VII), again in prose by Whetstone in his
Heptameron (1582). It also furnished the plot for Marston's *The
Insatiate Countess* (1613).

Another verse tale in this collection containing obvious variation on the Penelope theme also comes from Bandello. This is
"The Complainte of Lorde Alberto and Udissas, the two
Hungarian Barons That Unadvisedly Wagered Their Lands
to Winne the Lady Barbara to Wantonnesse: Who Having
the Foyle (Besyde the Losse of their Livings) for Their Slaun-
derous Opinions Were Condemned to Perpetuall Exile." This
condensation of Bandello's *novella* (I,21) combines the verse
romances with the *complaint*. Despite the limitations of space,
Whetstone retains the main events of the story.

> The nuptiall fest yfinished, Ulrico with his dame,
> Bids friends adewe, to castle his, they do their journey
> frame.[17]

After a brief sojourn with his wife, Ulrico is forced to go to
King Corvinus' court to seek his fortune. During an argument,
the two recreant lords wager their lands, confident that they
can conquer the virtue of his wife within two months. After
failing miserably in his attempt to seduce the faithful Barbara,
Alberto is imprisoned by her and set to spinning. Udissas also
fails and is made to reel yarn for his companion. They are discovered, banished, and obliged to forfeit their lands to Ulrico.
In "The Barons' Complaint," which follows this tale, Whetstone moralizes about the misdeeds of the pair, pointing to
their disgrace and to the menial tasks they are made to perform as a result of their uncouth action.

Whetstone's tales have an unmistakable bourgeois tone. His
characters are forever indulging in conversations of a practical
nature, typical of the circumscribed lives of petty country
gentlemen. Whetstone dwells on their daily occupations; he
shows wives eager to share the troubles of their husbands. The
attempt to glorify chastity and his healthy concern with the ac-
quisition of worldly goods are also constantly evident. The
disillusioned ex-soldier often creeps into his verse with ad-

. . . . .

[17] George Whetstone, *The Rocke of Regarde*, p. 151.

monitions against dicing, tavern-keepers and tailors. He voices aloud his bitter complaints against the court and the lack of reward given to soldiers for their heroic performances.

One may perceive, too, certain variations from Bandello's story, indicating that Whetstone either translated from memory or in hurried fashion. They are slight differences, such as calling the necromancer who assures Ulrico that his wife will be faithful, Pollacco; whereas Bandello merely alludes to him as "*un vegliardo Pollacco.*"

Another of Bandello's tales of violence reached the English public through Thomas Achelley's verse romance, *A Most Lamentable and Tragicall Historie, Conteyning the Outrageous and Horrible Tyrannie Which a Spanish Gentlewoman Named Violenta Executed Upon her Lover Didaco* (1576). However, the poet did not go straight to Bandello for his model; instead, he preferred to use Painter's version, retaining several of the variations from the original introduced by the author of the *Palace of Pleasure.* The tale begins:

Where Phoebus foming steedes their restless race doo ende,
And leaving our Horizon to th'Antipodes doo wende,
Right there dooth lye a famous soyle, whose farthest bounds of land,
Environed with the brinish floods of Ocean doo stand.[18]

Didaco, a noble Spaniard, the most valiant knight in Valencia, falls violently in love with Violenta, the daughter of a family of goldsmiths. Unable to win her through gifts, he marries her, asking, however, that the marriage be kept secret to avoid his family's displeasure. After a year, he tires of her and with great pomp weds a great lady. A true Spaniard, Violenta vows to be revenged. She succeeds in persuading Didaco to come to her, an easy task, since he is eager to explain his conduct. He tries to convince her that his other marriage was forced upon him by his relatives and that he will murder his other

. . . . .

[18] Thomas Achelley, *The Tragicall Historie of Didaco and Violenta,* lines 1 ff.

wife at some convenient moment. But Violenta is not swayed in her resolve. While he is asleep, her maid, Janique, fastens him securely, and the two women butcher him mercilessly with two chopping knives.[19] The body is then thrown into the street. Upon being arraigned, Violenta makes no secret of her bloody revenge, the highest duty of a Spaniard. Despite the extenuating circumstances, she is condemned to death. Following a variation introduced by Painter, Janique is made to escape to Morocco, instead of sharing the fate of her mistress.

Achelley revels in the brutality of the tale, dwelling at length on the butcherly details of the murder. His moralizing is typical of the genre. He does not show any concern for the betrayed woman or for the justification which might be offered for her actions. Ethical considerations leave Achelley unmoved. On the other hand, the poet stresses the fact that the tragedy was brought about by those senseless persons who allowed themselves to be overcome by blind passion. For, he adds, "in love nought is but vayne," a sentiment which is quite in keeping with the moralizing function of the verse romances. With all its deficiencies, however, Achelley's poem shows a smoothness and variety of verse which is quite unusual for the verse tales.

Bandello also served as a source for two of Turberville's *Tragical Tales*, which exploit episodes of violence so popular in Elizabethan literature. One of these offers the familiar story of the revenge taken by Rosamund, Queen of the Lombards, over the barbarous King Alboin, who forced her to drink out of a cup fashioned from the skull of her father. The story had wide diffusion in England, for, besides being found in *The Palace of Pleasure* (I,57), it furnished plots for several plays.[20]

· · · · ·

[19] One is forced to consider if the change in her name from Violante in the original to Violenta (the violent one) is after all a printer's mistake.

[20] Davenant's *Albovine, King of the Lombards*, Middleton's *The Witch*, and in the nineteenth century, Swinburne's *Rosamund, Queen of the Lombards*.

The second tale describes the revenge which the Eliensi took upon Aristotimus, tyrant of Macedon. It is one of the least known of Bandello's stories. In fact, doubt has been raised whether the author took this tale from Bandello, for proof has been advanced that Turberville may have found his source in another Italian collection of the time.[21]

During the last quarter of the sixteenth century, the tale of Diego and Ginevra,[22] appearing in both Painter's and Fenton's collections, was a great favorite. It was translated quite early by Whetstone in *The Rocke of Regarde* (1576) in conjunction with this author's general complaint against the court and the world's thanklessness. Complaining that his erstwhile "sugred voice forbids me now to sing," Whetstone cursed fate, love and the world in general. The author evidently wished to illustrate his own black mood through this tale of wantonness and female perfidy. Therefore, in order to suit his purpose, our versifier changed the original plot of the story in which Ginevra brings down her vengeance upon her poor lover. Instead of ascribing her behavior to jealousy, he attributed her sudden change to sheer wantonness. Not all the poem is in fourteeners, for part of it is in prose. Whetstone also makes use of a stanzaic form, soon to be encountered frequently, the sizain.

If there is little in Whetstone's poem to distinguish it from the dozen other *complaints* and little verse tales in his collection, it is a different matter when we come to Richard Linche's version, written some twenty years later as an appendage to *Diella*, a collection of sonnets. *The Amorous Poem of Dom Diego and Ginevra* (1596) is a finished piece, endowed with the grace and the refinements of verse typical of the sonnets of the time. In certain respects, this poem is almost a sequel to the sonnet sequence, since it recounts the tale of love, crossed

. . . . .

[21] The problem is discussed by Rene Pruvost in "The Source of George Turberville's *Tragicall Tales*." RES, X (1934), 29ff.
[22] Bandello, I, 27.

by apparently insurmountable obstacles, nevertheless, triumphant in the end. It begins:

> In Catalonia o'erpeered by Pyren mountains
> (A province seated in the East of Spain,
> Famous for hunting sports and clearest fountains,)
> A young heroic Gallant did remain:
> He Signior Dom Diego had to name
> Who for his constant faith had got such fame.[23]

Having lost his way during a hunt, this young Adonis finds a haven in the castle of Ginevra the Blonde, one of the fairest maidens in all Spain. The two young people carry on a conversation with their eyes, impeded not a whit by her mother, who approves of the very eligible youth. After a whirlwind courtship, the lovers are separated when,

> The gloomy curtains of the tongueless night
> Were drawn so close as day could not be seen.[24]

The romance proceeds apace; Diego becomes the accepted suitor, until one of her rejected suitors goes to Ginevra bearing a false tale. Diego is mocking her and has received as favor from another mistress a very beautiful hawk, of which he is inordinately proud. Ginevra immediately gives way to frantic jealousy. Her insane emotion blinds her to her lover's just complaints; she refuses to see him or to listen to his explanations. Even when he slays the offending hawk and sends her its head, she does not relent. At this fresh mark of cruelty, the unfortunate Diego takes to the woods where he gives utterance to his extravagant laments. It is only two years later that matters are righted. Hearing of Diego's plight, one of his friends goes to Ginevra, convinces her of her lover's constancy and succeeds in reuniting the estranged pair.

Thus the lesson which the author promised to rehearse for the benefit of his flint-hearted mistress is brought to a happy

. . . . .

[23] Richard Linche, *Dom Diego and Ginevra,* stanza 1 ff.
[24] *Ibid.,* stanza 20.

conclusion. Here Diella may see for herself that not all mistresses are obdurate, that even this Spanish maiden relented, restoring Diego to her good graces when she realized that his love was constant and true. The definite connection between the sonnets in *Diella* and the verse tale holds for us a measure of interest. Departing from the usual procedure in such works,[25] Linche tried to link the two poetic compositions by making the verse romance a sequel to his unfortunate love affair narrated in the sonnets. At first, we are shown the poet so weary of long serving his heartless lady that he has even contemplated going into exile. His life is dreary, for there is no hell as black as her disdain. The sequence ends in an unhappy key, and in the final poem he bids Diella:

> Hearken awhile Diella to a storie
> that tells of beautie, love and great disdaine,
> the last, caused by suspect, but she was sorry,
> For when she knew his faith to be unfained,
> Spotless, sincere, most true and pure unto her,
> She joyed as if a kingdom she had gained
> and loved him now as when he at first did woo her.
> I nere incur'd suspition of my truth,
> (fairest Diella) why wilt thou be cruell?
> impose some end to undeserved ruth,
> and learne by others how to quench hates fuell.
> Read all, my Deare, but chiefly marke the end
> and be to me, as she to him, a friend.[26]

Throughout the entire poem, the hand of the sonneteer is apparent. The exuberant descriptions, the piling up of conceits are all reminiscent of its companion piece, *Diella*. The extravagance of the joy and sorrow are typical of the sonnets. Linche describes the grief of the youth:

> Thus in these speeches would Diego sit,
> Bathing his silver cheekes with trickling tear;

. . . . .

25 For a discussion of this question see *ante* p. 70.
26 Linche, *Diella*, Sonnet XXXIX.

Which, often running down, at last found fit
Channels to send them to their standing meres.
Who at his feet (before his feet there stood
A pool of tears) received the smaller flood.[27]

The exuberance of the Renaissance, as well as his love of color
and display, mark the poet's verse; inevitably we are reminded
of Marlowe and of Drayton, as he describes Diego:

Clothed all in green, Sylvanus' livery,
He wore a low-crowned hat of finest silk,
Whose brim, turned up was fastened with a ruby,
And underneath a pearl as white as milke;
A sleeveless coat of damaske richly laced
With Indian pearl as thick as could be placed.

A glistering cutlass pendent by his side,
(He much esteemed that beast-dismembering blade;)
And half-legged buskins curiously tied
With loops of burnished gold full finely made:
Thus goes Diego, chiefest of his name,
With silver-headed spear to find some game.[28]

The entire poem has the facility of the sonnet sequences; it
marks a great advance upon the earlier versions of the tale, but
it has all the faults that can be imputed to the Petrarchists.
In narrative technique, it neither improves on its models nor
falls from the standard they set; for, if it lacks motivation and
character development, it is a failing which it shares with most
of the other narrative verse of the time. Its emphasis upon
artistic finish may be expected from a poem produced in the
nineties. As is to be expected, there is also a definite departure
from the heavy moralization to be found in Brooke's and
Whetstone's tales. No longer does the bourgeois tone of didacticism impinge upon the story. As will be seen again and again,
puritanism gives way to the pagan feeling of the end of the
century.

. . . . .

[27] Linche, *Dom Diego and Ginevra*, stanza 96.
[28] *Ibid.*, stanza 12ff.

Verse Romances Adapted
from Boccaccio

To BOCCACCIO, AS THE RECOGNIZED MASTER OF
the *novella*, the versifiers of this period turned with regular
frequency for inspiration and material for their tales. As has
already been pointed out, Puritan authors objected in no un-
certain fashion to some of the spicy humor to be found in the
Florentine; consequently, it is not surprising that the borrowings from Boccaccio are not so heavy as those from Bandello.
Many of the more decorous tales, however, were turned into
verse romances for the greater enhancement of Elizabethan
morals.

The tales of friendship, especially, were held in great esteem.
This theme engrossed many of the writers of the Renaissance,
for the virtue of friendship was regarded as one of the basic
requirements in the education of the complete gentleman. Boccaccio's story of Titus and Gesippus (*Decameron* X,8) had
already been translated several times during the sixteenth
century. A prose version of it was included in Sir Thomas
Elyot's *The Boke of the Governour* (1531), used by the great
courtier and educator to illustrate the perfect friendship be-

tween two men.[1] A year later, William Walter, who had versified other tales of Boccaccio, brought forth a metrical version
of the novella, *The History of Titus and Gesippus Translated
out of Latin into Englyshe.* Walter followed the Latin version
of this romance by Matteo Bandello, adhering quite faithfully
to his source.

This popular tale appeared again in metrical form as *The
Most Wonderful and Pleasant History of Titus and Gesippus,
Whereby Is Fully Declared the Figure of Perfect Friendship
Drawen into English Meter by Edward Lewicke, Anno 1562.*
This author makes little effort to disguise his source, admitting
from the outset that his work is merely a metrical paraphrase
of Elyot's version of the tale. His very first words:

> There was in the city of Rome
> A noble man hight Fulvius;
> A Senatour of great Wisdome,
> One of the chiefest, the truth is thus.
> He had a sonne named Titus,
> An apter child could not be found
> (As witty men did there discus)
> For learning going on the ground,[2]

are practically a versification of Elyot's:

> There was in the city of Rome a noble Senatour who sent his
> sone called Titus, being a child, to the cittie of Athens in Greece.

Throughout the poem, Lewicke follows Elyot's text faithfully;
the friendship of the two youths, the love intrigue, the final
surrender of Sophronia by Gesippus to his friend, the subsequent meeting in Rome, all being duly versified.

· · · · ·

[1] It has been long believed that the immediate source of Elyot's *novella*
was a Latin translation made by Philip Beroaldus about 1495. For a discussion of the subject, see H. H. S. Croft's edition of *The Boke Called
the Governour.* See also C. T. Goode's "Thomas Elyot's *Titus and
Gesippus,*" *MLN*, XXXVII (1922), 1ff.

[2] J. P. Collier, *The Poetical Decameron*, p. 77.

Occasionally Lewicke takes liberties with his source. Indulging in the favorite practice of the metrical versifiers, he inserts explanatory passages or moralizes upon the events. Thus, after Titus has passed by him without recognizing him, Gesippus departs heart sore:

> There in a sorie simple state
> Gysippus, thence away did trudge,
> Cursing his chance infortunate,
> Oh Lord, thought he, what man would judge
> Titus to have been such a snudge
> From whom I suffer all this smart?
> Gysippus thus at him did grudge
> Thinking forever to depart.[3]

Gesippus is determined to wander to the desert where he will exist as a wild beast. But having taken refuge in an old barn,

> Where he falling flat on the ground,
> Drew out his knife and thought it best
> To give himself a deadly wounde.

> But wisdome did his wil so drounde
> That from that acte into a sounde
> Or (as God woulde as he did slepe)
> Into a sad and slumbring sleepe:
> His knife, wherewith he would have slain
> Himself down by his side did stepe.
> In the meantime a thefe certain,

> Which was a commen ruffian playne
> And had both robbed and slaine a man
> Thought in that barn for to remaine
> To hide himself that night; but whan
> He sawe a wretche bewept wan,
> On slep and a knife by his side,
> He tooke the knife and quietly than
> Towards the dead man he did glide.[4]

. . . . .

[3] *Ibid.*, p. 79   [4] *Ibid.*, p. 81.

Compare this with Elyot's text:

And therewith drewe his knyfe, purposing to have slaine himselfe. But ever wysedome (which he by the studie of Philosophie
had attained) withdrewe hym from that desperate acte. And in
this contention between wisdome and wille, fatigate with longe
journeyes and watche, or as god would have it, he fell in to a dead
sleepe, His knyfe (wherewith he would have slayne himselfe)
fallynge down by hym. In the meane tyme a commun and notable
ruffian or thefe, whyche had robbed and slayne a man, was entred
into the barne where Gysippus laye, to the intente to sojourne
there all that night. And seeying Gysippus bewept and his visage
replenished with sorowe and also the naked knyfe by him, per-
ceyved well that he was a man desperate and supprised with
heavyness of heart was wery of his life. Whych the said rufian
taking for a good occasion to escape, toke the knyfe of Gysippus
and puttinge it in the wounde of him that was slayne, put it all
bloody in the hand of Gysippus, being fast asleepe and so departed.[5]

It seems hardly necessary to quote more extensively in order
to demonstrate the close resemblance between the two stories,
for it seems obvious that Elyot's story, rather than the Decameron, furnished the source for Lewicke's romance. Little
need be said concerning the poetic merits of the new version.
It is inferior even to Brooke's *Romeus and Juliet*, yet along
with this better known poem, it marks the movement towards
the Italian *novelle* as a mine for English narrative plots.

Another imitation of Elyot's account, which has not been
heretofore pointed out, appeared in 1574. We may assume for
it an earlier date, however, since it was entered in the Stationers' Register in 1566-67 under the title: *The Notable History
of Two Faithful Lovers Named Alfagus and Archelaus,
Wherein is Declared The True Figure of Amitie and Friendship. Much Pleasante and Delectable to the Reader. Translated into English Meetre by Edward Ienynges.* Despite the

. . . . .

[5] Elyot, *op. cit.*, II, 156-7.

author's assertion that he "translated," we need not read far into the tale to perceive its slavish adherence to Elyot's text. In his Preface, Jenynges imitates the example of his predecessor and, following Aristotle, terms friendship a very noble virtue, declaring it to be far better than silver and gold. The tale begins:

In Rome sumtyme a knyghte dyd dwell
Both noble, wise and good,
His stocke of auncient Romayne were
And not of Rascall blood.[6]

This sets the theme and gives a fair inkling of what to expect. Jenynges changes the names of his personages. The Roman youth is turned into Alfagus, while his father becomes Lypodus. Anxious to complete the education of his talented son, the old man, instead of sending him to Athens, sends him to Carthage, a city which is said to be a center of learning. In the African city, the boy soon becomes friendly with Archelaus, son of Olympus, and the two inseparable companions are so much alike that no one can tell them apart. Both are handsome and accomplished, famed throughout Carthage for their learning and wisdom.

In this version, too, upon the death of his father, Archelaus is urged by his friends to marry. Despite his wish to study Philosophy, for their sake he agrees. The plot unfolds in the usual manner. Taken to see his friend's future wife, Alfagus falls in love with her. He finally confesses to Archelaus, who has already guessed the nature of his friend's woes. Seized by pity for his unhappy friend, Archelaus immediately renounces his claims and proposes the familiar ruse of substituting persons during the wedding day. Everything goes off as scheduled; then on the following morning, exactly as Elyot describes it, the two friends reveal their stratagem to the Carthaginians who have to accept the *fait accompli*.

. . . . .

[6] Edward Jenynges, *The Notable History of Two Faithful Lovers*, Sig. B1ʳ.

The similarity of the two versions is striking, since Jenynges follows Elyot even more completely than does Lewicke. He divides his story into ten "fyttes," but copies the language of the older version. His amplifications are mere padding and add nothing to the plot. The poet strives constantly for realistic touches, such as stressing the likeness of the two youths as a means of later recognition. However, he nullifies his efforts by his verbosity and needless repetition of incidents. For example, though he narrates the events as they occurred in the cave when the murderer placed the weapon in Archelaus's hands, the entire story is again retold in court, practically word for word. Certainly Jenynges displays none of the vigor and incisiveness of Boccaccio. Again, the oration made by the two youths to the Carthaginians the morning following the wedding is identical with Elyot's. The same phrasing is used; the same arguments are repeated. In both speeches we find Alfagus's bold statement that, far from blaming his friend, the Carthaginians should erect a golden statue to Archelaus and place it in their largest square as a momento of a great friendship. In both versions there is the quiet but significant reminder to the Carthaginians of the invincible power of Rome. Still more convincing is the fact that in several places where Jenynges should be alluding to Carthage and the Carthaginians, he copies the text so closely that he forgets his locale and uses Elyot's "Athens" and "Grecians," instead. Could further proof be needed? What reasons may explain this dissimulation? It may have been the desire to tell an old story with new characters, under a new guise. Perhaps it was Jenynges' wish to make it appear a translation and gain readers through the appeal to a popular medium.

Another of the acceptable plots taken from Boccaccio appeared in 1569 as *A Notable History of Nastagio and Traversari, No Less Pitiful than Pleasaunt, Translated out of Italian into English verse by C. T.* This is the familiar tale in the *Decameron* (I,8), relating the method employed by Nastagio in reducing to submissiveness his intractable mistress. For a long time, neither his pleas nor her family's wishes can sway the wilful girl. Having wandered off by himself towards a ravine, Nastagio witnesses a spectacle that well-nigh makes his blood curdle, but at the same time proves very instructive. It is the scene of the spectre huntsman who chases a naked girl through the woodland and, having captured her, rips her body apart and feeds her heart to his mastiffs. C. T. describes the pursuit of the spectre knight:

> He sawe approache with swiftie foote the place where he
> did staye,
> A dame with scattred heares untrussed, bereft of her araye.
> Besides all this, two mastiffes great, both fierce and full he saw,
> That fiercely pinchde her by the flanke with greedily ravening
> rawe.
> And eke a knight, of colour swarthe, he sawe behind her
> backe,
> Came pricking after, flinging forthe upon a courser blacke:
> With gastlye threatening countenance, with armyng sword
> in hands:
> His looke would make one feare, his eyes were like a fiery
> brande.[7]

Just as he is on the point of interfering, Nastagio learns that this is a punishment for her senseless attitude towards the huntsman during their lifetime and her just retribution for causing his suicide. Profiting from the lesson, Nastagio arranges a banquet on the same spot to which he invites his refractory lady. When she witnesses the scene and hears its explanation, she soon changes her mind and agrees to wed Nastagio.

The poem is written in the familiar fourteener couplets, the same meter which Christopher Tye, the supposed author, used for his translation of the *Acte of the Apostles*. Although lacking in poetic brilliance, the verse is smoother and more pleasant than is usual in these romances.

. . . . .

[7] C. T., *A Notable History of Nastagio and Traversari*, Sig. Avʳ.

The same theme was also versified by George Turberville in the first poem of his *Tragical Tales* (1576). Turberville makes some slight changes to emphasize the situation. At first, Nastagio is depicted as a wild gallant who refuses to marry; then, having fallen in love with Euphymia Traversari, he tries every expedient to win her—all to no avail. He finally attempts to commit suicide, but at the last minute he reconsiders his decision and takes to drinking, instead. He forsakes the town for the country where he witnesses the gory but instructive scene. Except for such slight changes, Turberville retains the essentials of the story and often many of the phrases. In Lenvoy, in genuine Turberville fashion, he pauses to deliver his little sermon: he who bows at every woman's beck should receive due punishment, ill-treatment; however, let women who are vixenish curb their tempers and their vanity, lest they, too, reap the punishment that overtook Guy's beloved! [8]

A Pleasaunt and Delightful History of Galesus Cymon and Iphigenia, Describing the Fickleness of Fortune in Love. Translated out of Italian into English verse by T. C. Gent, (ca. 1570) is also adapted from the Fifth Day of the *Decameron.* Cymon, it will be remembered, is a Cyprian youth, the bane of his father's life because of his uncouth behavior. However, after beholding the beautiful Iphigenia, the young man changes his mode of living. Unwilling to return to his hunting and other loutish pursuits, within a short time he becomes the most accomplished gentleman on the island. When Cymon finds that Iphigenia has been promised to another, he kidnaps her. After a number of escapes and adventures the lovers are finally united. [9]

· · · · ·

[8] Another version of this tale is found in H. C.'s *The Forrest of Fancy* (1579).
[9] This novella has been ascribed both to Thomas Campion and to Thomas Churchyard. Campion, as Warton has pointed out (H. E. P., III, 378) could not have been its author, since he was born in 1567 and died in 1620. Neither is it likely that Thomas Churchyard was the author, though we know that he translated *novelle.* At this time,

Two of the less decorous stories from the *Decameron* found their way into a handbook of mirth and manners for meal time, Thomas Twyne's *The Scholemaster, or the Teacher of Table Philosophie,* published in 1576. This little book, in reality an adaptation of Macrobius' *Saturnaliorum Conviviorum,* contains four treatises, the last of which deals with "honest jests, delectable devises and pleasant purposes." Among other postprandial stories considered useful to good digestion, Twyne included the spicy tale of the abbess (*Decameron* IX, 2). The latter arises in haste to catch a nun who has been denounced to her. Mistaking the breeches of the priest who has been abed with her for her coif, she covers her head with them. Consequently, she is forced to forego punishment of the nun, who exploits to the full her superior's sad oversight. Also taken from Boccaccio,[10] the second tale recounts the woes which befall a jealous citizen after he hears his wife's confession under the disguise of a priest. Believing her feigned confession that she

---

however, he was interested in other things, and it was not until several years later that he began to versify Italian tales. Moreover, Churchyard was quite careful to enumerate and record at various times the list of his works, and nowhere do we find mention of any such tale. Nor does the story itself seem to bear his stamp. On the other hand, a good deal of the evidence points to Christopher Tye as the author. In the first place, the initials C. T. and T. C. are the same and from what we know, the printing practices of the day did not specify that the given name should be printed first. Both this tale and the version of *Nastagio and Traversari* by C. T. were published *circa* 1570. Moreover, both of them are drawn from the same group of stories in Boccaccio, the Fifth Day, a group dealing with very proper amorous subjects, such as would appeal to a person with Puritan leanings like Christopher Tye. Furthermore, each has a curious set of verses immediately following the title. *Nastagio and Traversari* is followed by:

> S'amor non puol a un cor ingrato & empio
> Giovanelli timore e crudel scempio;

while *Cymon Galesus* is accompanied by the following:

> Di rozzo inerto, e vil fa spesso amore
> Generoso et cortese, un nobil cuore.

These verses bear a strong resemblance to each other. We might almost assume them to be the device of an author.

10 *Decameron* VII, 5.

loves a priest who visits her every night, the jealous husband sets a trap for him. Meanwhile, she entertains her real lover in her home. It is quite likely that the first *novella* was introduced more as an illustration of a witty tale, conducive to convivial mirth, than to translate the spirit of Boccaccio's satire on the Church. At any rate, the licentiousness of the narrative would be excused by the fact that it pointed out the corruption of the Roman church and its clergy.

For a long time, however, such translations were more or less sporadic attempts, with little or no plan behind them. George Turberville was really the first to exploit the *Decameron* as a wholesale source for his versified narratives. In his *Tragical Tales* (1576), he included seven tales from Boccaccio's work. Writing in "the time of his trouble," as he tells us in the Preface, the poet says that he intended to translate "Dan Lucan's verse," but he thought better of it, for it seemed more fitting to leave this task to Lord Buckhurst.

> Than I to reading Boccas fell, and sundry others moe,
> Italian authors where I found, great stores of states in woe,
> And sundry sortes of wretched wights: some slayne by cruell
> foes,
> An others some that through desire and Love their lives did
> lose: [11]

Having taken this as his text, Turberville adheres to it quite faithfully. Most of the plots are drawn from the Fourth Day, which deals with lovers who came to unhappy ends.

As a rule, Turberville follows the *Decameron* as closely as possible within the requirements of his verse. In most cases, however, he leaves out the sharp details, the verbal flashes that characterize Boccaccio's version. Turberville's verse lumbers along, unmarked by any such distinction. Here is his picture of the scene when the Lady of Roussillon learns of the ghastly

 . . . . .

[11] George Turberville, *Tragicall Tales* (Edinburgh, 1837), "The Author to the Reader."

revenge her husband has wreaked upon her lover by feeding
her his heart:

> And therewithal upon her legges the loving lady stoode,
> Before a windowe, that was full behind her feete,
> And sodainly from thence she fell into the open streete,
> Which deed no sooner done the windowe was so hie
> But out of hand her breath was stopt and so the dame did die
> With carkasse all to crusht by reason of the fall,
> The knyght her husband seeying this (who was the cause of
>   all)
> Stoode like a man amazed and then misliked sore
> Both of the Ladies loose and eke the murthred knight be-
>   fore.[12]

What a contrast this is to Boccaccio's swifter and more dramatic handling!

In these tales, Turberville seems to have had in mind a
double purpose: to portray the overpowering mastery of love,
and to inculcate in his readers some definite moral lessons.
Naturally, such moralization is quite foreign to Boccaccio.
Since both aims, however, were in consonance with the spirit
of the time they must have made Turberville's collection a
favorite. Sometimes he feels justified in altering Boccaccio's
intent for the sake of pointing a moral. For example, in Lenvoy
to the "Historie of Gerbino" he says:

> Who works against his sovereign princes word
> And standes not of the penalty in awe,
> Well worthy is to feele the wrathfull sword
> And die the death appointed of the law.[13]

Citing several examples of Roman obedience to authority, he
observes sententiously, "For Kings are second Gods in earth
belowe." It may be seen that Turberville uses the tale primarily
to expound the lesson of submissiveness to properly constituted
authority. This was hardly Boccaccio's purpose, who was con-

· · · · ·

[12] *Ibid.*, p. 136.   [13] *Ibid.*, p. 180.

tent to place the *novella* among those dealing with loves which came to an unhappy end. The Italian poet concluded his tale: "Thus have I told you did these two lovers within a few days die miserably a violent death, without having tasted any fruit of their loves."

Although he is a sentimentalist, Turberville always sacrifices love in the interest of his moralizing. This often prevents him from being consistent and able to follow a logical course. For example, in the tale of Isabella (*Decameron* IV,5), later to acquire further poetic fame at the hands of John Keats, he recounts the woes of the unfortunate girl whose lover was slain by her unfeeling brothers. Here Turberville's motto is: "*Amor vince ogni cosa.*" Love's supremacy is shown over the lives of the greatest heroes, Caesar, Hannibal, the very gods; therefore, he blames the brothers for attempting to make "the wench from fixed fansie stay." The author sheds a tear for the unfortunate lovers in the tale of Jeronimo and Silvestra (*Decameron* IV,7), in which the noble youth is forced by his wealthy relatives to forego his marriage with a poor tailor's daughter. The poet regrets that the lovers had to die of a broken heart, especially when, true to her marriage vows, Silvestra refused the advances of a man she really loved. In his "Lenvoy," Turberville declares that it is folly for parents to try to restrain their children for the sake of gold. No one can halt the stroke of Cupid's arrow. Yet he blames this love which runs counter to law and the dictates of religion. He admonishes his readers:

> Renounce the love of such as are forsped
> Forgoe those frends whom law forbids to lyke.[14]

Such a course can only bring woe and death! And in "Lenvoy" to his tale of the Knight of Roussillon, he pursues with bitter intensity this same tenor of moralizing, advising the reader to trust neither brother nor companion, for each man seeks only to serve himself. Trust even less those who are hidden, because

. . . . .

[14] *Ibid.*, p. 140.

the snake bites more poisonously than the dog. He points to the obvious moral to be drawn from witnessing a man betraying the friend who trusts him. Women, too, feel his censure, as he exclaims:

> So are those dames exceedingly to blame
> Whose glaveryng glee to lewdness doth entice.[15]

But the gods vent their just wrath upon such people, for:

> Note, here are the fruites of treason and of lust,
> Forbeare the like, for God is ever just.[16]

Thus the puritan tendency which, during the third quarter of the sixteenth century, loved to moralize Ovid and insisted upon fashioning *mirrors* from the conduct of evil magistrates for the edification of Christian citizens, may be seen working in full force also in the verse romance. Boccaccio's amiable satire and joyous atmosphere are transformed into Turberville's gloomy moralizing. The Florentine's examples, distorted and given a coating of didacticism, are used to point the way to salvation. This results in a confusion of intent in which love is made to appear as a snare, leading to corruption. Consequently, earthly passion must be regulated and made to conform to the dictates of established society and true religion. This attitude will be even more readily perceived when contrasted with the spirit of the following tale which, though edited in 1597, was written much earlier in the century, before the puritan tendencies began to ferment.

This poem, one of the numerous versions of the story of Guiscardo and Ghismonda (*Decameron* IV,1), was included in a publication called *Certayne Worthye Manuscript Poems of Great Antiquitie, Reserved Long in the Studie of a Northfolke Gentleman and now First Published by J. S.* Dedicated to "the worthiest poet, Maister Ed. Spenser," it includes two typically medieval satires, *The Northern Mothers Blessing* and

. . . . .

[15] *Ibid.*   [16] *Ibid.*, p. 141.

The Waye to Thrifte. The other work is *The Statelie Tragedie of Guistard and Sismonde.*

> Tancrede the noble Prince of Salurne,
> Flowre of knighthood and myrrour of prowesse,
> The whiche long time his people did governe
> Wittilie by benignitie and gentlenesse.
> Iche man reioyced in his great noblesse
> Discreete in all thing that was iudiciall
> And evermore Prince like in thing imperiall.[17]

The tale goes to great lengths in describing Tancred's pedigree, his marriage, the birth of Sismonde who excelled Helen and all the other famed beauties of antiquity. Upon reaching the proper age, Sismonde is married to the Duke of Champagne; but the sun has hardly set on her wedding day, when her husband dies. Back once more in Tancred's court, the young Duchess falls in love with Guiscardo, an accomplished squire of low lineage. Their love is discovered by her father, who condemns the youth to death and sends her his heart. The story follows the *Decameron* with certain variations. As Miss Scott has suggested,[18] this poem appears to be a reprint of a metrical version of the romance made by William Walter about 1530. Walter's poem, which is in octave stanzas, is itself based, not on Boccaccio's tale, but on the Latin *Epistola Leonardo Aretini de Amore Guistardi et Sigismunda.*

It is hardly likely that if J. S. knew Painter's and Boccaccio's accounts, he availed himself of them, for he differs radically from these two versions. To begin with, he elaborates on the original by adding detailed descriptions of feasts, long comparisons, and so forth. A great deal of padding is noticeable, *viz.* the following passage:

> So dayly in her mind she was full diligent
> For to note eche man in his demeanance,
> . . . . .

[17] J. S., *The Statelie Tragedie of Guistard and Sismonde,* Sig. B1ʳ.
[18] M. A. Scott, *op. cit.,* p. 150ff.

But Guistard to love is her only intent,
And he right wel knew by the appearance
Of her chere and her chaunged countenance,
That of brennyng love she daunced in the trace,
Which hath bound her heart with goldin lace.[19]

Again in this version, immediately before the King is to discover the intrigue between her and Guiscard, Sismonde has a
troubled sleep during which she dreams that her lover is holding a cup with a heart in it; he is all bathed in blood, and in
vain she begs him not to leave her. Tancred comes to his senses
too late and dies with the two lovers, a detail which occurs
neither in Painter nor in Boccaccio. J. S. depicts Sismonde as
more resolute than she is in other versions. Here, she makes all
the advances. Blaming the senseless oath which her father
caused her to take, for it prevents her from remarrying while
he is alive, she takes the initiative and plans all the steps necessary to bring about the meetings with Guiscard.

The story suffers from a lack of characterization, a fault
common at this time, of course. There is evident in it, however,
the easy-going attitude towards love, not to be found in the
stories versified by the Puritan poets. Its tone is medieval. We
may perceive in it a tranquil benevolence towards the intrigue,
such as Chaucer might have taken, the feeling that lovers
will be lovers, and that the temptations of the flesh, as well as
the darts of the Lord of Love, are wellnigh impossible to resist. It is the spirit of Boccaccio, a spirit, however, which the
Puritan versifiers warped or completely destroyed in their
verse romances.

. . . . .

[19] J. S., *op. cit.*, Sig. B5r.

XII

Verse Romances from Ariosto

As **a** source of plots for verse romances
and other translations, Ariosto was not so popular as Bandello
or Boccaccio, obviously because of the continuity of his epic and
the nature of the characters of *Orlando Furioso*. Nevertheless,
we find that some of the lighter and more romantic incidents
provide a nucleus for full-fledged poetical narratives.

One of the episodes in question, utilized also by numerous
other poets, was used by Peter Beverley in *The Historie of
Ariodanto and Jenevra Daughter to the King of Scottes*
(1565?). This is merely a versification of cantos IV and V of
Ariosto's *Orlando Furioso*. Following the custom in the verse
romances, Beverley modified somewhat Ariosto's version, altering especially its order. Though Ariosto began his tale with
Rinaldo's rescue of Dalinda, Beverley commences in chronological fashion, with the visit to Scotland of Lurcanio and
Ariodanto, two Florentine brothers. Tired of a life of ease at
home, the two youths visit the court, impress the king with
their fine mien, and are allowed to stay. Lurcanio wins the
king's favor by saving him during a lion hunt; at the same
time, the younger and well-favored Ariodanto charms Je-

nevra, the king's daughter. In true metrical-romance fashion, the lovers spend months sighing for each other, concealing their love, wasting away. They employ intricate ruses in order to correspond. When they finally succeed in declaring their love to each other, their joy is but short-lived, for the Duke Polinesso plans to wreck the romance in order to marry the princess himself. Polinesso sows suspicion in Ariodanto's mind by securing a token which the latter has given the Princess. He is aided in his schemes by Dalinda, one of the Princess' women whom he has secretly promised to marry. Aided further by Dalinda, who clothes herself in her mistress' garb and allows him to embrace her on a balcony where Ariodanto can see them, Duke Polinesso convinces the youth that he is Jenevra's lover. Mortally hurt, Ariodanto disappears from the court and becomes a hermit, upon which, believing that his brother has drowned himself, Lurcanio swears to obtain revenge. After he reveals the supposed intrigue to the king, who reluctantly agrees to a trial by combat, Lurcanio beats Jenevra's champion, leaving her liable to punishment. When news of her plight reaches his hermit's cave, Ariodanto is torn between the desire to save Jenevra and his reticence to fight against his beloved brother. Meanwhile, having planned to remove Dalinda whose knowledge of the intrigue might become too dangerous, Polinesso asks her to meet him in a wood, under the pretext of wishing to have their wedding performed. Just as she is about to be slain, Raynaldo appears, rescues her, and hastens to the city, arriving just in time to witness the fight between the two brothers, each, ironically enough, motivated by noble intentions. In a later combat, Polinesso is wounded by Lurcanio and before he dies, confesses to the black plot. Dalinda is exiled and the lovers united.

The numerous highly dramatic situations latent in the tale are left unexploited. Any poet with a sense of the dramatic would have brought out the conflict in the mind of Ariodanto, struggling between a desire to defend his lady and love for his brother. Any other poet would have exploited the balcony scene. Beverley is content to leave such situations to themselves. His habit of retelling events which have preceded, without modifying the details, sparing no description is even more tedious. His chief concern seems to be to develop the tale in logical sequence, regardless of dramatic interest or climax. The verse is little better than doggerel, with little poetic refinement. But with a public unaware of such subtleties, the tale of Ariodanto in its various versions was a favorite.[1]

Inspired perhaps by Harington's success with his translation of *Orlando Furioso*, Robert Tofte, an italianate Englishman, also tried his hand at translating Ariosto, and in 1597 brought forth *Two Tales, Translated out of Ariosto, the One in Dispraise of Men, the Other in Disgrace of Women*. Upon his return to England, after extensive travel in Italy, Tofte had compiled a series of translations and adaptations of Italian works. He had translated one of Varchi's works as *The Blazon of Jealousie*. His poetical miscellanies, *Laura* and *Alba*, reveal the influence of the *strambotti* writers such as Serafino. In one of his prefaces, he further claims to have translated Ariosto's *Satires*. More ambitious was his version of Boiardo's epic, *Orlando Innammorato, the Three First Bookes of that Famous Noble Gentleman and Learned Poet, Mathew Maria Boiardo Earle of Scandiano in Lombardie, Done into English*

• • • • •

[1] Similar versions are found, not only in Bandello who used the window intrigue in his *novella* I, 22, but also in the ninth *novella* of Cinzio's *Ecatommiti*. M. A. Scott lists another version in Belleforest's *Histoires Tragiques*, while the use of the intrigue in Shakespeare's *Much Ado*, in the tangle between Hero, Claudio and Don John is universally known. Spenser used it in the story of Phedon, *Faerie Queene*, II, iv, 17. A version of this tale is reported to have been composed in English by George Turberville, but no trace of it is found in the extant works of this poet. Miss Scott also lists the presentation of *A Historie of Ariodante and Geneura* by the boys of the Merchant Tailors School under the direction of Richard Mulcaster, on Shrove Tuesday, 1582. Scott, *op. cit.*, p. 229.

Heroicall Verse by R. T. Gent. An examination of the foliation of these two translations has shown quite conclusively
that *Two Tales* was intended as an appendage to the translation of Boiardo.[2] Taken from Canto 43, these two episodes
illustrate the avarice of women and their frailty in resisting
the lure of gold.

The first is the tale which the Doleful Knight narrates to
Rinaldo in the first part of Canto 43. The Knight, being
pleasing of person, awakens the passion of the enchantress
Melissa. She has desired him for a long time, yet he has been
loath to do injury to his wife, a very virtuous woman. By
subtle reasoning, however, Melissa questions his wife's chastity on the grounds that it has never been tested and thus
begins to sow the seeds of suspicion in his mind. Melissa proposes that he feign going on a trip, leaving his wife alone.
Then she transforms the Knight into one of his wife's unsuccessful suitors and herself as his squire. The disguised
husband approaches his wife and by wooing her with the
promise of untold wealth, succeeds in seducing her. When
he accuses her of falseness, she turns from him and leaves
him forever.

The second episode is the story of Anselmo, Argia and
Adonio, also found in the same canto. Insanely jealous of his
wife, Anselmo takes all precautions that she remain faithful
during his absence. Meanwhile, Adonio, an admirer who has
gone bankrupt in trying to win her good graces, has returned
to his native city. Manto, an enchantress whom, years before,
he saved from certain death, offers him aid. After securing
for him great wealth, she even turns herself into a dog which
can perform wonderful tricks. Entranced by the dog, Argia
offers to buy it, but Adonio's price is her yielding. Finally,
spurred by her greed and by the urgings of her nurse, she
consents. Having become aware of his wife's unfaithfulness
through a soothsayer, Anselmo orders a servant to slay her;

. . . . .

[2] F. B. Williams, "Robert Tofte," *RES*, XIII (1937), 24ff.

but when the henchman tries to commit the deed, Manto makes Argia disappear. Upon learning this, Anselmo goes to the forest to ascertain if Argia may be hiding there. He finds, instead, a great palace, rich beyond belief. An ugly Ethiopian paces outside and at Anselmo's inquiries reveals that he is the owner of the palace. Anselmo is astounded at this assertion, for the African is ugly, foul, and clad in rags. He is even more astounded when the caitiff offers to give him the palace, provided Anselmo will submit to him. The latter's greed finally overcomes his repugnance. Whereupon, Argia leaps out of a thicket and confronts her husband with his admission, pointing out to him how much more reprehensible his conduct was than hers. Thus the two are eventually reconciled.

Tofte and his printer evidently tried to clear themselves of any suspicion of having copied Harington's version, for they are careful to explain that these two *novelle* were composed in Italy in the year 1592. In general, we find that Tofte is a faithful translator, who keeps to the original and translates stanza for stanza. His verses reflect the Italian influence of the sonnet writers and his continental predilections.

Casting a glance backwards upon the mass of Italian material, the reader is enabled to pick up certain threads which link these widely scattered tales. To begin with, it is clear that the verse romances formed part of the great bulk of middle class reading material and served to open up the fertile field of Italian popular literature to the English reading public. Though the majority of English readers was distrustful of the dangers inherent in the satirical writings of Boccaccio and his fellow-novelists, the verse romances drew the venom from the snake, as it were; and while sedulously avoiding stories whose morality might be questionable, they offered only those tales which would edify the reader. These compositions, then, became strong factors in the plan for a godly education, since they brought to Englishmen the writings of famous foreign authors, yet censored them so effectively that even Roger Ascham could not have found fault with them.

In accordance with this design, the romances sought only to exalt the lofty emotions, friendship and nobility in love, or to satisfy Elizabethan England's passion for tales of violence. The appeal to the middle class was further strengthened by the bourgeois tone so prevalent in them. Time and again, the venality of women is scored; repeatedly, the dangers of unwise marriages are pointed out. Obedience to family and to social custom is stressed at every turn; the tragic end of transgressors is eloquent proof of the wisdom of such conformity. Only seldom do risqué stories intrude. When they do, there is always some good motive behind them, perhaps the feeling that from these lewd tales, the good Christian may learn to shun the wiles of Popery which fostered them.

This purely utilitarian aim of the verse romances retarded their artistic development. Since only the solid, instructive qualities were esteemed, there was little clamor for such refinements. Style mattered very little, for, after all, the tale and its moral were the main object. In addition, the lack of well-planned translations of the Italian *novelle* further hindered the development of the verse romances as works of art. Few of the early authors seemed to profit from the work of their forerunners, although, judging from their prefaces, they give every indication of having known the earlier works. Consequently, each tale tended to repeat the faults of its predecessors, and it was not until the end of the sixteenth century that the verse romances showed any real artistic improvement.

It is quite difficult to explain why only a few Italian authors, the major ones, were used as sources for the verse tales, especially since the prose translations made ample use of the minor *novellieri*. Was this choice due to the urgent need for translations for the middle class? Did the translators feel that since their scope was limited, they might as well offer only the best known tales? These are questions which must be left unanswered; the obscurity of many of the authors and the lack of biographical data shroud them and their motives in complete darkness.

As we have observed, in the process of versification many of the plots were altered in atmosphere and mood. Often an author like Turberville changed Boccaccio's intent to make it coincide with his desire to expound a moral or to bring home a lesson to the reader. Through these verse translations, Italian tales and settings also acquired a curious, neutral quality, neither English nor Italian. Having taken on characteristics which are a mixture of English and Italian and yet belong to neither nation, they seem to exist in a sort of no man's land. We get the same feeling from some of Shakespeare's plays, for example, *Twelfth Night* or *Two Gentlemen of Verona*. It is the first step in the process of producing indigenous stories—the stories which we shall see evolve in the following chapter.

X I I I
Verse Romances of Native Origin

THERE EXISTS ALSO A GROUP OF TALES WHICH
follow the general pattern, but give every indication of being
products of the invention of English poets themselves. In some
cases, the authors attempt to gain importance for their work by
asserting that they "translated" out of some foreign language,
but the absence of proof and certain inconsistencies discernible
in the stories tend to contradict their assertions. Most of these
tales exhibit the faults of the verse romances, long windedness
and tedious moralizing, to a greater degree even than the preceding poems.[1]

One of the first native verse romances appeared in 1563,
hard on the heels of Brooke's *Romeus and Juliet,* as *The Tragicall and True Historie Which Happened Between Two English Lovers.* Its author was Bernard Garter, an obscure poetaster
of unmistakable Puritan leanings. Its preface is interesting be-

. . . . .

[1] Among the many lost works dealing with such subjects, we find:
The Famous Historie of Two Spanish Lovers, entered in the Stationers'
Register to R. Jones, 1569, and *A Proper Historye of Two Dutche
Lovers,* entered to Purfoote in 1567.

cause of the decided appeal made by Garter in the interests of morality and filial duty, sentiments exactly like those expressed by Brooke in his poem. Garter asks the reader's attention:

Note (loveing friend) the matter succeeding is of two English lovers, both young; of lynage like substantiall enough, maried by the parents consent of equall troth in keepeing the honorable bedde of matrimony undefyled what should I say, both virtuous and loving: and yet their doings not prospering. I must think good readers (but I leave the judgment to God) that he was offended, because they both at first sight, rashely, unadvisedly, unknowen and without friendes consent durst thrall themselves in the desire of unclean lust (But I must terme it cleanlye Cupid's flamme) and did not call upon God for the meeteness of the match nor sought parents consent till, (had the same been never so unmeete) they must have graunted or elles the love growne from follye, and thought from love, would have wrought the lovers ende.[2]

He shakes a warning finger at his readers and cautions them: if you are a father, look for such conditions in your family; if a child, remember your parents always come first.

We thinke that the faulte was committed because without the feare of God and friends consent craved in the beginning, they durst love and in themselves contracted a marriage.[3]

The beginning of the tale presents a situation somewhat similar to that of *Romeus and Juliet*, without, of course, the tragic elements to be found in Brooke's story. Garter begins in the conventional pseudo-Chaucerian manner:

When that bousterous Borias, and hiemps hory frost:
By iust return of lady Ver, their pinching power had lost:
That lady stayede the fyne of March, in comely course and
    hewe:
And left her seat to Estas then, and bade the Pryme adewe.[4]

. . . . .

[2] Bernard Garter, *The Tragicall and True Historie, which Happened Between Two English Lovers*, Address to the Reader.
[3] *Ibid.*, Sig. A3ᵛ.
[4] *Ibid.*, Sig. A6ʳ.

The laments of two love-stricken young people, who have met by chance in the fields, take up the entire first part of the poem. Their moanings are interminable. No advice, no attempt on the parents' part to help them is of any avail. Finally, there comes to the rescue a shrewd physician who, with a few questions, diagnoses the situation correctly and immediately discovers the secret of the two lovers. He astounds the girl when he tells her the length of her illness and its cause. At the same time, he revives her spirits by informing her that her swain is wealthy, comes from a good family, and loves her beyond measure. After a meeting is arranged, the match is made with all due propriety, and the wedding takes place. But happiness lasts only a brief while. War having been declared, the young man enlists and, despite the pleas of his young bride, goes off with his company. Created a knight after glorious encounters, he is preparing to return, when he is slandered by a malicious old man. During the combat which ensues, the old man is wounded and confesses his guilt. But our hero also has received a serious wound, and, in spite of his wife's care, dies. Inconsolable, she wails her bitter fate:

> Since that my cursed chance is such as neither I can have
> My love alive, nor yet myselfe be buried in his grave,
> Wel, wel oh, lord, remyt my sinnes even through they mercy most.
> Wherewith she stretched forth her armes and yielded up the gost.[5]

To complete the mass slaughter, her mother is overpowered by grief and also dies; only the father is left, ostensibly to execute their dying requests.

One would be hard put to discover the point of the tragedy or the underlying causes which bring it about. No reason is given for the fatal quarrel which finishes our hero, beyond the mention that it was to justify a malicious accusation. The

. . . . .

5 *Ibid.*, K7r.

author devotes most of his pains to minute details of the courtship and the anguish of the lovers. These two are mere abstractions; no name is given either one, nor have they any traits
which might stamp them as individuals. The only bit of individuality in the entire poem is the reaction of the mother after
the girl has complained interminably about her husband's departure to the wars. The young bride has apparently been con-
soled by the mother. But for no discernible reason, she relapses
once more into her tearful state. The mother then breaks out
with a healthy berating, reminiscent of old Capulet's outbursts
and refreshing in the extreme after the inanities which have
preceded it. The author introduces a new note in making use
of a conventional device. As he pens a letter to his wife just
prior to the crucial attack, the youth uses a quill dipped in his
blood instead of ink.

If the poem has no merit from a dramatic point of view, it is
of some value in depicting the family life of the English middle
class. Garter's painfully detailed descriptions of the carefully
planned first meeting of the two lovers at the girl's home, the
obvious, vapid small talk between the father and the lover, the
girl's sly piercing of a hole in the tapestry in order to catch a
glimpse of her lover, all may have some sociological value. And
there may be some significance in the description of the wedding preparations, the setting out of the plate, the arrival of
the minstrel, the grooming of the lover, the viewing of the
presents, the tips to the waiters, the music, the dainties, the
afternoon sports, such as leaping, weight-lifting, running and
dancing which last for days, but it is a value which is hardly
poetic. Still, if we must make apologies, we may always ascribe
such mediocrity to the generally low level of the Muse during
this period.

A few years later, John Drout, a gentleman of Thavis Inne,
supposedly "translated out of Italian" *The Pityful Historie of
Two Loving Italians, Gaulfrido and Bernardo Le Vayne:
Which Arived in the Countrey of Grece, in the Time of the
Noble Emperour Vespasian* (1570). Based on the popular

theme of friendship, this metrical romance utilizes some of the more conspicuous situations of the Titus and Gesippus story. In fact, in the "Preface to the Reader," Drout expresses his hope that these two friends will be numbered in the illustrious company of perfect friends who have been recorded in the pages of history.[6]

The tale begins:

> In pleasant moneth of this (my frendes)
> Eche man doth ioy by kinde,
> And every man doth practise what
> Were best to please his minde.
> As Gaulfrido here (th'Italian Books
> Do shewe his name to be)
> Doth seeke and search in rotten boat
> Straunge countries for to see.[7]

In the course of his wanderings, he arrives in Greece where he encounters Bernardo, a kinsman. Having recognized each other, they proceed to tell of their vicissitudes. Bernardo explains that after being chased by Turks, he managed to reach these shores. As they are thus discoursing, two enemies meet by chance upon this street. A quarrel ensues, a tussle, then:

. . . . .

[6] Beholde (gentle reader) how I have depaynted and set forth unto thee this wofull historie of two Italians (al for thine ease as I hope) whiche by thy diligente reading thou shalt finde them nothing at all inferious (concerning amitie) to the two turtles, Titus and Gysippus and that thou shalt thinke them worthie to be received into the troupe or to bee committed amongst the crue, which are already rehearsed of Maister Underdonne: also I have as great admiration (as ever he had) what they should bee that do not rejoyce to heare of the unspeakable friendshippe and amitie which was betweene Orestes and Peliades, Theseus and Perithous, Achilles and Patrocles, Nisus and Eurialus, Castor and Pollux, Damon and Pithias, Achates and Aeneas, Alexander and Ephestio, Celius and Patroclus, C. Lelius and Scipio Africanus, Darius and Megabisus, and last of all, that be not glad to heare of our Gaulfrido and Segnior Bernardo, who for true amitie may be annexed and adjoyned with the rest. John Drout, *The Pityful Historie*, Preface to the Reader.

[7] *Ibid.*, Sig. B4ʳ.

Gan they their shivering blades to drawe:
And to be shorte, the one did thruste
The other though the mawe,
The guttes, the lungs, the intrayls all,
But stryght away he went
That didde the fact: [8]

Friends rush to the scene of the fray and, seeing Gaulfrido looking out of the window, seize him and accuse him of the slaying. The two friends are cast into a dismal, gloomy dungeon, "where toads do keepe and adders dwell," there to await trial. Some time later, haggard and worn by their confinement, they are brought to the square where the gallows has been erected. Bernardo protests their innocence and is freed, but his friend is declared guilty. Each of them tries to assume the blame. However, struck by remorse, the real murderer, who has witnessed the scene, confesses to the murder and shows the bloody sword to prove his guilt. Then, a new assize having been called, the foreman brings in a new verdict and the real culprit is hanged.

Freed by the sudden fortunate turn of events, the two friends are enjoying the town, when, at a banquet, Bernardo sees the beauteous Charina and is smitten. A typical lover, however, he is struck dumb, and all he can do is to look at her. During the festivities, a minstrel comes and plays a "jest of Robin Hood," but throughout the dance Bernardo can only gaze dumbly at his divinity. It is the sprightlier Gaulfrido who catches her up as soon as the minstrel has done.

When they had done he toke the mayd,
A galliard he did bid:
The minstrels play in comely sort,
He led her twice about,
Then her he capt, she cursie made
Afore the open rout;
He trips about with sincopace

. . . . .

[8] *Ibid.*, Sig. C4ᵛ.

He capers very quicke;
Full trimly there of seven aleven
He showeth a pretty tricke.[9]

Such a show pleases her family mightily, especially since the youth is well-favored; Amasina, her mother, declares that "he shall beare the bell."

Realizing that he is the loser in the affair, Bernardo goes to his room and pens a letter describing his woe. Gradually becoming more desperate, he finally commits suicide. Gaulfrido returns, perceives the corpse of his friend and, upon reading the letter explaining his action, also stabs himself to death. The action now sinks to bathos, for when the host finds the two corpses, he is struck by the melancholy situation and hangs himself. The lovely Charina flings herself in despair out of a window; Tibine, her father, also commits suicide; and the destruction is complete when Amasina drowns herself. To add to the tragedy, every one of the sailors, who had perceived this bloodshed from a nearby ship, drown before they have proceeded two leagues on their journey. Despite the ordeal of witnessing all this blood and death, the author has the strength to praise his sovereign at the end of the poem:

God save our noble Queene,
That she may vanquish traitours all,
Which seeketh her decay:
The goodly and the godly so I knowe
Continually will pray.[10]

The wretchedness of the verse, the lack of poetic inspiration and execution do not detract from a certain amount of historical interest to be found in this unfortunate poem. Certainly, we must state at the outset that the author showed a more than usual abiliy in penning mawkish verse, even at a time when wretched poetasters were rampant. The following will speak

· · · · ·

9 *Ibid.*, Sig. F2ʳ.
10 *Ibid.*, Sig. G4ʳ.

more eloquently than any comment. When the two friends recognize each other:

> The one imbrast, the other kist,
> They weepe for joy in place:
> Gaulfrido could not speake because
> All myred was his face,
> With driveling drops of lukewarme teares,
> Which trickled down apace
> His paled face: his friends in deede
> As fast did poure agayne
> His dryry teares: incontinent.[11]

Certainly the gruesomeness of the ending, the unnecessary bloodshed are matched only in a piece like *Gorboduc*.

Yet the poem is interesting because, despite the author's assertions to the contrary, it seems to be native, a thoroughly English, attempt to create a plot which would resemble those of the Italian *novelle*.[12] To begin with, the author asserts in the very title that the tale is a translation. Several of his friends who wrote gratulatory poems corroborate this statement. J. F. calls Drout "this translator"; T. S. says:

> The Italians they themselves do love
> And dayly praise our Drout
> Who hath so aptly turned to verse
> Verbatim thorowe out.[13]

. . . . .

[11] *Ibid.*, Sig. B4ᵛ.
[12] J. P. Collier, the editor of the poem, recognized this ruse on Drout's part and stated in his preface, "The author professes to have 'translated the story from the Italian,' but although some foreign words are introduced as he proceeds, such as 'pup' for ship, 'oselly' (*ocelli*) for eyes, we doubt whether he was not endeavoring to secure for this small volume an artificial recommendation on account of the *frequency and popularity* at that time of stories derived from Italian novelists. The poem does not read like a translation and the curious incident of calling in a minstrel who plays the tune of *Robin Hood* is evidently merely national. One peculiarity is the use of Prefixes to various speeches to give dramatic value to what, in fact, is a mere narrative." Drout, *op. cit.*, Editor's Preface.
[13] *Ibid.*, Sig. A4ᵛ.

We may discount such assertions as in keeping with the author's wishes to maintain the fiction. But a similar example may be perceived in the case of George Gascoigne who, in order to give added weight to his *Tale of Master F. J.*, said that it had been "translated out of the Italian of Bartello." No one has ever heard of any such *novelliere*, and it is doubtful that he will ever be unearthed. It seems reasonable to assume that, as in the case of Gascoigne, Drout was merely making use of a device to catch the popular fancy and attempting to avail himself of the reading public's predilection for such translated tales. To carry this fiction a little further, in his "Dedication" to Sir Francis Jobson, the author says that he translated the tale as an exercise for those trying to learn Italian:

> I considered myselfe first how profitable it would be to those which be desirous to learne the Italian speeche: ageyne in my minde how pleasant a thing it is to read this hidden historie (which not without little paine) I have translated out of Italian into English verse, very plainly for those which shall have means to give their whole indeavour and industry to the attaining of so pleasant a language.[14]

All these statements, however, cannot minimize the numerous touches in the poem which stamp it as indigenous. For example, when Gaulfrido is relating his wanderings, he gives a very rough but graphic description of the sea and sea life, its perils and the terror of the waves:

> Then every man doth hale and pull,
> The halliards all a row,
> Behold thy foresayle it is up,
> How Auster do thou blow
> A huffing gayle: and by and by,
> Because thou wouldst be gone,
> Thy foretop and the mayne top sayle,
> Thou placest even anone.[15]

. . . . .

[14] *Ibid.*, Editor's Preface.   [15] *Ibid.*, Sig. C2ʳ.

Such passages are rarely, if ever, encountered in Italian *novelle;* they are far more common in the descriptions penned by Englishmen whose familiarity with sea life was proverbial. Again, to quote the "minstrel" passage:

> The minstrell he was called in
> Some pretty jest to play,
> Then Robin Hood was called for
> And malkin ere they went.[16]

Certainly, these allusions could hardly have come out of an Italian *novella.* Glancing once more at the trial of the culprits, we shall find that the foreman of the jury calls a new assize and when the jury brings in its verdict, the murderer is hanged. The sergeant and the yeomen are described as standing by. No one will dispute the English touches here. Certainly, the atmosphere of the romance is not Italian; moreover, no such *novella* is to be found in any of the collections with which the investigator is usually familiar. Consequently, until more conclusive evidence is unearthed, one may safely assume that Drout did not translate his tale from Italian sources, but that he merely imitated the plot found in Boccaccio's *Titus and Gesippus* or in Elyot's version of the tale.

William Averill's *An Excellent Historie Both Pithy and Pleasant Discoursing on the Death of Charles and Julia, Two Brittish or Rather Welsh Lovers* (1581) is another tale probably of native origin.[17] It displays some of the characteristics of the verse romances and even exaggerates certain of their more objectionable traits. Although the author does not state it, there is the implication that the story existed in some other form, since he says that he has "reduced this historie into

. . . . .

16 *Ibid.,* Sig. F1ᵛ.
17 This tale is declared lost by A. Esdaile in his *List of English Romances Before 1740* (London, 1912), p. xxxiv. Although it is entered in the *Short Title Catalogue,* no copy is listed as being extant in any library. A copy does exist in the Huntington Library at San Marino. I have used a microfilm reproduction of this specimen.

savorie verse." We meet again the tedious, conventional "Address to the Reader," in which the latter is exhorted to profit by the mistakes of these two lovers who flouted parental authority. This is the usual moralizing, an indication that the first half of Elizabeth's reign was open season on romance.[18]

Wishing, no doubt, to give a firm foundation to his tale, the author dips into legendary lore to seek the origins of his protagonists. We are taken back to the days of the Trojan struggles and the subsequent wanderings of Aeneas. In this wise, the beginning of this tale becomes one of those popular chronicle histories which trace the familiar legendary origins of the British race to Brutus. One of his sons, Camber, having received Wales as his portion of the kingdom, eventually begets a sturdy son, called Charles, the hero of our tale. At the same time, Owen, the ruler of Flint, has a daughter named Julia, famed throughout the land for her beauty. Each year at Saint Winifred's well a festival is held at which the lame, the blind and the afflicted are relieved of their ailments. Here, during the general merriment which follows the religious ceremonies, the two young people meet and fall in love. Unable to endure delay, Charles proposes that they marry immediately. But the strain of even a short delay irks Charles so much that he falls ill. Sensitive as all romantic lovers must be, however, he will not reveal to his family the cause of his illness. Consequently, when he does not appear at their tryst, Julia imagines all sorts of mishaps, even suspects another woman.

Finally, having learned of his illness, she writes him, assuring him of her unending devotion. She goes so far as to pen her own epitaph. The rumor now spreads that Charles is dead, whereupon the inconsolable Julia journeys once more to St. Winifred's to make her peace with God. Then, entering a

. . . . .

[18] Averill also published *A Dyall for Dainty Darlings Rockt in the Cradle of Securitie* (1584), a group of moralized short stories intended to edify the reading public of England and to cause them "to eschewe Love's madness."

sealed casket she floats off to join Charles in death. Fortunately, she is picked up in a very weakened condition by some sailors and conveyed to a religious house in Albany.

Unaware of her desperate step, her lover immediately sets out to see her. Overcome by the news of what she has done, he attempts to drown himself, but a kindly priest succeeds in preventing this rash step. Instead he sets off with Charles on lengthy wanderings. After numerous adventures, they land in Albany where Charles becomes the leader of a band of soldiers. Eventually, having ended up in the town where Julia has taken refuge, he spies her from the fortifications. He contrives to meet her, and when finally she obtains her discharge from the nunnery, the two lovers are reunited.

We need not dwell on the lengthy rejoicing, the return to their homeland where they obtain their parents' consent and are finally wed. But evil Fate pursues them. His father having died a few months after the wedding, Charles sets out for his realm. Julia follows him and is drowned. Unable to bear this tragedy, the lad sails to the spot where she drowned and takes poison, thus, according to the legend, finding death in her arms.

This tale seems to combine the elements of the love verse tale with some of the features of the saint's legend. There is the usual amount of sententiousness and moralization, as for example:

> Where femine do prefixe their love,
> No measure they observe:
> They fasten then theyr faith so sure,
> That they doo never swarve.[19]

His ethical premise in the Address to the Reader is, of course, far-fetched; one feels that the deaths are absolutely unnecessary and merely brought in to satisfy the exigencies of this stock moralizing. As in Drout's verse romance, we find here

• • • • •

[19] William Averill, *The Historie of Charles and Julia*, Sig. C5ᵛ.

an engrossing interest in the sea, further proof that the tale
may be indigenous. For it is remarkable that such passages are
found largely in this type of story. For example, in describing
the progress of the ship:

> The carving keele doth cutte the wave, the maynsaile, top-
> sayle and
> The missen spreete sayle further course, aloft the flag doth
> stand;
> The pilot markes his compasse well, and carde with tentive
> eye:
> The masters mate dooth guide the sterne of Rudder right-
> fullie.[20]

The numerous details of the feast at Saint Winifred's, as well
as the description of the dances and the festivities accompanying the religious ceremony, also appear to be English. It is
possible that the tale may have been written to celebrate an
actual festival at this famous well in Flint. Aside from such
historical interest, however, the tale has the usual faults of
repetitiousness and piling up of superfluous detail.

The prolific Thomas Churchyard, who with his writings
spans the last half of the sixteenth century, also left several
romances of this type. They are usually found in his miscellanies among a variety of topics such as satires on the court's
ingratitude towards veterans of his stamp and descriptions of
military operations. Making use of situations from his own
adventurous career, Churchyard has left a voluminous list of
works of which he was inordinately proud. We have already
observed how strenuously he laid claim to *Shores Wife;* in all
his volumes he repeatedly stated his authorship of various compositions. Indeed, in his *Challenge,* he took pains to list all the
works which he had fathered in thirty-odd years of writing,
tracing the wanderings of several of them, not omitting to
mention others, lost through the carelessness of persons to

. . . . .

20 *Ibid.,* Sig. F8ᵛ.

whom they had been sent. So careful was he of claiming his work, that he employed a device amounting to a trademark in his choice of titles. These invariably begin with "ch" to correspond, no doubt, with the first two letters in his own name. Thus we have *Churchyards Choice,* his *Chips, Challenge, Charge,* and so forth. Many of these miscellanies repeated, either in their original form or in some altered fashion, stories which he had already used. One moment he imitated an Italian tragedy of blood and vengeance, the next he essayed his hand at a *fabliau* which might have come out of Chaucer.

One of these satirical tales, included in *Churchyards Chips* (1575), is *The Tale of a Freer and a Shoemaker's Wife.* Its protagonist is a jolly Welsh friar:

> This freer was fat and full of fleash, a jolly myrry knave,
> Who with the gossips of the town himself could well behave;
> Those wealthy wives and thrifty dames could never make
>   good cheer
> Nor well dispute of Peeters keis, if absent were this freer.[21]

This prankish wight is carrying on an intrigue with a shoemaker's wife. In order to provide himself with a little amusement, he chooses an occasion when she is visiting him to invite her husband to his dwelling, under the pretext of ordering a pair of shoes. Then he calmly has his measurements taken while the wife quakes in bed. Eager to please the friar, the shoemaker returns with his own wife's shoes, whereupon the latter is so angered that she swears revenge. Later, during one of the friar's visits to her home, she finds her opportunity. When her husband comes home unexpectedly, she hides the friar in a chest in which the shoemaker has hidden some brandy. She then feigns illness, and the friar passes a few trepidant moments while the shoemaker is preparing to break the locked chest in order to find some remedy for his wife. Saved only at the last moment when she suddenly recovers,

. . . . .

[21] Churchyard, *The First Parte of Churchyardes Chips,* Sig. L4ʳ.

the friar is sent on his way with an admonition to curb his waggish wit.

A different brand of humor is exhibited in *A Fayned Fancie of the Spider and Gowt,* a charming beast fable narrated in a lively manner:

> Tenne thousand years agoe at least,
> I meane when everye bird and beast
> And everye thing that we can name
> Could talke and reason in good frame . . . .[22]

A spider and a gowt[23] contend that each of them stands lower in Fortune's graces. In order to settle the question, they agree to select a master and meet a year hence. The spider goes to a gentleman's home, while the gowt seeks out a husbandman. It is an unhappy choice for the spider; his life is made miserable and he is given no rest because of a busy maid who goes about

> With swapping besome in her hand,
> A jolly bontch of keys she wore:
> Her petticoet fine laest before,
> Her taile lockt up in trimmest gies,
> A napkin hanging o'er her eyes
> To keepe the duste and drosse of walles
> That often from the windowe falles
> Though she was smog, she took smal ease.[24]

This busy creature never rests, for she arises by candle light to spin and card. As a result of her industry, she can boast of

> Two fair new kirtles to her back,
> The one was blue, the other blacke;
> For holy days she had a gowne
> And every yard did cost a crowne;
>
> . . . . .

---

[22] *Ibid.,* C2ᵛ.

[23] The origin of this word is not to be found in the *New English Dictionary.* An examination of the text, however, indicates that the *gowt* must have been a parasitic insect closely allied to a flea.

[24] Churchyard, *The First Parte of Churchyardes Chips,* Sig. C3ʳ.

. . . .

> She would go barefoote for to save
> Her shoes and hose, for they were dere.[25]

Pretty, despite her chapped hands, this paragon of domesticity, who can cook and still look graceful, makes the poor spider very miserable, pursuing him in the darkest of corners, tearing down his scaffolds, until he wishes himself well out of her range.

Meanwhile, the gowt has gone to the country where he has perched upon an honest man who has many mouths to feed and who cannot muster five pounds. But all these handicaps cannot upset his jollity:

> His face as red as any brick
> Whear in there stood a bottel nose,
> A couple of corns upon his toes
> He had, which made him cut his shue;
> He never put on garment new
> But when that to the waeks he went,
>
> . . . .
>
> A velvet night cap half thread baer,
> But herein must be understood
> His wief was come of gentyll blood
> Which would not have him clad in clouts
> But when he moyld with other louts
> Then caerd she not what he put on.[26]

Despite his unpolished verse, Churchyard gives us quite a vivid description of an Elizabethan yeoman's home: the scampering children and the capons, the dogs and cats, the bacons hanging from the walls. We are shown the entire household in bustling activity; no one is idle but the infant.

> The maidens to their wheels they song,
> The cardders myrry wear also
> The hyends about the fields they go,
>
> . . . . .

The oxen champped in their stall,
The pigs lay gronting by the wawll,
The capuls fed upon their hay,
The hens full many an egg did lay.[27]

At first the gowt feels that he will have an easy life; but he is rudely jolted when the wife begins to berate her husband, accusing him of laziness, while she slaves all day, ill-clothed, pinching and scraping, trying to make ends meet. The landlord is dunning them for money. So the gowt must accompany the yeoman on all the chores of the farm, tilling the fields, tending to the animals. Churchyard gives a truly charming picture of the entire household and the relationship of master and maids, their larks, their happy frolics, their dinners. They go to market, where the gowt watches them barter and haggle; he attends their innocent games upon feast days. But this is not the life for him. At the end of the year, the gowt changes places with the spider; the latter goes to the farmhouse to weave his webs in peace, while the gowt returns to nestle in the furs and cushions of the city gentleman whom he rules in ease and comfort.

Churchyards Chips contains "A Dolefull Discourse of Two Strangers, a Lady and a Knight," a poem encountered again in *Churchyards Challenge*. The poet informs us that the tale was "translated out of Frenche." Its undramatic plot deals with the misfortunes of a lord and lady who fall in love, but fail to win "Caesar's consent"; whereupon, the gentleman has no other recourse but to flee the kingdom. Most of the poem merely records their moans. The lady finally dies, asking the prince's pardon. In the end, the offending lord wins the forgiveness of his sovereign.

Churchyards Choice (1579) includes "A Pitifull Complaint in the Maner of a Tragedie of Seignior Anthonio Dell Donaldoes Wife, Sometyme in the Duke of Florences Court.

. . . . .

[27] *Ibid.*, Sig. C6ᵛ.

Translated out of Italian Prose and Putte into English Verse."
This verse tale has many of the characteristics of the *mirrors*
and reminds one quite forcefully of some of George Whet-
stones' bourgeois romances. We meet the same story, enlarged
and recast, in *Churchyards Challenge* under the title: "The
Tragicall Discourse of the Dolorous Gentlewoman." The poem
presents the lament of a wretched lady who was once a virtuous and seemingly contented gentlewoman. Suddenly, her
husband having gone off to the wars, she finds her love for
him cooled. After having spread the word that her husband
is dead, she chooses a younger man for herself. During this
unexpected transformation, she becomes a combination of
Cressida, Moll Flanders and Messalina, for when her unfortunate husband returns, she refuses to admit him to her bed
and even brazenly presents him with a bastard girl. In addition, she plots against his life, complaining that "he's too sick
a foul for mee." Finally, having prevailed upon him to sell all
his possessions so that they may go out in the world, she and a
maid set themselves up in town, surrounding themselves with
lusty youths. She poisons her husband, commits all sorts of
excesses, and instead of mourning for him, she "braves the
world in silks and velvets gay." But she can foresee her own
end, a Cressid pursued by remorse, scorned by all the good
women; she hears her own boys proclaim her infamy. She recalls incidents out of her past. Once, hearing that she was ill,
though bitterly maltreated her husband came to proffer aid
and reconciliation to her, but she scorned him. She now de-
spises herself, and viewing the abjectness of her life, she vows
to pursue a better course. She accuses Love as the cause of her
crimes:

> Love stayes not long, it is but one yeares birde,
> A foolish fitte that makes wild wittes goe madde!
> .   .   .   .
>
> Love must have change to season sweete delite,
> Love's minde will range like Spaniel in the field:

> Love likes to rule, she hath no minde to yeelde,
> Love will have scope, love is restrained seelde:
> If Love lacks ought, she showes a lowring eye
> And then for nought the babe will pule and cry.
> Love must go gaye and paynted like a poste,
> Love must be peecest and patched with many a clout,
> Love is a sprite, a shadow or a gost.[28]

And she closes her woeful tale with an exhortation to the good dames of England not to repeat her errors, for she has wandered twenty years without finding peace.

Several other poems appear to have originated from Church-yard's own experiences, even though he claims to have translated them. Here we suspect once more the familiar device designed to obtain favor for a poem by ascribing it to a foreign author. From some of these sketches we may gather, perhaps, a truer view of the author's experiences than from the poem which seems to be his "official" life. In this, *A Tragicall Discourse of the Unhappy Mans Life,* he berates fate and the court for the unjust treatment handed him. Churchyard relates his adventures in Scotland, in France and in Flanders. He weaves a long tale of broils, of hair-raising escapes and heroics. It is Churchyard's odyssey, but it seems to glorify the poet too much; and one is inclined to think that more than once he gave himself the benefit of the doubt. On the other hand, *A Heavie Matter of an English Gentleman and a Gentlewoman* seems to come closer to the truth. It is the episode of a prisoner who has been lying in a foul jail for many months, pursued by the malice of a dreadful duke, undergoing taunts and vile usage. To make matters worse, he falls in love with a widow of "gentle race and seed," thus adding to his other miseries that of a hopeless love.

"A Storie Translated out of Frenche" apparently deals once again with personal experiences. A young man of good family chooses to go to the wars instead of settling down, only to find

. . . . .

[28] Churchyard, *Challenge,* Sig. Kk3r.

himself disillusioned by the rigours of campaigning. He suffers privations; he is imprisoned and forced to pay a ransom he can ill afford, so that when he returns, he is broken in health and penniless. His household is dispersed, his father gone. The court gives him little hope and less help. Resolved never to return to that paradise of sycophants, he goes off to Picardy. An attempt to win a wealthy widow fails, for she prefers "a merchant with a grounded trade." Then he's off to the wars once more, only to be captured and imprisoned. Though good fortune smiles upon him momentarily when a kind lady aids him in escaping, he is forced to cleave his jailer's head to avoid pursuit. After walking three score miles, he reaches his own lines and safety. Then, unable to settle down, he engages in another campaign and is captured. Once more, a noble lady saves him from the fate that awaits spies—beheading. The poem ends by trailing off into a lengthy discourse on wealth and the lack of rewards for soldiers.

One does not need to go far into Churchyard's verse to discover the pedestrian vein in him. Hopelessly bourgeois, he seldom rises to an elevated mood. Yet, at times, he shows astonishingly keen powers of observation. Much of his jingling verse must be ascribed to the exigencies of hack-writing, by means of which he was trying to eke out the living which neither his soldiering nor the court would provide him. There are times when he shows a freshness and originality which belie the epithet "croaking voice" given him. For a certainty, his works gain in stature when compared to those of a Lewicke or a Garter. Despite his obvious limitations, Churchyard remains one of the small band of experimenters, such as Gascoigne and Whetstone, who paved the way for the great figures of the Elizabethan age.

As the sixteenth century draws to a close, however, a new temper may be observed creeping into literary works, the inevitable reaction to the strict morality of previous decades. It is not difficult to lay a finger on the reasons for the change. Chief among them was one of Elizabeth's customary shifts in policy.

Having finally come to the conclusion that the Puritan party was no longer essential to the pursuit of her statecraft, the Queen had definitely decided to curb the pretensions of the militant reformers with whose aims she was hardly in sympathy. The policies of general education and widespread reform sponsored by this group tended to give the common people too clear a view of church and government, a fact which Elizabeth, wily despot that she was, certainly did not favor. Consequently, we find that after 1585, the Puritans fell further and further into disfavor, until a point was reached where they felt that any measures sponsored by them must be taken without the aid of the sovereign.[29] There were other reasons, notably the rapid influx of foreign literature and the increase in travel. In addition, the feeling that Spain was defeated also brought an added sense of security. No longer could the major Catholic power and the Wolf of Rome threaten England, either politically or with their nefarious propaganda. Henceforth, the venom having been drawn from the serpent, England had little to fear.

Whatever the reasons, the change was significant and evident. It could be witnessed in the great outburst of amatory literature which broke out in the last two decades of the century. How the righteous Puritans must have writhed at the flood of sonnets and poems like *Caltha Poetarum* and *Venus and Adonis!* No longer was Ovid "moralized" and expurgated through the chaste, revising pen of Golding; it was brought forth in all its naked frankness to the chagrin of scandalized reformers, who loudly voiced their indignation.

So many pieces of dubious morals and questionable taste made their appearance during this period, that a number of them were publicly consigned to the flames in 1599 by order of Archbishop Whitgift and Bancroft, Bishop of London. This was the great purge in the Hall of Stationers as a result of

. . . . .

[29] M. M. Knappen, *Tudor Puritanism* (University of Chicago Press, 1939), p. 283ff.

which Marston's *Metamorphosis of Pygmalion's Image*, Marlowe's translations of Ovid, the satires of Hall and Marston, the *Epigrams* of Davies and Thomas Cutwode's *Caltha Poetarum*, together with a number of like poems were all condemned to the fire. Besides banning specifically the works of Nashe and Harvey, the decree further directed that no satires or epigrams could be printed in the future. Plays must be inspected by and receive the sanction of the prelates, who also reserved the right to pass on all "Englysh hystories." Among these, no doubt, were included many of our verse romances. Any work of this nature found without a license was to be brought before the scrutinizing eye of the church and punished accordingly. Thus an effective censorship was established on literary production in order to purify the new mood which had crept into poetry.

As an example of the change in the attitude towards morality which took place at this time, we may glance at Thomas Nashe's *The Choice of Valentines* (1592). The poem is one of those "unedifying toys for gentlemen," which Nashe admits having been forced to write. There is great likelihood that it may have been written for some convivial gathering of gentlemen. In the "Epilogue," he addresses the Earl of Southampton to whom the poem is dedicated and says:

> My mind once purg'd of such lascivious witt,
> With purified words and hallowed verse,
> Thy praises in large volumes shall rehearse
> That better may thy graver view befitt.[30]

Written in a frank spirit of fun, it describes the poet's visit to a brothel where his "Valentine" has been forced to take sanctuary, following the persecutions of the god Justice, Dudgeon-haft. As soon as he enters, the poet is made to leave his offertory; he refuses the advances of a pair of votaries of Venus, asking, instead, for "jentle mistris Francis." She is delighted

. . . . .

[30] Thomas Nashe, *The Choice of Valentines* (London, 1899), p. 24.

to see her "Tomalin," and Nashe embarks upon a lively, merry description of the concrete form which her joy takes. No details are spared; nothing is left for the reader to imagine. As he takes his departure:

> I paie our hostess scott and lothe at moste,
> And looke as leane and lank as anie ghoste.[31]

The poem closes with his farewell to the company:

> And so good night! unto you everie one;
> For loe, our thread is spunne and plaie is donne.[32]

Henry Petowe's *Philochasander and Elanira, the Faire Lady of Britaine* (1599) is hardly less piquant, although it is veiled under delicate, if rather transparent, allegory. It attempts to relate "the miserable passions of Love in exile, the unspeakable joy at being again received into favor, with the deserved guerdon of perfit love and Constantie." Restating this in less flowery terms, the poem describes the conquest of a hesitant but willing maiden by a persistent young man. We are plunged into the language of the sonnets, antitheses, conceits. The poet tells us that for two years he has been in love with this cold beauty, who casts him not so much as a tender glance to salve his misery. Her name is White:

> From Tuskane came my Ladies worthy race,
> Faire Florence was sometimes her antient seate,
> The wester Ile whose pleasant shore doth face,
> Wild Camberr cliffes did give her lively heate,
> Fostred she was with milke of Irish breast,
> And now in famous Britaine she doth rest.[33]

With all the usual sighs and moaning of a sonnet sequence, the poet describes his unsuccessful attempts to frighten off his

. . . . .

[31] *Ibid.*, p. 23. [32] *Ibid.*
[33] Henry Petowe, *Philochasander and Elanira*, sig. B1[r]. The reader will, no doubt, have recognized the source of this quotation as Surrey's sonnet to Geraldine.

rivals. Having killed four of them in a melee, he is banished from her presence; he must watch while:

> They eate the honny, I must hold the hive:
> I sowe the seede, and they must reape the corne,
> I wast, they win; I drawe and they must drive,
> Theirs is the thanke, and mine the bitter scorne,
> I seeke, they speede; in vaine my winde is spent,
> I gape, they get; I pray and yet am shent.[34]

Heretofore, the wooing has been conducted on a strictly decorous plane. The change in mood soon becomes apparent, however, as the poet gives vent to a frankly ribald outburst. Still, though the narrative deals with decidedly risqué material, Cutwode manages to preserve a definite air of delicacy.

One day the lady's horses become frightened, her coach is disabled, and she is thrown to the ground unconscious. While she is lying about in disarray, the birds flock about her, thinking her Flora. Petowe relishes the situation and gives us a lively description of her charms as the birds fly about her. Having ventured near her, the poet covers her up; when she awakens, she is thankful and, with a kiss, restores him to favor. There follows the usual ecstasy; the young man goes about entranced while she takes him to her palace, a Renaissance young man's dream, filled with treasures, pearls and costly stuffs. All this shall be his, she promises, if he will aid her in her plight, for her bane is "a proud Brittaine dame, Silla my foe."

> This dame (quoth she) a neighbring castle by
> Doth keepe, whose faire indeede I must confesse,
> Is too too faire grac'd with a wanton eye,
> Whose beautie then my faire is nothing lesse,
> Were she but dead, then I should never mone,
> For with her death my heavie woes were done.[35]

. . . . .

[34] *Ibid.*, Sig. C2ᵛ.
[35] *Ibid.*, Sig. E3ʳ.

Whereupon, he promises to do her bidding, to murder the enemy slowly, to be "slow in his cruelty," shedding as little blood as possible. By making use of the conventional language used in storming a medieval castle, Petowe describes the situation delicately, it is true, but unmistakably. Soon, Silla and her virgins are reduced to submission, and Elanira is enabled to enjoy life to the full. As a conclusion the author asks:

> How many dames affords this wilfull age?
> How many Sillas is there to be found,
> How many women can revenge aswage
> And bury mortall anger underground?
> As Silla did, for which as erst before,
> Faire Elanira did her joyes restore.[36]

Petowe, who is probably better known as the author of a second part of *Hero and Leander* (1598),[37] writes in the typical manner of the time, with a light touch, reminiscent of the Anacreontic imitations which were just becoming popular. A love of color and display is prominent throughout the poem. Despite his questionable subject, he succeeds in surrounding his work with an air of delicacy and lightness which dispels most of the objectionableness generated by the theme.

One needs only to scan the entries in the Register of the Stationers' Company and compare them with the extant pieces to realize how many have been lost during the passage of time. Poems such as *The Unluckie Firmentie,* composed by G. Kyttes (*circa* 1585), were doubtless very numerous. They must have been written for a reading public gifted with strong stomachs and a not-too-high degree of intelligence. This typical fragment celebrates the mishaps into which one Beede falls during his wedding night, when he finds himself unable to sleep because of his hunger. He finds a "pott of Furmentie"[38] and gorges himself, but encounters woe after woe in trying to

. . . . .

[36] *Ibid.,* Sig. G2ʳ.   [37] See p. 246.
[38] Frumentie, a porridge made of wheat and milk.

return to his bed. At the conclusion of the adventure, there are several broken heads, a good deal of wounded dignity and other such disasters. The piece displays the coarsest kind of humor and an unspeakably bad taste, both in poetry and subject matter.

Perhaps more than any other group, the native romances embody the characteristics and all the faults of the entire genre. Definitely bourgeois in tone, they attempt to bring home the cardinal points of middle class conduct—the lessons of thrift, industry and sobriety. We are shown young men who forsake their gainful occupations to seek a soldier's laurels but come to woeful ends. The evils of leading a wastrel's life and not applying oneself to commerce are vividly pointed out.

With the exception of a few tales like Nashe's and Petowe's, these verse romances are even more strikingly puritan in their attitude towards love. Everywhere the passion of love is decried and deprecated as a temporary aberration. Love is a snare, and matrimony is a remedy to be applied only with the greatest caution, with the due aid of parents and kinsmen. It is fitting, therefore, that maidens be wary of sudden passions, for betrayal lurks at every turn. Consequently, every heroine from Juliet to Catanea is made to pause and calculate with prudence and foresight just what the intentions of the lover may be. For purity is quickly lost, and the path to perdition thereafter is inevitable. Despite occasional exceptions such as Nashe's and Petowe's, the verse romances stress again and again the necessity of correct behavior on the part of children. This is best accomplished by allowing parents to choose mates for their offspring, because youth is obviously unable to exercise judgment in such matters. Again, author after author insists that marriages between people of unequal social status are unwise. Those who flout social conventions may expect the censure of the world and divine wrath to fall upon them.

Thus were the moral lessons brought home to the good burghers of England.

The Pseudo-Greek and Oriental Romances

A CERTAIN NUMBER OF VERSE TALES WHICH draw their origin from Greek and Oriental material differ but little from their prose counterparts so common at this time. Some of them have definite sources in Greek literature, but a large number merely imitate the popular Greek romances of Heliodorus and Longus or content themselves with using pseudo-Greek names and locales. For the most part, they are characterized by the same episodic structure, with adventure following upon adventure, little thought being given to arranging their innumerable events into an organic structure.

One of the earliest of these tales, by Edmund Elviden, a poet from the north country who flourished *circa* 1570, is *The Most Excellent and Pleasant Metaphoricall History of Pesistratus and Catanea*, dedicated to Edward de Vere, Earl of Oxford. We are taken to the land of the Aganetians, where two rulers, the brothers Kenedoxus and Pesistratus, are warring against the treacherous Tetimetians. Anteres, leader of the enemy, offers them a combat with his two sons, arranging to resort to treachery, however, should his side be the loser. Suspicious of his intentions, the two Aganetians post guards, so that the combat turns into a pitched battle in which the enemy is routed. During the victory feast, Kenedoxus begins to bluster, and his younger brother is forced to defend himself. A duel follows:

> But now began the broyle so hot, that who had seene the
> blows,
> The deadly thrustes, the desperate foynes that eache the other
> showes,
> The battring bangs, the thumping thwacks that eche the
> other lent,
> With stayned field of brothers blood so carelessly spent.[1]

It is not long before the valiant Pesistratus has overcome his brother, who, weakened by his wounds, falls to the ground. The victor is about to kill himself from remorse, when he is persuaded by friendly knights to flee the wrath of the avengers.

Having landed in Italy, Pesistratus rescues a hermit from a maddened lion, thereby winning the admiration of Pecipater, a knight of Tarentum. Together with his new-found friend, he makes a triumphal entry into the city and meets Catanea, his friend's sister. Inevitably love is kindled. Inevitably the two lovers go off to be miserable and to assail love bitterly. They will accept no help, nor will they reveal their love to their friends. Catanea, prudent and calculating, reviews all the advantages of love with the cold appraisal of a gambler placing a bet. Meanwhile, under the name of Antropos, Kenedoxus, who is thirsting for revenge, takes service with his brother. Having discovered the secret of his love for Catanea, he persuades Pesistratus to write her a letter. By this means, they are finally brought together, but armed with the letter, the treacherous Antropos-Kenedoxus goes to her uncle and warns him that the two lovers are plotting against him. During the resulting trial, Pecipater acts as their champion, kills the traitorous brother and the woes seem to be at an end. But

. . . . .

[1] Edmund Elviden, *The Most Excellent and Pleasant Metaphoricall History of Pesistratus and Catanea*, Sig. B8ʳ.

Phetratus, the uncle, seizes the throne, after poisoning Pecipater, and exiles Pesistratus. The latter is prevented from committing suicide by a friendly shepherd, just as couriers from the Aganetians summon him to his throne. Finally, he returns to avenge his friend and to claim Catanea.

Certain of the elements of *Gorboduc* are evident in this metrical romance; at the same time, its pastoral locale reminds us vaguely of the settings made famous later by the *Arcadia*. The quality of the verse is pitiful, however, and the author shows little awareness of the dramatic value of the tale.

Matthew Grove tried his hand at something more ambitious than his usual "songes and sonnets" in bringing forth *The Most Famous and Tragicall Historie of Pelops and Hipodamia* (1587), a versification of the famous chariot race. The "Argument" will suffice to give an impression of the poem:

> Onomaus, King of Archadia, unto whom it was told by the soothsayers that whensoever his only daughter, Hipodamia, did marie, he should die, she coming to her ripened years, he proclaimed a prize of running with chariots that whosoever did vanquish him therein should marry Hipodamia and have the realme with her, but the vanquished should die. Many of the wooers were slayne: at last Pelops promised privily to Myrtilus that if he should winne the prize, Myrtilus should lye with Hipodamia the first night: whereupon the latter made the axiltree of wax, by reason whereof in the race course, the charet fell downe, which Onomaus then perceiving, slew himselfe and Pelops enjoyed the lady. And Myrtilus requiring that which was promised, Pelops threw him into the Sea, which ever after was called Myrtonum.[2]

The tale has little to distinguish it from its predecessors; the verse is boring; the love element is hardly exploited; and several dramatic opportunities are overlooked. The race, for example, is told in two lines, whereas the preparations for it are

. . . . .

[2] Matthew Grove, *The Most Famous Historie of Pelops and Hippodamia*, Argument to the Poem.

discussed endlessly. Despite all attempts to make a hero out of Pelops, he is a miserable caitiff. The story might have provided an interesting "question of love," such as the Renaissance courtly audiences would have loved to discuss had they felt in a cynical mood. Who was to blame? Who deserved the reward? Pelops, for his transparent casuistry in accusing his friend of intended lechery and treason, using this as an excuse for having him drowned? Or Myrtilus, for his shrewdness and wit? Certainly the ironic salve given to the victim, by naming after him the sea into which he is plunged, is nothing short of genius.[3]

We have already seen that two of the tales from Turberville's 1587 collection also have Greece for a locale. These are based on accounts in Plutarch's *Moralia* and reached England by way of Italian translations. They are respectively the tale of the tyrant Nicocrates and the tale of Muzio and Micca.[4] In neither of these, however, is there the atmosphere and the type

· · · · ·

[3] Grove was the author of many shorter poems, all undistinguished; we might quote one, however, for its intrinsic utilitarianism. It is called "A Perfect Trick to Kill the Little Black Flees in One's Chamber."

> Take half a quart of barly graine,
> A quart of strongest beere,
> And boyle withall in earthen pot,
> A pint of water cleare,
> Till all these three consumed bee
> To ounces twelve or lesse,
> And then the place to which you will
> These fleas in heaps to presse,
> Anoynt with that; this water hath
> In it this virtue saw,
> That all the flees will thither come:
> Then take a slender strawe,
> And tickle them on the small ribs,
> And when you see one gape,
> Thrust then the strawe into his mouth
> And death he ne shall scape.

A recipe, no doubt, worthy to take its place with the salt-on-the-tail-of-a-bird method!

[4] This tale is to be found also in Bandello, III, 5.

of incident found in Elviden, where we get a definite feeling that we are breathing the air of Heliodorus' *Aethiopica*.

The widespread favor which pastoral romances found in England brought forth many imitations, among which is to be noted Francis Sabie's *The Fisherman's Tale of the Famous Actes, Life and Love of Cassender, A Grecian Knight* (1595). Sabie has given us a fantastic mixture of anachronistic material which confuses Sidney, Greene and the original source, Diodorus Siculus. Cassender, the son of Antipater, was a celebrated Greek warrior who lived *circa* 300 B.C. Prominent in the Macedonian wars, he was regent of Macedon and Greece until Alexander the Great became of age.[5] Sabie, however, gives us a far different characterization. We have a short introduction in which the narrator is shipwrecked on an island. Here, he meets an old man who tells him the following story: He comes of "Achilles race," and his name is Cassender. In his youth, he performed great deeds among pagan folk, warred under the mighty Philip of Macedon, against the "flintie Getes." Returning thence through "Boheme land," he finds King Mathias warring with the Turks, aids him in rescuing his daughter, Lucian, kept prisoner by Amurath, and turns the tide in favor of the Christians. After refusing the hand of the princess, he proceeds on his journey and falls in with a group of "nymphs." Captivated by the most beautiful of them, the foundling daughter of old Thirsis, he throws away his arms and turns shepherd. Later, having found out that the maid loves him and that she is about to marry another, he abducts her, only to be separated from her during a storm.

Their subsequent adventures are told in the second part of the poem, *Flora's Fortune*, published the following year. Grieved at the loss of her lover, Flora has attempted to kill herself, but Thirsis has prevented her. Later, she receives a measure of comfort when the oracle of Apollo reassures her that her

. . . . .

[5] Charles Anthon, *A Classical Dictionary* (New York, 1883), article on Cassender.

lover is alive. The plot becomes more and more involved, but
finally, it is revealed that Flora is the daughter of the king of
the land. Eventually, the lovers are reunited.

Sabie departs from the customary fourteener couplets, using
instead the lighter pentameter line. Thus, even in the last
decade of the sixteenth century, we see blank verse being used
as a narrative medium. Here is Sabie's description of a storm:

> This said, an huge, tempestuous blast of wind,
> Fraught with a mighty garison of waves,
> Laid so hard siege against our fortrest pine
> That cables crackt and sailes in sunder tare.
> Out cride the keepers, now we are undone,
> But fully bent unto our endlesse wracke
> Fierce Adria remunified his force:
> A roaring cannon he again dischargde
> Which rent our shippe against the craggie rockes,
> Then might you see an heart-lamenting hap;
> Some hang on boards, some swimming in the deepe,
> All laboring to save and keepe their lives.
> I held in armes my true and dearest love
> Thinking with her to end my lothed life,
> When suddenly we were by fate disjoyned:
> I thrown by force all headlong in the seas,
> Yet laboring my life still to preserve
> For who so wretched but desires to live?
> These twinding armes caught hold upon a board
> Which drew me to this life preserving rocke.[6]

Like many other authors of verse romances, Sabie is fond of
such descriptions of the sea, and in these he often succeeds in
writing his best verse. Many of the details of this tale are
drawn from Greene's *Pandosto*; it has been shown that he also
borrowed from Ovid and Mantuan.[7]

. . . . .

[6] Francis Sabie, *A Fisherman's Tale*, quoted from J. P. Collier, *The Poetical Decameron* (Edinburgh, 1820), I, 137.
[7] M. D. Mawdsley, *The Use of the Latin Sources in the Writings of Francis Sabie* (University of Chicago, 1936).

Most of the remaining tales, like the preceding ones, offer little variety of incident and are very similar in treatment to those already discussed. A few words might be spared, however, for John Partridge who composed several of these romances. One of them, *The Most Famous and Worthy Historye of the Worthy Lady Pandavula, Daughter to the Mighty Paynim, the Great Turke* (1566), makes use of Oriental material and recounts the story of the beautiful daughter of Sylewma, King of Turkey.

> In every place the comely corps of this Princess to see,
> The lusty gentell knights, on foaming steades on hie,
> Her love to wynne, their manly force full often there do trie.[8]

During the tournament, Alfine, her beloved knight, distinguishes himself by his valor and his modesty. Though he tries to avoid Flaccus, another of her suitors who is determined to provoke an incident, he is finally forced to unhorse him. Much of the tale describes the pangs of the two lovers, since the king refuses to grant them permission to marry. During the struggle with the Christians, Alfine is taken prisoner, but his captors release him upon condition that he will not bear arms against them. Later, taunted by Flaccus, who accuses him of cowardice, Alfine kills his foe. Just as he is about to embrace the princess, the king plunges a fatal blade in his body. Pandavula throws herself into the fire at his cremation, and the despondent king ends his days by falling on a sword. The poem has many of the qualities of a ballad, especially its extreme naiveté.

Partridge was evidently quite active about this time, for besides publishing *The History of Astyanax and Polyxena*, in the same year, he also composed *The Worthy Historye of the Most Noble and Valiant Knight Plasidas, Otherwise Called Eustas* (1566), a redaction of the well-known medieval saint's

. . . . .

[8] John Partridge, *The Most Famous and Worthy Historye of the Lady Pandavula*, Sig. A1ʳ.

tale. We are given an account of Plasidas' conversion, his subsequent impoverishment, his departure for Egypt, the loss of his wife to the master of the ship, who keeps her in lieu of payment. Though beset by endless trials, Plasidas is finally summoned by the emperor and reunited with his family. Upon their refusal to adore the pagan gods, however, they are placed in a brass ox and burned to death. The story was extremely popular during the Middle Ages, versions of it being found in Caxton's *Legenda* and also in the *Gesta Romanorum*.

Even a brief summary of these romances of Greek origin clearly reveals their chief characteristics. None of them achieves distinction as a work of art, but, as in the case of other verse romances, this was not their aim. Knowing that their middle class readers would not be exacting in this respect, the chief interest of their authors lay in piling incident upon incident, in building up a tale of endless adventures, without thought of organic construction. Following the example of the popular medieval romances of chivalry, they introduced fantastic incidents and anachronistic absurdities which could have pleased only an undiscriminating class of readers and which drew the cynical sneers of more sophisticated critics like Thomas Nashe and Henry Fitzgeoffrey.[9] But their themes and settings, drawn from far-away lands, their revival of the saint's adventures delighted bourgeois readers and made this type a great favorite of the middle classes.

. . . . .

[9] See Wright, *op. cit.*, p. 92ff.

PART THREE

Mythological
Narrative
Poetry

X V

Mythology in England

LEAVING ROMANTIC TALES AND THE BLOODY
broils of history, we come to even richer pastures for poetical
fiction—the world of pagan mythology. It is the world of the
old Roman and Greek gods, condemned and denounced by the
Church as heathen, yet forever strong in the minds of men
even during the Middle Ages. It is the fabled kingdom in
which Venus and Jove run counter to ascetic Christian doctrine, but gaze indulgently with their Olympian serenity at
the strangely barbarous requirements of the new religion. For
no matter how strongly the myths of Christianity established
themselves in the Western world, they never succeeded in
eradicating the old gods of Olympus; and even in their greatest
heyday, the Virgin and saints had to reign side by side with
Venus and the demigods of the Pantheon. Just as the old
Grecian gods had been made welcome at the side of the Roman
Lares and Penates, so Apollo and Diana became acceptable to
the minds of the Middle Ages. We have only to look at the
complete acceptance of the Virgilian heroes,[1] at the enthusi-

· · · · ·

[1] Domenico Comparetti, *Virgilio nel Medioevo* (Firenze, 1896).

189

asm shown for Homeric figures, to realize that the Middle Ages wisely, if unconsciously, had not rejected the rich inheritance of the preceding cultures. Virgil himself became Dante's ideal mentor, and the pathetic Trojan warriors, fleeing from the burning ruins of their city, were eagerly claimed as the legendary ancestors of many of the leading dynasties in Europe.

During the intervening centuries, the poets in Europe had kept alive the old myths. Sir Orfeo had become a knight of the Middle Ages, Pyramus and Thisbe, typical lovers of the thirteenth century. At the same time, Cressida had been conjured up from supposedly classical origins to represent the faithless, weak, thoroughly feminine heroine of romance. Aided by handbooks of mythology like Boccaccio's and Waley's, every literate person became saturated with this lore and with the various interpretations which the Fathers of the Church attributed to the old myths. With the approach of the Renaissance and its revival of interest in the classical world, the old mythology gripped more and more the minds of the people. Mythological phrases and comparisons were constantly heard on everyone's lips. Mythological characters were dramatized and became household figures. The very pastry cooks, well versed in the history of the ancient gods, decorated their huge pastries with scenes from the *Metamorphoses*.[2] We find the various guilds, which formerly had delighted in representing scenes from the Old Testament in their interludes, discarding these figures for Venus and her retinue. At her coronation in 1533, Anne Boleyn is greeted with rich pageants suggested by the mythological world, while the choirs which welcome her sing not hymns but gay ballads, inspired by the old, profane poetry.[3] The sumptuousness in England is beginning to rival that of the courts at Paris and Ferrara.

With the crowning of Elizabeth and the stabilizing of political conditions, with the incipience of the tremendous adula-

. . . . .

[2] Warton, *op. cit.*, III, 396.
[3] For accounts of these festivities, see Hall's and Holinshed's chronicles.

tion paid the Virgin Queen and the innumerable festivities, pageants and masques given by courtiers in her honor, courtly England began to live in a veritable mythological world. The Queen herself was raised to the status of a goddess; she was addressed as one of Diana's nymphs and received a final coronation as a divinity at the hands of Spenser in the *Faerie Queene*. The concern with theology was minimized or subordinated; Christianity's harsh doctrine was forgotten for the time being; and the Renaissance introduced a world replete with the Panic feeling, a pagan world, saturated with life and color and emotion. Despite the howlings of reformers—and in England they were plentiful—there came to reign a frankly sensuous delight in color and in song. Everywhere rang the Anacreontic motto, "Let us concern ourselves with today, for tomorrow—who knows?"

The generation of Shakespeare, Drayton and Spenser reveled in color and in imagery. It took great delight in the magnificent hues of brocades, in the exotic gleam of jewels, rich beyond the imagination. To the Elizabethans an Orient pearl was not a culture pearl, but a fabulous jewel, conveyed from romantic lands by caravans which had sweated over the trade trails that straggled endlessly across the desert. In their poems, we are taken to a world of flocks, grazing peacefully in green pastures. Shepherds draw forth tenuous sighs from their flutes and enchant nymphs who are flushing with languid desire. And it is in the mythological poems that all this love of color and the senses is distilled and refined. They reflect the passionate worship of beauty, the voluptuous concern with the world of the gods, and the sensuous enjoyment of the physical values of life. They are the culmination of the Renaissance, the final triumph of the pagan spirit.

Despite all the languor of this type of poetry, there is in it a nervousness which is typical of the Elizabethan age. The Italian mythological poems of the late sixteenth century convey an impression of enervation, of spent lassitude. Lovers go through the same weary motions which they have been rehearsing for the past three centuries. On the other hand, Marlowe's Leander is a lusty youth whose desires will not be denied; Hero, a young woman who believes, fundamentally, that virginity is not the most desirable of human conditions. There is a tired feeling in Continental poetry which does not seem to exist in its English counterpart. Granted that almost invariably the young poet is singing with the aid of Petrarch and Ovid, still, the singing is joyful and spontaneous, not at all like the artificial, if flawless, chant of Marino.

In view of the great profusion of Continental mythological poems, one might be tempted to believe that English poets dipped freely into these sources, as was the case with the sonnet and the epic, but the evidence seems to preclude such a conclusion. This independence was the result of their familiarity with classical literature. Because Ovid and other popular writers from which the mythological poems chiefly derive were school texts, young poets had no further to go for inspiration than to these originals. Moreover, the greater part of the classical authors had been made available through translations, during the first part of Elizabeth's reign. Therefore, by this time, the introduction of mythological material in poetic compositions had become a convention. A glance at a typical miscellany, *The Gorgeous Gallery of Gallant Inventions* (1578), will show many of the mythological characters to be the subjects of brief lyrics and part of the common literary heritage.[4] The absence of the usual acknowledgments of sources which Elizabethan authors used so freely furnishes additional proof of the independence of this genre from foreign models. European poets are seldom, if ever, mentioned; and the student is well aware that there would have been no reticence on the part of English writers to admit that they had "translated" or imitated. Plagiarism was an unknown sin in those days; and one of the rare voices which cried out in the wilderness was

. . . . .

[4] *A Gorgeous Gallery of Gallant Inventions,* ed. H. E. Rollins (Harvard University Press, 1926).

Sidney's when he exclaimed, "I never drank at Aganippe's well."

Because of this widespread familiarity with classical models, English mythological poets went straight to the originals for their materials. The favorite work by far was Ovid's *Metamorphoses*. But the rather frank episodes of the *Metamorphoses*, as well as some of the other lascivious gambols of the Olympians, were bound to draw the fire of the Puritan element in England. John Marston, in satirizing them, alluded to the writers of this type of poetry as "lewd Priapians." Likewise, Bishop Hall recognized the popularity of the type in his satires, but decried its immorality, including in his censure, Marlowe, Cutwode, Marston and Shakespeare.[5]

In spite of their licentiousness, these poems were considered speedy remedies for "melancholy, heart qualmes and such dumpishness."[6] Nor did censure deter feminine readers from perusing this amorous poetry; women were constantly berated by Puritan critics for their addiction to such bawdy writings; and it is recorded that Shakespeare's *Venus and Adonis* and other such poems formed part of the library of a lady of pleasure.[7] The effort to purge English minds of such lewdness continued, but we must admit, with no great success. Towards the middle of the century, however, strong attempts were made to purify Ovid and to present myths in moralized guise, by concealing the grosser passages under a mantle of allegorical significance.[8]

An examination of mythological poetry will reveal little novelty of incident, for, after all, in these poems the action is minimized to insignificance and their entire scope lies in the

. . . . .

[5] The reaction to these amoristic poems was evinced by many writers, among them Southwell and Nicolas Breton. A discussion will be found on p. 279. See also Marston's *Metamorphosis of Pygmalions Image*, A. H. Bullen edition (London, 1887).
[6] L. B. Wright, *Middle Class Culture in Elizabethan England*, p. 233.
[7] *Ibid.*, p. 113ff.
[8] For a further treatment, see p. 213ff.

creation of a mood. Description no longer serves as background for action, but becomes an end in itself. The poems develop into a series of tableaux, brilliant in imagery and redolent with the luxury of the Renaissance. We are transported to a magic world of color and music where pain is banished and only joy and inebriated pleasure exist. We are brought to a land of nymphs and satyrs, gods and goddesses, a world of light loves and broken hearts which leave us sad but not despondent, a world of gay intrigue where anguish and deception are transitory and are quickly dispelled by the eternal gladness which reigns over it. It is the momentary triumph of the paganism of the Renaissance over the morality and the strict Christianity of the Reformation.

In the subsequent pages, we shall observe the development of mythological poetry, from the ineffectual gropings of a Peend or a Hubbard to the superb mastery over verse and myth of a Marlowe and a Drayton. We shall see these compositions serve as the trial horses of young poets who climbed Olympus. But we shall also watch the gaiety and the airiness, the youthful delight which the early poets took in consorting with the gods, alter with the new mood which overtakes the seventeenth century and turn into bitter satire. When this happens, the new poetry gives the impression that poets, ashamed of earlier, childish games, are repudiating their former exuberance and are now playing at a masquerade with the obvious self-consciousness of adults, fearful of being caught indulging in such trifles.

XVI

The Continental Background

BEFORE PROCEEDING TO THE ENGLISH MYTHO-
logical poems, however, it will be well to cast a brief glance
at the background of this poetry on the Continent itself. There
is little doubt that some of the Italian and French mythological
poems gave the incentive to English poets to essay their skill
in this type, although, as we indicated, England preferred to
work independently of actual European models.

In Italy the mythological poem was even more popular than
in England. Literally hundreds of poems, dealing with mythological material, were written in Italy during the three centuries from 1300 to 1600. Their popularity did not cease with
the end of the Renaissance, for they enjoyed favor well into
the nineteenth century.

As is usual, Homer, Virgil and Ovid served as the foun-
tainheads from which all this material derives. The latter's
Metamorphoses were by far the favorite hunting ground of
poetasters, for the individual incident or metamorphosis provided an ideal nucleus for the composition of a poem. Thus in
Italy, as in England later on, practically every budding poet
dipped into Ovid, seeking poetic material for his Muse. His

195

reputation for immorality during the Middle Ages notwithstanding, the genial author of the *Art of Love* kept a very strong hold upon the affections of the poets of Italy, drawing praise even from such a stern moral critic as Dante.

For Boccaccio, Ovid had a veritable fascination, and many of the Florentine's works either reproduce him literally or are permeated with his spirit. In the final analysis, Boccaccio himself may be considered as a Tuscan Ovid. Today, because of the greater emphasis laid upon the *Decameron*, we are inclined to forget that during his own day and throughout the Renaissance, Boccaccio was held in repute mainly for his Latin works. In *De Genealogia Deorum*, *De Casibus*, and *De Claribus Mulieribus*, he chronicled legendary or semi-legendary characters as Ovid had done purely mythological material. Boccaccio himself had a good deal of the myth-maker within him. A good example is furnished by his *Ninfale Fiesolano*, a typically Ovidian metamorphosis in which is told the pitiful deception of Mensola, one of Diana's nymphs, by a youthful shepherd, Affrico. Unable to bear her remorse, the nymph flees from her lover and is transformed into a body of water. The shepherd drowns himself in the little brook which now bears his name. Here is the true Ovidian idyll, with its ingenuous atmosphere so vital to this type of composition.

Boccaccio's later works include among others the *Amorosa Visione*, which treats many of the mythological fables, and *La Caccia di Diana*, a series of charming mythological inventions of Ovidian flavor. In Boccaccio, however, the myths retain an allegorical significance, for the Florentine still believed that the aim of poetry was to expose life under a veil of poetic fiction.

It would be impossible to cite all the mythological material left by various poets.[1] Suffice it to mention the graceful *Orfeo*

. . . . .

[1] For a useful treatment of the subject, see A. Belloni, *Il Poema Epico e Mitologico* (Milano, 1912), p. 349ff. See also A. Schiavo-Lena, *La Poesia Mitologica nel Secolo XIV, XV, XVI* (Caltagirone, 1907).

by Poliziano, told more as a dramatic interlude than as a narrative poem. Luca Pulci (1431-70), eldest of three brothers all famous for their poetic efforts, made his *Driadeo d'Amore* conform more to the narrative models. This popular poem which ran through numerous editions is strongly reminiscent of Boccaccio's *Ninfale Fiesolano* as well as of Ovid. The tale narrates the love of the satyr Severo for the nymph Lora and their subsequent transformation into clear streams.[2] It has relatively little poetical value, outside of the interest it holds in the development of this type. Pulci employed the *ottava rima* for this poem, although in his *Pistole*, imitations of Ovid's *Heroides*, he made use of *terza rima*. The favor enjoyed by these short mythological compositions was so widespread that even Pulci's more famous brother, Luigi, tried his hand at two of them.

Many of the humanists of the fifteenth century used Ovidian material for Latin poems of this type. The celebrated Lorenzo de Medici fashioned *L'Ambra* on the models of Ovid and Boccaccio. In it, he traces the origins of his villa of Poggio a Caiano, the site of the loves of Lauro and one of Diana's nymphs, Ambra. The poem has all of Lorenzo's warmth, his love of color and his sensuous enjoyment of the world about him; it shows not only his idyllic strain, but also his acute sense of realism. *L'Ambra* is a worthy specimen of Lorenzo's famed artistry in mythological poetry. Giovanni Pontano, another famous humanist, also contributed to the genre his *Lepidina* and *Urania*. Though it professes to be an astronomical treatise, *Urania* has a strong mythological tinge because of Pontano's description of the myths of the various pagan divinities from which the constellations derive their names. The name of Girolamo Vida (1485-1566) will not be unfamiliar to English

. . . . .

[2] Many of these poems were composed with the idea of creating myths of locality, a process very favored by Renaissance poets. For a study of this interesting aspect, see Rudolf B. Gottfried's "Spenser and the Myths of Locality," *Studies in Philology*, XXXIV (1937), p. 107ff.

readers. This poet is perhaps better known today for a religious epic, *Christias,* than for his mythological poem on chess, *Ludus Scacchiae,* which in its day enjoyed a wide reputation and was translated into English in 1597.[3]

Numerous translations of the *Metamorphoses* attest to the increasing interest in Ovid during the sixteenth century in Italy. These make use mostly of *ottava rima* rather than the blank verse advocated by later critics. Prominent among them are Niccolo Agostini's version in 1537, G. A. Anguillara's in 1561, and Fabiano Maretti's in 1570. Another translation by Lodovico Dolce in 1553 reads like a romance; it has an introduction, links between the fifteen books and moral reflections at the end of each division.

Despite these frequent translations, the individual episodes of the *Metamorphoses* continued to furnish poetic material, and we may note Bernardino Martirano's Ovidian *Aretusa* which suggested certain passages to Tansillo's *Clorinda.* Martirano, a counsellor of Charles V, is chiefly remembered for his anachronistic treatment of Narcissus who is made to go to war against the Turks. The poems of Luigi Tansillo, which convey vignettes of truly idyllic freshness, have far greater poetic merit. This poet, a native of Horace's birthplace, wrote a *Clorinda* reminiscent of Petrarch and Sannazzaro. He exhibited a more rugged and lively mood in his *Vendemmiatore* (*circa* 1532), inspired, perhaps, by the bacchanalian customs common around Naples. A strong tinge of Ovid's *Ars Amatoria* is noticeable in his exhortations to women to make the most of their youth and in his actual lessons on how to achieve "love's

· · · · ·

[3] We cite also Giovan Maria Filelfo (not Francesco, the humanist), who composed a *Marziade,* a very encomiastic piece; Baratella's *Polidoreis;* Maffeo Vegio's *Velleris Aurei Libri* IV, relating the intrigues of the gods and the adventures of the Golden Fleece; and Basini's *Argonautica,* which remained unfinished. This poet also composed *Meleagridos Libri III,* dealing with the adventures of Meleager in Caledonia, and also *Hesperides,* an epic poem in praise of the Malatesta family in which the author dips freely into Homer.

sweet end." In his more sentimental moods, Tansillo is color-ful and akin to Bembo and Ariosto.[4] Luigi Alamanni's *Favola di Fetonte* and *Favola d'Atlante*, are very close to Ovid in manner and mood. From Alamanni's pen comes a *Favola di Narcisso* in hendecasyllables, as well as an ingenious *Diluvio Romano*, cloaking in mythological language the story of the great Roman flood of 1530.

Bernardo Tasso's paraphrase of Musaeus's *Hero and Leander* loses a great deal of its effectiveness as a result of the poet's interpolations. Here, the ancient Greek account is dressed in Platonic and Petrarchan garments which by no stretch of the imagination measure up to the excellence that Tasso assumed them to possess. It will be remembered that the elder Tasso boasted to Melin de Sainct Gelays that he, a modern Orpheus, with his lyre had caused the winds and the sea to be still.[5] Tasso's poem was highly regarded by his contemporaries, how-ever, and it served as the model for Boscan's Spanish version of the tale.[6] Unwilling to rest upon these laurels, the father of

. . . . .

[4] Mention might also be made of F. Maria Molza's *La Ninfa Tiberina* (1538) an Ovidian idyll in praise of the poet's mistress, reminiscent of Theocritus. Others are Lavezzola's *Le Nozze di Cerbero e Megera* (circa 1570); *Amor Prigioniero* by Mario di Leo; Coppetta's *Favola di Psiche*, Rocco Lando's *Favola della Rosa*; G. F. Bellentani's *Favola di Piti, Peristere Anassarete*, and also several versions of the Adonis story by Dolce, Parabosco and Turcagnota.

[5] *Quasi canoro cigno*
lungo le vaghe sponde di Meandro,
e d'Ero e di Leandro
piansi'l fato maligno;
ed ebbi il ciel si grato e si benigno,
che'l sordo mare e i venti
rabbiosi poser giu l'orgoglio e l'ira
al suon della mia lira,
e ster cheti ed intenti
alle mie voci i liquidi elementi.
          B. Tasso, Ode XXXVII, stanza 12.

[6] For a study of these two versions of the tale of Hero and Leander, see Francesco Flamini, *Studi di Storia Letteraria* (Livorno, 1895), p. 385ff.

the poet of *La Gerusalemme Liberata* tried his hand at several other such poems, among which is a *Piramo e Tisbe*.[7]

Mythological poetry finds its highest development in *L'Adone* by Giambattista Marino. Here, the mythological world receives its supreme embodiment in a poem, graceful, idyllic, enchanted, yet artificial. Already the spirit of the seventeenth century begins to weigh upon writers; and though the work represents the very perfection of such art, its decadent tone is unmistakably evident. Marino labored at this work for many years, preparing himself by writing other mythological idylls. Taking as his central theme the tale of Venus and Adonis, the author weaves about it countless other mythological incidents; he paints numberless tableaux of pagan myths and enchanted gardens, inserting, at the same time, strange bits of incongruous scientific poetry, which foreshadow the new interests of the age. But with all its color, its music, its sensuousness, the poem is pervaded by a cold, artificial spirit. It belongs to an age of false morals and false religion; it belongs to a world moribund and yet incapable of dying. Evidently these drawbacks were not apparent at the time, for Marino's poem was wildly acclaimed by his contemporaries and was regarded as the standard of perfection for centuries afterwards. Literally hundreds of such poems poured from the refined but sterile minds of *abbés* and decadent noblemen. To the detriment of Italian letters, the genre persisted down to the last century, when it received new stimulus at the hands of such great poets as Foscolo and Manzoni.

In general, the French mythological poem developed very much in the same manner as it had in Italy. The creative, original work was preceded by an outburst of translations of the classics during the first half of the sixteenth century. One has only to remember Amyot, who made of Plutarch a complete

. . . . .

[7] For a list of other poems of this nature, consult Flamini, *op. cit.*, 256ff.

French gentleman, to realize how delightful such translations could be upon occasion.[8]

In France, as in the rest of Europe, Ovid was the most popular poet during the fourteenth and fifteenth centuries. Although he must have been widely read in the original, he was known chiefly through a paraphrase provided with a moral commentary which attempted to explain in terms of Christian doctrine the objectionable passages of the Latin poet. In 1531, Clement Marot reintroduced the *Metamorphoses* by translating two of its books into French verse. From then on, there was no halting the flood. Earlier, in 1515, Marot had tried his hand at *Le Temple de Cupidon* and later translated Moschus's Greek story of the flight of Eros. Not inconsiderable in the list of his translations is *Hero and Leander* versified from a Latin version of Musaeus. The literary activity of the numerous Italians at the French court was very influential in spurring the efforts of French poets in the composition of mythological poems. The personal friendship between Alamanni and Bernardo Tasso and many of the French poets was especially significant.[9]

The example set by these Italians produced a good many fruits, among which may be noted M. de Sainct Gelay's graceful *Deploration de Venus*, written in imitation of Bion's idyll. Baif's *Le Ravissement d'Europe* (1552), a narrative poem imitated from Moschus and generally acknowledged to be one of his best efforts, is also notable.[10] The vogue of the mythological poem in France, however, was not as great as in Italy or in England, for French genius, modelling itself upon the Petrachists, remained mostly lyrical or spent itself upon the great satirical works that distinguish French letters of this age.

. . . . .

[8] A detailed discussion will be found in Arthur Tilley's *The Literature of the French Renaissance* (Cambridge, 1904).
[9] See Flamini's excellent article "Le lettere italiane alla corte di Francesco I," *op. cit.*, pp. 199ff.
[10] Tilley, *op. cit.*, II, 6.

In Spain, the close relations carried on with Italy as a result of Spanish political domination in the Italian peninsula helped to spread the literary ideas which the Renaissance had fostered. Widespread imitation of Ovid's works is noticeable throughout Spain, evidenced not only by translations, but by prose tales, plays and narrative poems.[11] Lope de Vega and Calderon composed many mythological plays, and there is a wealth of narrative mythological poetry.

Again the personal relations between poets contributed to the popularizing of the genre. Andrea Navagero's and Bernardo Tasso's numerous visits to Spain as ambassadors left a powerful imprint upon Spanish letters. Bernardo Tasso's *Favola di Leandro et Ero* had a direct influence upon the work of Juan Boscan. This poet, already known for a translation of Castiglione's *Il Cortegiano,* published *La Historia de Leandro y Hero* in 1543. He followed his model by introducing the Italian *versi sciolti* into Spanish for the first time.[12] Boscan's version of Musaeus is even more prolix than Tasso's, for he expands the original 340 hexameters to almost 3,000, retaining none of the simplicity of the original. Traces of other Italian poets, such as Poliziano and Bembo are evident.[13] Although Boscan's attempt deserves praise because of a certain amount of grace and an occasional fine line, he wanders far from the true classic vein. His digressions and needless expansion of material destroy utterly the proportion found in Musaeus. The most one may say for it is that it has more psychological fidelity than true poetic quality.[14]

Among other compositions of this type, we find Fernando
. . . . .

[11] See R. Schevill, "Ovid and the Renascence in Spain," *University of California Publications in Modern Philology,* IV (1913).

[12] George Ticknor, *History of Spanish Literature* (Houghton Mifflin Company, 1888), I, 477ff.

[13] A complete account of Boscan will be found in M. Menendez y Pelayo's critical study of the poet in *Antologia de Poetas Liricos y Castellanos* (Madrid, 1919), Vol. XIII.

[14] Flamini, "La Historia de Leandro y Hero," *op. cit.,* p. 385ff.

de Acuña's blank verse version of the contest between Ajax and Ulysses, some mythological poems on Pyramus and Thisbe by Antonio Villegas written about 1550, and also a group of narrative poems, not without merit, written in the Italian manner by Gregorio Silvestre, another contemporary poet.[15]

But we must close this brief survey of European mythological poetry and proceed to England to observe the mythological poem develop into a type of truly artistic rank.

. . . . .

[15] Ticknor, *op. cit.*, II, 63ff.

XVII

Mythology in England: Virgil, Homer, Ovid

THE ENTHUSIASM GENERATED IN ENGLAND BY
humanism gave rise to anxious pleas from many learned men
for the translation of the works of antiquity and those of more
recent European production as well. Constantly the cry was
heard that English letters did not adequately fulfill this demand and that classical lore must be made available. The call
did not go unheeded; before long, translators set to work and
achieved results that are still astonishing for their vitality and
freshness. The sixteenth century in England may proudly
boast of its translations, which rival in excellence the best that
France and Italy can offer; and the names of Florio and North
may well go down beside that of Amyot.[1]

Thus the first three quarters of the sixteenth century witness
a feverish activity in rendering the works of Greece and Rome
into the English vernacular. During these years, England as-
similates the classical knowledge necessary for the outburst of
creative energy which characterizes the last twenty-five years

· · · · ·

[1] F. O. Matthiessen, *Translation, an Elizabethan Art* (Harvard University Press, 1931), p. 71.

of the Elizabethan age. Translations of Seneca multiply; there are brave, if rare, attempts to bring Greek drama to the consciousness of English readers; Horace, Virgil and Homer are finally brought within the range of all. Sometimes, the attempts are ambitious and include the translation of an entire work; at other times, they involve only a fragment; they may be the new version of a licentious *novella* or a versification of the Psalms. The translations are at once the product of a hesitant schoolboy and the magnificent attempt of an erudite scholar; now they flow from the pen of the verbose pedant, again from that of the exultant poet. Everyone translates, court officials, poet-soldiers, great lords, humble tradesmen, dissolute courtiers and pious clergymen; the result is a tremendous flood of material that defies cataloguing or description. Since we are chiefly concerned with the classical or mythological narratives, however, these may be conveniently, if roughly, divided into three main categories: the works deriving from Virgil, Homer and Ovid.

Knowledge of Virgil had been copiously handed down throughout the Middle Ages, but during the process, the Roman poet had ultimately suffered from the too protracted intimacy and had been debased just as King Arthur and Charlemagne had been. The indignities heaped upon the Augustan poet had turned him into the undignified wizard of the *fabliaux*, but at the same time, he had also been transformed into a Christian prophet.[2] He was at once the enchanter and the theologian whose works were used to buttress Christian doctrine. With the coming of humanism, however, these accretions, the debris of the Dark Ages, were gradually cleared away, and the clear outlines of the Roman poet emerged once more. In this process of purification, the translations of Virgil's works played a most potent role.

Among the first translators of the *Aeneid* may be ranked Thomas Phaer, one of the contributors to the *Mirror for Magis-*

. . . . .

[2] Comparetti, *op. cit.*, Chapter V.

trates, who completed seven books of the *Aeneid* in fourteener couplets in 1558. He subsequently translated two more books and was at work on a third when he was halted by death. Phaer made use of the manuscript copy of Surrey's version of Book IV.[3] Since it offered a faithful translation of the text, Phaer's work remained one of the favorites with Elizabethan readers and was frequently reissued. Thomas Twyne, already familiar to us as the compiler of *The Schoolmaster or Teacher of Table Philosophie*, completed Phaer's unfinished version, but did not improve on the work of his predecessor. Nor did the translation of the first four books of the *Aeneid* by Richard Stanyhurst in 1583 better it, even though the new translation attempted to substitute English hexameters for the usual cumbersome fourteener couplets. Consequently, he was soundly berated for his pains by Thomas Nashe in *Pierce Pennilesse*, where his work was called "a foul, lumbring, boisterous, wallowing measure."

Other works of Virgil translated at this time include versions of the *Georgics* by William Webbe and Abraham Fleming. The latter also translated the *Bucolics* in 1575. The *Eclogues* and some of the minor works were translated at various intervals. Edmund Spenser's translation of the pseudo-Virgilian *Culex*, which in its amplifications heralds the later handling of such classical material in the mythological poems, is also worthy of note. Spenser's *Culex* closely renders the spirit of Virgil, despite the English poet's fondness for introducing lavish description.

The relative ignorance of Greek in England during the sixteenth century proved no serious hindrance to the knowledge of Homer. The tales of the exploits of Ulysses and the wanderings of the survivors of Troy reached the English public through manifold channels. Anyone familiar with the sources of Chaucer's poems will recognize instantly such names as

· · · · ·

[3] O. L. Jiriczek, *Specimens of Tudor Translations from the Classics* (Heidelberg, 1923), p. 57.

Dares, Dyctis Cretensis, Guido delle Colonne, and Benoit de Saint Maure. A glance at Lydgate's ponderous *Troy Book* and Caxton's *Recueyll of the Histories of Troye* will convince the reader that the English did not lack information concerning Homer. Whether or not these versions manifested the pure Homeric feeling is another question, for England had to wait until almost the end of the sixteenth century in order to obtain a full translation of the Greek bard.

Meanwhile, there was no lack of translations of isolated portions of Homer's works. In these, the Homeric characters took on attributes certainly never intended for them. We observe the introduction of romantic incidents, foreign to the original, as well as the development of interesting but certainly un-Homeric attachments, such as the Troilus-Cressida interlude. Some of the characters are exalted, while others, like Achilles, are debased. In some instances, the individual preferences of authors play tug-of-war with the character of these legendary figures; and in Cressida's case, we have several interpretations, ranging from the benign, forgiving attitude of Chaucer to Henryson's severe arraignment. It is true that in this tendency to alter source materials lies danger, but there is also the potentiality of imaginative creation, which is one of the essential qualities of literary art. It must be recognized from the very beginning, however, that the pieces to be discussed in the subsequent pages often show little of this quality and are mere preparation for the translations of Homer made by Arthur Hall in 1581 and by Chapman at the beginning of the seventeenth century.[4]

About 1500, the Scottish poet Henryson brought forth his *Testament of Cressid,* in which he continued the woeful story told by "worthy Chaucer,"

. . . . .

[4] Chapman began his numerous translations of Homer with *The Shield of Achilles* (1596); he followed this with seven books of the *Iliad* in 1598, completing the entire 24 books in 1611. The first twelve books of the *Odyssey* appeared in 1614 and the entire *Odyssey* in the following year.

When Diomed had all his appetite
And more fulfilled of this fair ladie,
Upon another he set his haill delyte.

Cressida has had the imprudence to upbraid the false gods, Venus and Cupid. Angered, they call a council of the gods, who pass judgment upon her and condemn her to be a leper. Among other early poems of Homeric origin may also be numbered Nicholas White's *Jason's Argonautica* (n.d.), Sir Thomas Chaloner's *Epistle of Helen to Paris*,[5] and an anonymous ballad, typical of many such pieces, *The Wandering Prince of Troy* (*circa* 1564).[6] We might also list John Partridge's *Astyanax and Polyxena* as being derived from Homeric legend, although the poem belongs more properly with the verse romances than with mythological poems.

One of the popular miscellanies of the time, *Fennes Frutes* (1590), rehashes the whole Homeric question and seeks to prove to Englishmen: "That it is not requisite to derive our pedigree from the unfaithful Trojans who were the chief causes of their own destruction; whereunto is added Hecuba's mishap, by way of apparition." Most of the poet's material is taken from Dyctis Cretensis, and Fenne passes very severe judgment upon the legendary ancestors of the British. *Hecuba's Mishap*, the long poem appended to Fenne's work, has nothing but its length to distinguish it. The tragic events of Troy, related from Hecuba's point of view, might have been developed into a great poem as was done in the *Trojan Women*, but Fenne was no Euripides. As the work stands, it is an interminable repetition of details, out of which Achilles emerges as the villain of the piece.

Richard Barnfield, author of *The Affectionate Shepherd*,

. . . . .

[5] We have met Sir Thomas Chaloner as a contributor to the *Mirror for Magistrates*. He is also praised highly by both Puttenham and Meres for his pastoral poems, being ranked by them next to Sidney and Spenser.
[6] Bush, *op. cit.*, p. 59.

made use of a popular theme in *Hellen's Rape* (1594),[7] a short poem in hexameters, describing the well-known meeting of the two lovers. He pursued the same vein in the *Legend of Cassandra*, appended to his collection of sonnets, *Cynthia* (1595). We shall not linger over John Trussel's *The First Rape of Fair Helen* (1595), a poem in sizains, bearing strong resemblances to the *Rape of Lucrece*.[8] A word of description might be permitted, however, for the *Lamentation of Troy for the Death of Hector* (1594), in which a number of ghosts from the unhappy city appear and wail their fate. Hecuba, Andromache, Cassandra, all tell their versions of the tale with copious tears. Repentant of his rash adventure, Paris swears that he will no longer be the minion of Venus but rather Hector's avenger. Helen, on the other hand, is fearful for him and wishes to keep him near her, for already too many of his brothers have fallen.[9] The poem has little merit beyond a certain smoothness of verse, but even this is marred by the lack of variety and its long and tedious repetitions. However, we must leave these Homeric imitations in order to consider a far more important source of material, the world of Ovid and his *Metamorphoses*.

Scholars have aptly named the beginning of this millenium "aetas ovidiana," for the poet of Corinna came into his own with the beginning of the eleventh century and has held his ground throughout the successive centuries. Whereas in the

. . . . .

[7] This story had been made popular through a Latin translation of Coluthus's poem by Thomas Watson in 1586. An English version was supposedly made by Christopher Marlowe in 1587 (see p. 237n). However, Barnfield's account appears to be merely a short exercise in hexameters and gives little evidence of definite borrowings.

[8] *T L S*, July 9, 1931, p. 552.

[9] An interesting reference to Sidney's "Stella" occurs in one of the passages:

> Such were the tears of Albion's Stella faire,
> Which in continual raining she did shed,
> And such her sighs which ecchoed in the aire
> When she did say her Astrophell was dead.
> *The Lamentation of Troy*, Sig. D2ᵛ.

previous ages Ovid had been subordinated to Virgil, being regarded somewhat suspiciously because of the immoral nature of some of his writings, the Renaissance elevated him to great heights and he was quickly turned into a school manual, one of the essentials of a liberal education. Glosses and reinterpretations deposited a thick layer of pedantic dust upon Ovid's original text, until the meaning was well-nigh invisible. Nevertheless, he was studied and hailed as a classic; he was culled for elegant passages or *florilegia;* he was expurgated for the use of nuns;[10] he was turned into a theologian, and finally debased into a magician. Later, he was even forged [11] and, at last, became the handbook of imaginative writers who, brushing aside all the far-fetched interpretations, turned to him for the pure gold to be found there—the stuff of romance.

For the great writers of the Middle Ages, Chaucer, Boccaccio, Petrarch, even Dante himself, were all steeped in Ovid. The *De Genealogia* is, after all, another handbook of mythology. Petrarch himself did not disdain to dip his hand into Ovidian material. These poets, keen critics as well, recognized the grand conception of the *Metamorphoses,* seeing in it the distillation and supreme refinement of the grandest myths of the pagan world, comparable in its sphere to Homer's achievement in the world of the epic. They admired the grand panorama of mythology in which the gods wandered through the world, picking up earthly tidbits behind their consorts' backs, more often than not, caught and made to pay for their adventurousness. They revelled in this world of pleasant intrigue and light loves, a world in which servants like Mercury often forgot their masters' business to attend to their own pleasures. They saw the grand sweep of every human emotion in Ovid's portrayal of all the varieties and moods of love, jealous, conjugal, libertine, narcissistic, incestuous.

· · · · ·

[10] For a study of Ovid's fortunes through the Middle Ages, see E. K. Rand, *Ovid and his Influence* (Boston, 1925), p. 135.
[11] *Cf.* the medieval *De Vetula, De Pulice,* Rand, *op. cit.,* p. 128ff.

Ovid's manifold talents did not go unrecognized. His ability to analyze human character and especially his sensitiveness to feminine psychology were greatly appreciated. Above all, Ovid's great gift for story-telling was prized. Gilbert Murray penetratingly comments that among all the poets who take rank merely as story tellers and creators of a mimic world, Ovid still stands supreme. Consequently, Ovid remained the most popular author throughout the Renaissance, imitated, paraphrased, translated, his world of mythology popularized by means of innumerable compilations such as those of Natalis Comes and Cartari.[12] In his definitive examination of the subject, Douglas Bush has summed up Ovid's great contribution, stating that "a history of mythology and the Renaissance tradition must be largely an account of the *Metamorphoses* of Ovid." [13] This work forms, as it were, the focus of all the mythological material and stands practically as the sole source of all the mythological poetry of the Renaissance.

The ingenious scholiasts of the Middle Ages, however, had been quick to perceive that even the obvious immorality of this

・　・　・　・　・

[12] Tilley, *op. cit.*, p. 37. For a fuller account of Ovid's position, see the introduction to Leo Rick's *Ovids Metamorphosen in der englischen Renaissance* (Munster, i.w., 1915). Unfortunately, this work which promised to investigate the position of Ovid during this period was not published in its entire form and the printed part takes the investigation only through the moralizations of Ovid and the translations of the *Metamorphoses* down to George Sandys. Leo Rick had promised to make available the complete work in a later publication, but he was evidently unable to carry out his plan. One has only to recollect the years in which he was working, 1914, 1915, to realize that more powerful events must have stepped in to interfere with his purpose. He says, *"mit erlaubnis der Fakultät erscheint hier nür ein Teil der Dissertations, die in den Munsterschen Beitragen zur englischen Literaturgeschichte ganz vorliegen wird."* Publication of this periodical was discontinued, however, and all attempts to ascertain what happened to the project have proved unavailing.

[13] Bush, *op. cit.*, p. 6. One cannot stress too strongly the value of this work which unites scholarly effort with an ease and polish rarely met in critical works. The reader is directed to Chapter IV, "Ovid, Old and New," where the question is fully developed.

work could be turned to account; thus, little by little, various reflections of serious character to be found in Ovid had been added to the sententious literature of Christianity. Slowly, lines from the *Amores* and the *Fasti* had crept into moral works like the *De Contemptu Mundi* of Innocent III, and even the great Abelard did not disdain to refer to "Ovidius ethicus" in mustering arguments for his teachings.[14] Gradually, there emerged during the Middle Ages and even into the late Renaissance, a twofold function for Ovid, that of the teacher of the most refined phases of amatory art and its direct opposite, the role of ethical and theological guide in Christian asceticism. In addition, Ovid was pushed into a theological bath, even as his predecessor Virgil, and emerged not only expurgated for the chaste eyes of religious recluses, but also cloaked with a veil of allegory which identified many of the mythological figures with the Virgin and the saints. Manifold interpretations of the various myths flourished, and the *Metamorphoses* soon could rival the *Divine Comedy* in the number of its allegorical significances.[15]

In this process, Petrus Berchorius (Pierre Berquire), who paraphrased the *Metamorphoses* as part of one of those frighteningly encyclopedic works of the Middle Ages played an important role. Through one of the frequent mistakes of the period, his work was attributed to Thomas Waleys, an English monk, a misconception which prevailed throughout the sixteenth century.[16] Numerous other compilations of moralized

. . . . .

14 Rand, *op. cit.*, p. 132.
15 For a fuller treatment see Rick, *op. cit.*, p. 22ff. The more philosophical phases of this material will be found discussed in Walter F. Schirmer's *Antike, Renaissance und Puritanismus* (München, 1933).
16 Tilley, *op. cit.*, I, 37. Colard Mansion helped to spread the error, and we find that Thomas Waleys had the work ascribed to him as: *Metamorphosis Ovidiana, Moraliter a Magistro Thoma Waleys Anglico de Professione Predicatorum Sub Sanctissimo Patre Dominico: Explanata.* Warton (H. E. P. I, clxxxiv) states that Turpin's romance was to be found on the same shelf with Thomas Waleys's work on the Psalter in Croyland Abbey.

mythology like Cartari's, as well as actual translations of Ovid, aided materially in spreading these distorted views. This tendency for moralization was especially prevalent in England where there were very strong Puritanical influences at work; and we observe constant attempts to explain away the immorality of Ovid, first by attacking the works which translated him faithfully, and also by minimizing his eroticism. We cannot be too critical of these efforts if we recollect that even a great story teller and able critic like Boccaccio, who saw in mythological tales the most potent source of fiction, admitted that the old gods were false and hastened to clothe them with a semi-Christian veil, not only when treating classical material, but even in tales of contemporary events.[17]

Space obviously prevents us from indulging in a thoroughgoing discussion of all the moralized pieces extant.[18] A typical example may be noted, however, as representative of such work. This is *The Fable of Ovid Treting Narcissus, Translated out of Latin Into English Mytre, with a Moral Thereunto, Very Pleasant to Rede,* compiled by T. H. in 1560.[19] The two hundred-odd lines of narrative reproduce the original *Metamorphoses* very closely; then, the author plunges into a lengthy moralization wherein is stated his purpose:

> I meane to shewe accordynge to my wytte,
> That Ovid by this tale no follye mente,
> But sought to show the doyngs far unfytte
> Of sundry folke whom natuer gyftes hath lente;
> And gather Ovids reason straunge
> That wsydom hydeth with some pleasant change.[20]

In accordance with this plan, Narcissus is represented as gifted with beauty, but doomed by his vanity. The poet warns his

. . . . .

[17] Belloni, *op. cit.,* p. 350.
[18] See E. Witz, *Die Englische Ovidübersetzungen des 16 Jahrhunderts* (Leipzig, 1915); also Rick, *op. cit.*
[19] The piece is reprinted by W. E. Buckley in his edition of Thomas Edwards's works (Roxburghe Club, 1882); see also Rick, *op. cit.,* p. 29ff.
[20] T. H., *The Fable of Ovid Treting Narcissus,* Sig. T3ʳ.

readers: Honors and riches may be desirable things, but "they wracke them that possess." Misuse of them will bring about a tragic downfall. In this sermon, the author cites the examples of Goliath and Sampson and quotes Boccaccio's interpretation of Echo as the voice of human flattery which lures men to destruction. Not content with this, he presents Ficino's neo-platonic explanation as well as Waleys's moralized interpretation. Its wretched verse and tedious moralization, however, void any but the historical value of this tale.

A more notable effort, Golding's translations of the *Metamorphoses*, appeared in 1567, dedicated to the Earl of Leicester, in whom the hopes of the Puritans of England were centered. This monumental work, worthy of a place among the best translations of the ancients, even in an age of great translations, filled a great need, for the entire *Metamorphoses* had not been turned into English since Caxton's version. Golding, a translator-general, was well known for his renderings of the classics. Since he was a very stern Puritan, he took great pains to render palatable Ovid's plainly heathen philosophy. In the preface he presented his readers with elaborate moralizations based on the philosophy of Pythagoras:

> These Fables out of every book I have interpreted,
> To show how they and all the rest may stand a man in stead:
> Not adding over curiously the meaning of them all,
> For that were labour infinite and tediousness not small.[21]

Further on, he states that if rightly approached these heathen tales may have some significance even for the good Christian,

> But if we will reduce their sense to right of Christian law,
> To signify three other things these terms we well may draw
> By gods we understand all such as God hath placed in chief
> Estate to punish sin, and for the godly folks relief:

. . . . .

[21] Publius Ovidius Naso, *Metamorphoses*, ed. W. H. D. Rouse (London, 1904), Prefatory Epistle.

By fate the order which is set and 'stablished in things,
By God's eternal will and word, which in due season brings
All matters to their falling out, which falling out or end
(Because our curious reason is too weak to comprehend
The cause and order of the same, and doe beholde it fall
Unawares to us) by name of Chance or Fortune we do call.[22]

Enough has been written of Golding's translation to warrant foregoing a discussion of it. Its rapid, fluent style, its concise and faithful reproduction of Ovid's matter, if not of his spirit, served the Elizabethans well. Thus Golding became the chief interpreter of the Roman poet until Sandys replaced him with his translations in the seventeenth century. If only for his making Ovid available to Shakespeare, he deserves unstinted praise.

Directly in this tradition of moralizing Ovidian material lies Thomas Peend's *Hermaphroditus and Salmacis* (1565). This author will be remembered for his verse romance, *John, Lorde of Mandosse*. Following closely Waleys's version of Ovid, he allegorizes Hermaphroditus as youthful purity and Salmacis as unbridled vice.[23] As we have already observed, Peend was hardly a great poet, and the present attempt adds little luster to his dull reputation. It does, however, contribute to his fame as a mysogynist by his bitter attacks on women, stating that he,

> the mad desyres of women now,
> theyr rage in folysh fits I wyl display.

Thomas Underdowne's *The Excellent Historie of Theseus and Ariadne* (1566) follows the same mysogynistic vein. The poet takes every opportunity to berate the feminine sex, singling out especially Phedra for her attempts to win Theseus away from her sister. But he uses the Ovidian model very judiciously, and, as Collier points out, never does the poem sink to

. . . . .

[22] *Ibid.*
[23] Consult Rick, *op. cit.*, p. 32ff. See also Bush, *op. cit.*, p. 303. Peend states that he had planned to translate the *Metamorphoses*, but "was prevented by another," possibly Golding.

mere imitation.[24] The latter believes that Underdowne, translator of Ovid's *Ibis* and of Heliodorus's *Aethiopica*, was far in advance of his age in poetic ability and terms the piece a "highly creditable performance."[25]

The same critic has a word of praise also for William Hubbard's *The Tragicall and Lamentable Historie of Two Faithfull Mates: Ceyx, King of Trachine and Alcione his Wife* (1569). In this poem, Hubbard obtains unusual metrical ease through his use of run-on lines and of a novel stanza form, consisting of eight tetrameter lines. His introduction of marine details, encountered frequently in the verse romances, is also unusual. The absence of the moralizing strain, so characteristic of the versions of Ovid at this time, adds in no small measure to the simplicity of the poem.[26] This lack of edification in so early a poem is rather uncommon, but it foreshadows the mood which we have already seen sweeping over England during the latter part of Elizabeth's reign. Once again, the change which took place in the *mirrors* and the verse romances may be perceived operating, this time in the mythological poems, which in the nineties came to be conceived in a purely pagan spirit.

A word might be spared, at this point, for a compilation of Ovidian material, Abraham Fraunce's *The Third Parte of the Countesse of Pembrokes Ivychurch: Entituled Amintas Dale. Wherein Are the Most Conceited Tales of the Pagan Gods in English Hexameters, Together with Their Ancient Descrip-*

. . . . .

[24] Collier, *op. cit.*, IV, 185.
[25] For the sake of brevity, we only list other pieces dealing with Ovidian material, such as Thomas Howell's *The Lamentable Historie of Cephalus with the Unfortunate End of Procris* (1568); *A Boke Entituled Perymus and Thisbe* (1562); B. G., *Helens Epistle to Paris* (1570); *The History of Pyramus and Thisbie Truely Translated*, found in Proctor's *Gorgeous Gallery* (1578). In William Fulwood's *The Enemie of Idleness* (1568) is found also a model poem, "The Story of Pygmalion's Ill," in which the ancient fable is applied to the case of the poet. The list could be lengthened considerably.
[26] Reprinted by Collier in *Illustrations of Old English Literature* (London, 1864); see also Collier, *A Bibliographical Account*, II, 143.

tions and Philosophicall Explanations (1592). The title itself explains the nature of the work, for here we have sixteen verse tales, paraphrasing Ovidian material from the *Metamorphoses,* but with not the slightest intention on the author's part of re-capturing its spirit. There is the inevitable moralization, drawn largely from Natalis Comes and Golding. In fact, the borrow-ings from this author are so heavy that, at times, Fraunce merely turns Golding's fourteeners into the equally ungainly hexameters.[27] In most cases, however, Golding's fairly concise rendering of Ovid is expanded without any noticeable im-provement in the process. Nevertheless, Fraunce was merely following the contemporary literary fashion of expanding and decorating Ovidian material, a tendency which leads us di-rectly to *Hero and Leander.*

The layer of moralization superimposed on mythological narratives was cleared away only towards the last decade of the sixteenth century. But an undercurrent of pagan feeling must constantly have been present, else there would be little ex-planation for many of the virulent attacks which preachers and moralists uttered at various intervals against these accounts. The qualms were often caused by innocuous pieces like *La Conusance d'Amours,* printed by Pynson early in the century, and illustrating the all-powerful influence of love by means of the tale of Pyramus and Thisbe.[28] Again, tales like Henryson's *Traitie of Orpheus,* which exhibited the Ovidian spirit with increasing force, began to multiply and spread, to the eminent horror of reformers. Another work denounced by the moralists was *The Court of Venus* (1557).[29] Although to us the poem

. . . . .

[27] Compare *Metamorphoses,* ed. cit., XIII, 929ff. with Fraunce's *Amintas Dale,* MLA Rotograph No. 75, p. 20, lines 37ff.
[28] See Bush, *op cit.,* p. 302; see also Collier, *op. cit.,* IV, 161.
[29] For further accounts of the *Court of Venus,* see A. K. Foxwell's edi-tion of the poems of Sir Thomas Wyatt (University of London Press, 1913). See also R. H. Griffith and R. A. Law, "A Book of Balettes and *The Court of Venus," University of Texas Bulletin, Studies in English,* No. 10, July, 1930.

seems harmless enough, it attracted their animosity because of its alleged looseness, and brought forth indignant replies from John Hall in the guise of a *Court of Vertue*. This antidote sharply reproved its predecessor:

> A booke of songes they have
> And Venus Court they do it name:
> No fylthy minde a song can crave,
> But therein he may find the same:
> And in such songs is all their game.
> Whereof ryght divers books be made
> To nouryshe that most filthy trade.[30]

More angry blasts were let loose at the poem by Thomas Bryce, compiler of the *Register of Martyrs*, in *The Courte of Venus Moralized* (1567). To such efforts must be added another of the same type, *The Ungodlyness of the Hethnicke Goddesse or the Downfall of the Ephesians by D.J., an Exile for the Word, Late a Minister in London* (1554), in which the methods of educating the youth through study of the Roman poets are bitterly attacked as leading to idolatry and immorality.

Little more need be said about the remainder of the Ovidian material, beyond pointing out that it was translated profusely. Turberville's *Heroicall Epistles* (1566), Churchyard's *Tristia* (1580), and Marlowe's translation of the *Amores* are eloquent proof of the universal interest in Ovid, which culminates in the creation of the mythological poems. It is of these that we shall speak in the following pages.

．　．　．　．　．

[30] Quoted from Warton, *op. cit.*, III, 342n. Warton prints a specimen of the piece which is more noted for its rarity than for its poetic merit.

XVIII

The Early Poets: Lodge, Spenser, etc.

THE MYTHOLOGICAL POEMS OF THE LAST QUAR-
ter of the sixteenth century did not spring full-blown upon an
England eager for the color and the exuberance of the Renaissance, but were, as we have already seen to some extent,
the result of a slow and measured process, through which Ovidian imagery and myth were gradually cleared of the layers of
medieval moralization, and became once more visible in all
their original beauty, ready for the creative magic of Marlowe
and Shakespeare.[1] First, there was the increasing influence of
the sonnet literature, providing imagery which, though often
hackneyed and artificial, at the same time fostered a love of
color and decoration. Then the increasing appreciation for the
true Ovidian spirit and the yearning for what we must call,
lacking a better phrase, the pagan feeling were becoming very
strong in an England that had labored for almost a century

· · · · ·

[1] Even as early as 1567, Turberville in *Epitaphs and Epigrams* gives us
a poetic trifle after the style of Anacreon, in which Venus promises a
kiss as reward for news of her lost son and "greater bliss for his return."
A charming and elaborate description of the wandering Cupid is given.

through a period of religious struggle and moral reform. England was regaining its appreciation of the sensuous and found
it both beautiful and pleasurable; but, before the cycle was
complete, many efforts were made, many failures were regis-
tered.

Among the early attempts to relate Ovidian material must
be included George Gascoigne's *Complaint of Phylomene*
(1575). It might well be expected that Gascoigne, whose pioneer work in literature has already been discussed, should be
found among the earliest essayers in this genre. He tells us
that the poem was composed in 1562 while "I was riding by
the high way between Chelmisford and London and being
overtaken with a soden dash of Raine, I changed my copy." [2]
As a result, the *Complaint* was left incomplete until 1575. The
poem is framed in the medieval dream setting and has none of
the decoration so prominently found in later pieces; it has
rather the bare, narrative quality of the verse romances:

> In Athens reignde somtimes
> A king of worthy fame,
> Who kept in courte a stately traine
> Pandyon was his name.[3]

Even its meter is the well-known fourteener couplet. Gascoigne
relates the Ovidian episode (*Metamorphoses* VI, 412 ff.), the
bloody tale of Tereus's guilty passion for Phylomene and his
cutting out her tongue to prevent discovery of his crime. He
narrates Phylomene's and Progne's savage revenge by feeding
Tereus the corpse of his own son, and their final transforma-
tions: Progne into a swallow, Phylomene into a nightingale
and Tereus into a lapwing. There is no Italianate manner
here; on the contrary, the tale moves with the speed of a ballad. Though not lacking opportunities to paint conventional

. . . . .

[2] George Gascoigne, *The Complaint of Phylomene*, ed. J. W. Cunliffe
(Cambridge University Press, 1907), II, 189.
[3] *Ibid.*, 182.

vignettes, especially with such events at hand as the wedding of Progne, Gascoigne prefers to hurry on. All his images are wisely taken from everyday life and indicate his keen observation. Yet one feels that had the author fashioned his poem a few years later, we should have had a far different description of Phylomene's tapestry, the means of revealing her cruel fate to Progne. Instead, Gascoigne merely states very barely:

> With curious needle worke,
> A garment gan she make,
> Wherein she wrote what bale she bode
> And al for bewties sake.[4]

Compare this passage with Chapman's elaborate description of Hero's scarf (*Hero and Leander* IV, 40 ff.) and one may realize what changes in poetic fashion were wrought in two decades. Gascoigne chooses, on the other hand, to dwell at length on an exposition of the various notes of the nightingale.

Some notice must be given at this time to George Peele's *Tale of Troy*, appended to *A Farewell to Norris and Drake* (1589).[5] This work, in reality, a rehashing of the old Trojan material, is described by the author as "an old poem, a pleasant discourse, fitly serving to recreate by the reading of the chivalry of England." It was written with the purpose of inspiring the gallant citizens of England to draw example and courage from their renowned predecessors, the Trojans. It merits some attention because of its tendency to use sources freely and its frequent interpolation of new material. Paris wanders to Menelaus's court and finds Helen so beautiful that he calls upon Venus to keep her word and help him woo Menelaus's queen. Venus fulfills her promise by causing Menelaus to leave on some expedition. There follow long descriptive passages, picturing Helen's delight in her guest's courtly graces. There are

· · · · ·

[4] *Ibid.*, II, 192.
[5] This poem was composed before 1584, however, before the *Arraignment of Paris*.

endless debates on the propriety of her lapse from virtue. The end is inevitable:

> From her heart was from her body bent,
> To Troy this Helen with her lover went.[6]

But the Ovidian tradition did not crystallize and the genuine Italianate style was not infused into the mythological poem until Thomas Lodge brought forth in 1589 his *Glaucus and Scilla*. Like Gascoigne, this poet was constantly experimenting with new forms. Despite all his experiments with blank verse, controversial pamphlets, prose romances and heroic satires, in none of them, however, can he be said to be pre-eminent. He was destined always to be overshadowed by some greater figure. Nevertheless, he must be given credit for his pioneer work, for pointing the way to the mightier poets who were to follow him. Today *Glaucus and Scilla* is forgotten, pushed into oblivion by *Venus and Adonis* and *Hero and Leander*. Still, when we compare this poem with the pieces which immediately preceded it, one realizes to what extent Lodge developed the type and just how close he brought it to the Italian models. In a certain sense, Lodge's work is the first true English mythological poem and, at the same time, the most typical of the Italianate type. While in later compositions, the personality and characteristic qualities of the authors were too strong to allow them to follow their models closely, in Lodge, on the other hand, there reigns the true pastoral atmosphere, with wailing shepherds and obdurate nymphs, a gentle melancholy spirit, the feeling of sad unreality, so typical of the Italian pieces. Never again is this sweet-sad style approached, either in the passionate, headlong verse of Marlowe or in the gay eroticism of Petowe. Lodge always exhibits this spirit, even in poems where it may be inconsistent with the subject. We have seen, for example, how in the *Complaint of Elstred*, the *mirror* spirit was abandoned and the mood of the sonnets replaced that of the *Mirror for Magistrates*.

. . . . .

[6] George Peele, *A Tale of Troy*, lines 178-79.

Lodge abandoned also the common tendency to pack a great number of episodes into a poem, preferring to concentrate upon a few scenes. He devoted all his powers of description to painting colorful tableaux, a practice common in the Italian pieces. He abandoned forever the temptation to moralize Ovid.[7] Instead, he took the Ovidian framework and expanded it either by fusing into it new details or decorating the old incidents with gorgeous elaborations. Consequently, the familiar Ovidian tale of Glaucus's unhappy pursuit of the nymph is expanded from a scant one hundred and fifty lines to almost six times as many. It will be remembered that, in Ovid, Glaucus goes to Circe and demands to be revenged upon the heartless nymph. After taking good-naturedly a refusal of herself as a substitute, the sorceress provides him with a potion which transforms Scilla into a monster: henceforth, she is made to vent her anger upon the unfortunate mariners who venture in her waters. Lodge expands this simple framework through significant alterations. However, not all his changes may be called improvements. His use of the medieval setting, in which we see the author pensively wandering about, meditating on his own wretchedness, only to be regaled with Glaucus's tearful story, is artificial. The description of this scene is a pompous affair in the best sonneteering fashion, for the author calls upon the roseate morn to aid him in his grieving. He goes about lamenting:

> When midst the Caspian seas the wanton played,
> I drew whole wreaths of corrall from the rocks;
> And in her lap my heavenly presents laid:
> But she, unkind, rewarded me with mockes.[8]

Angered by Scilla's unfeeling attitude, Thetis goes to Venus, demanding that Glaucus be cured and that the nymph be pun-

. . . . .

[7] Although Lodge indulges in an occasional gnomic line, viz., "And youth forspent, a wretched age ensu'th."
[8] Lodge, *Glaucus and Scilla*, stanza 57.

ished for her cruelty. She accompanies her plea with a graceful
song:

> Born of the sea, thou Paphian Queen of Love,
> Mistris of Sweete conspiring harmonie;
> Ladie of Cipris, for whose sweet behove,
> The shepherds praise the youth of Thessalie,
> Daughter of Jove and suster to the sunne,
> Assist poor Glaucus late by Love undone.[9]

With a well-dispatched arrow, Cupid obligingly cures the
love-lorn Glaucus, who resumes his sport with the gladsome
nymphs; at the same time, Scilla is made to fall in love with
the lover she previously scorned. It is her turn to sigh now,
her turn to feel his disdain.

> How oft with blushes would she plead for grace,
> How oft with whisperings would she tempt his eares,
> How oft with chrystall did she wet his face;
> How oft she wipt them with her amber heares,
> So oft me thought I oft in heart desired
> To see the end whereto disdaine aspired.[10]

Thus she moans; and, as her final transformation takes place,
she thirsts for the blood of men:

> The waters howle with fatal tunes about her,
> The air doth scoule when as she turnes within them,
> The winds and waves with puffs and billows skout her,
> Waves storme, aire scoules, both winds and waves begin them,
> To make the place this mournful nimph doth weepe in,
> A hapless haunt whereas no nimph may keepe in.[11]

Lodge's poem has been severely criticized because of obvious structural flaws, yet most of the poets who followed him
did not disdain to borrow or imitate many of his innovations.
Several of its passages are echoed in *Venus and Adonis*.[12] At

· · · · ·

[9] *Ibid.*, stanza 81.   [10] *Ibid.*, stanza 105.   [11] *Ibid.*, stanza 124.
[12] See *Venus and Adonis, ed. cit.*, Introduction, xvff.,where a complete list is given.

the risk of reproducing a stanza which finds its way in every
article written on the subject, we quote the following lines
which compare favorably with anything produced before 1590
and much that was written later:

> He that hath seene the sweete Arcadian boy,
> Wiping the purple from his forced wound,
> His pretie tears betokening his annoy,
> His sighes, his cries, his falling on the ground,
>   The Ecchoes ringing from the rockes his fall,
>   The trees with tears reporting of his thrall.

> And Venus starting at her love-mates crie,
> Forcing her birds to haste her chariot on;
> And full of grief at last with piteous eie
> Seene where all pale with death he lay alone,
>   Whose beautie quaild, as wont the Lillies droop
>   When wastfull winter windes doo make them stoop:

> Her daintie hand addrest to dawe her deere,
> Her roseall lip alied to his pale cheeke,
> Her sighes, and then her looke and heavy cheere,
> Her bitter threats and then her passion meeke;
>   How on his senseles corpse she lay a crying,
>   As if the boy were then but new a dying.[13]

These lines are echoed in Venus's grief in Shakespeare's poem,
(lines 1027 ff.).

Marlowe and Drayton also dipped into "Goldey's" honeyed
stanzas and drew forth, not only phrases, but numerous suggestions for their poems. Lodge himself had no compunction
in making use of his models, his poetry being well-larded with
passages from French and Italian poets, especially Ronsard
and Desportes. It will be remembered that the latter's *Ber-
geries* furnished the model for the song "Most happie blest
the man." [14]

. . . . .

[13] Lodge, *op. cit.*, stanza 21ff.
[14] For Lodge's use of foreign models, see Janet Scott, *Les Sonnets Elizabethains* (Paris, 1929).

To compare Lodge's halting and ill organized poem with
Venus and Adonis, as C. K. Pooler has done, is in a certain
sense to damn it, for few poems, after all, will stand up against
such a comparison.[15] It is true that Lodge inserts a good deal
of padding, that much of his action is mere convention, that
the characters are stock, and that a large portion of the poem
is given over to unnecessary wailing; but these are the faults
of the time and they arise from Lodge's acquiescence to convention. Fundamentally, the poem is the usual tearful lament
of the lover for his mistress. One cannot read a few stanzas of
Glaucus and Scilla without feeling that he is dwelling in the
world of the sonnets, that the nymph is merely another of the
long line of hard-hearted mistresses who draw their origins
from the Petrarchan tradition. Lodge is, above all, the sonneteer; all his emotions are expressed by means of Petrarchan
conceits. Scilla's hair is lovelier than Hibla's honey; Glaucus
has been caught by the snares in her eyes:

> Her polisht necke of milke white snowes doth shine,
> As when the moone in winter night beholdes them
> Her breast of Alabaster chere and fine,
> Whereon two rising apples faire unfolds them,
> Like Cinthias face when in her full she shineth
> And blushing to her love mates bower declineth.[16]

It is in the creation of colorful, languorous pictures that we
must look for the best in Lodge's art. Here, for the first time,
appears the charmingly portrayed vignette, the word-painting
which forms so integral a part of the mythological poem. Pictured for us are many graceful scenes which we have come to
term "Spenserian." We watch the dying Adonis, the nymphs
trying to comfort the forlorn Glaucus. Their tears fall to the
ground and form a crystal-clear brook. We see Angelica, the

· · · · ·

[15] *Venus and Adonis,* ed. cit., Introduction.
[16] Lodge, *op. cit.,* stanza 51.

fair, fleeing from her lovers; we watch Venus and her lovely
son hastening to heal Glaucus:

> The stately roab she ware upon her back,
> Was lillie white, wherein with cullored silke;
> Her nymphs had blazed the young Adonis' wracke,
> And Laeda's rape by swan as white as milke,
> And on her lap her lovely sonne was plaste,
> Whose beautie all his mother's pompe defaste.
>
> A wreath of roses hem'd his temples in
> His tresse was curlde and cleere as beaten gold,
> Haught were his looks, and lovely was his skin,
> Each part as pure as heaven's eternall mold,
> And on his eies a milk white wreath was spred,
> Which longst his back with prettie pleats did shed.[17]

It is soft poetry, languorous and beautiful; its words fall slowly,
caressing the ear; it is not great poetry, but it has all the qualities which we expect of the genre; and we shall see how it de-
velops beneath the skillful hand of a Drayton; we shall see to
what heights it can be brought by the imagination and fire of
Marlowe.

Although Edmund Spenser was ideally equipped for writing mythological poems, he tried his hand at the genre only
once, in *Muiopotmos*, found in the *Complaints* volume of
1591. This composition has received various interpretations.
It has been scanned for clues to Spenser's relations with Lady
Carey, his poetic mistress. It has also been interpreted as the
complaint of Spenser, the courtier, caught between the enmity
of Burghley and Leicester. Whatever meaning we read into
the poem, it remains a graceful play of the fancy, another
specimen of the Italianate poem introduced by Lodge, which
Marlowe and Shakespeare were to perfect.

Briefly, the story is a composite one, made up of several
Ovidian elements to which are added some graceful inventions

. . . . .

[17] *Ibid.*, stanza 86ff.

from Spenser's own fantasy. Its four hundred lines relate the fate of Clarion, son of the butterfly, Astery, who falls into the toils of Aragnoll, son of Arachne. The only apparent reason for this assault seems to be that Aragnoll is still burning for revenge over his mother's punishment, as a result of the famous needlework contest with Pallas. It will be remembered that Arachne was bested and changed into a spider. Aragnoll has ever since held an unquenchable hatred for all butterflies whom he considers to have been the cause of his mother's downfall. Spenser gives every indication of mastery over the genre from the manner in which he handles even this very tenuous plot. He draws upon the *Metamorphoses* for the story of Pallas and Arachne, but weaves into it the detail of the butterfly in order to provide a motive for Aragnoll's enmity.[18] Then, in a fanciful story which would not be out of place in the *Metamorphoses* itself, he invents the myth of Clarion.

The poem has all the characteristics of the mythological narrative, the interpolated tableaux, picturing the metamorphosis of Astery and the well-known contest between Arachne and Minerva being especially graceful. Although it does not have the ecstatic qualities of Marlowe nor the color of Drayton, *Muiopotmos* is marked by the typical Spenserian grace and subtlety.

Spenser's failure to try more of such poems is not surprising in view of the constant recurrence of the mythological incident in his other work. In certain respects, Spenser's entire poetry is cast in this vein. One has only to glance at sections of the *Faerie Queene* such as the house of Busyrane (Bk. III, canto 2), and the temple of Venus (Bk. IV, canto 10), to see how effective he could be. Like all great artists of the Renaissance, he considered decoration and ornament as the background of a great canvas, the setting for more significant work, rather than an end in itself. In this respect, Spenser's method is akin to

. . . . .

18 H. S. V. Jones, *A Spenser Handbook* (New York, 1930), p. 116.

that of Raphael and Leonardo da Vinci, who worked on the theory that landscape was, after all, secondary in the treatment of their themes. It is only later, in the seventeenth century, that these subordinate motifs are developed into the arts of landscape, decoration and still life.

Mythology plays an important role in William Vallans's *A Tale of Two Swannes* (1590), written by the author to publicize his birthplace, Ware, famous even today for its multitude of the birds sacred to Venus. The author gives us an account of the founding of Ware, the antiquarian material being taken principally from Polydore Vergil's history. This composition follows the conventional lines of the topographical poem, of which there were numerous specimens in English literature, notably, Leland's *Cygnea Cantio*, Camden's *De Connubio Tamis et Isis*, and others.[19] Having observed the beauty of the fields of Hartsfordshire, Venus conceives the plan to breed her favorite birds there. Later, she plans a progress through her dominions, and we follow her on a regular visitation, patterned on Elizabeth's frequent tours of her realm. At the climax of the ceremonies, we witness the marriage of the two rivers, the Thames and the Lee. Besides "eternizing" his birthplace, Vallans seizes the opportunity to shower praise upon local noblemen, among whom are the all-powerful Burghley and the Careys of Hunsdon, well known in the literary world. But as a poem, *The Tale of Two Swannes* is interesting chiefly through its use of blank verse and an occasional graceful line.[20]

In following the evolution of Ovidian material, the reader must have doubtless realized the definite changes which it

. . . . .

[19] See R. B. Gottfried, *op. cit.*, p. 109ff; also F. I. Carpenter, *A Reference Guide to Spenser* (University of Chicago Press, 1923), p. 128.
[20] There exists a considerable amount of this poetry, for example, Spenser's *Prothalamion*, Drayton's vast body of work, and a piece such as E. Wilkinson's *Thameseidos*, which describes Neptune's pursuit of Thamesis. See H. Taylor, *Topographical Poetry in England During the Renaissance*, University of Chicago Abstracts of Theses, Humanistic Series, V, (1926-7).

underwent at the hands of English poets. As we have so often seen, the temper of the time exerted a powerful influence on the attitude towards poetry and its functions. Towards the end of Elizabeth's reign, poetry shook off the bonds of a too strict morality, thus freeing the Ovidian myths of their layer of moralization. This reaction was not altogether new. At various intervals during the sixteenth century, scattered poets had represented Venus in her frank nakedness; even before 1570 Hubbard had foregone the customary ethical veneer in his mythological tales. With Lodge and the poets that followed, the change became definite. Perhaps one further example will indicate the tendency more vividly.

We have already spoken of Abraham Fraunce's *Amintas Dale*, and the reader must have noted its heavy, frequently word-for-word borrowings from Golding's *Metamorphoses*. Despite this imitation, Fraunce shows to a marked degree the tendency of the time to amplify mythological material for the sake of portraying sensuous scenes. Of the numerous examples, only one need be cited; it is the familiar account (*Metamorphoses* IV, 207ff.) of Venus and Mars being caught *flagrante delicto* by means of Vulcan's net. Ovid is simple and direct in his narrative, but Fraunce makes the most of his opportunity to dwell on the details, to smack his lips over this juicy tidbit:

> And in a secreate place expects polluted adultresse,
> And hot, raging Mars: who there lay lonely together,
> Either on others breast, and either in armes of another.
> When sweet tickling joyes of rutching came to the highest
> Poynt, when two were one, when moysture fully resolved
> Sought for a freer scope, when pleasure came to a fulness,
> When their dazeling eyes were over-cast with a sweete cloude,
> And their fainting soules, in a sleepe, in a swoune, in a love
>   trance,
> Then was Mars cooled, cooled was dame Cytherea.[21]

. . . . .

[21] Fraunce, *op. cit.*, p. 39.

All this, Golding had dismissed soberly with:

> Now when that Venus and her mate were met in bed
>   togither,
> Her husband by his new found snare before convoyed thither,
> Did snarle them both togither fast in middes of all theyr
>   play.[22]

Fraunce is obviously paying mere lip-service to morality; his feeble "polluted adultresse" is but perfunctory. Only the swooning ecstasy of the passions interests him. We have definitely arrived at the spirit of Christopher Marlowe.

. . . . .

[22] *Metamorphoses, ed. cit.,* IV, 220ff.

Marlowe and His Imitators

LIKE A BEAUTIFUL WOMAN WHOSE SHORTCOM-
ings are forgotten in beholding her, Marlowe's *Hero and
Leander* compels us to forget all its faults and remember only
its profound beauty. Douglas Bush aptly summed up its true
nature by saying "all the best qualities of the Italianate tradition are embodied and transcended in *Hero and Leander*." In
the same breath, he also qualified this statement, adding, "it
is equally true that the poem exhibits in high relief all the vices
of the tradition." [1] In reading this poem, we feel that for once
Marlowe achieved that true Renaissance feeling for myth
found in Poliziano and in Lorenzo de Medici. Its rapturous
verse makes us forgive Swinburne's exuberant appraisal of
Marlowe, when he says: "He, alone, was the true Apollo of
our dawn, the bright and morning star of the full mid-summer
of English poetry at its highest." [2]

The poem is incomplete, a mere fragment of eight hundred

. . . . .

[1] Bush, *op. cit.*, p. 124.
[2] George Chapman, *Works,* ed. A. C. Swinburne (London, 1875),
p. lxiv.

lines, yet in it are encompassed some of the most ecstatic lines ever written in English poetry. In it is told one of the most frankly sensuous, yet incredibly graceful and human love stories of the world. Though the poem was not published until 1598, together with Chapman's continuation, we know that preparations for its publication had been made in 1593, when John Wolfe entered it in the Register of the Stationers Company on September 28, just a few months after Marlowe's sudden death. Because of its unfinished state, it raises many pertinent questions which still defy answer.

We may be fairly certain that, despite the existence of several versions of the story in European literature, Marlowe hardly glanced at the versions by Tasso or at Marot's French translation of Musaeus. Even the text of this Alexandrine poet, which had received a great deal of well-merited attention during the sixteenth century, only served Marlowe as a mere framework upon which to weave his conception of the love story of Hero and Leander. It has been argued that perhaps it might have been better had Marlowe followed the more classic lines of the Greek version, but it seems pointless to demand that genius constrict itself in moulds foreign to it. As it stands, Marlowe's fragment seems almost a personal experience, the dream of a sensuous, imaginative young Elizabethan, projecting himself into a Greek setting. It may be criticized for its anachronisms, for its unconscious transformation of a Greek youth and maiden into Renaissance gallants, but after such comments subside, one only remembers that it is a pure song of youth, the very embodiment of the romantic mood.[3]

The Greek poem of Musaeus is the essence of simplicity. A scant 340 lines in length, it contains only the story of the en-

. . . . .

[3] It is believed that Marlowe may have used a Greek-Latin edition for his version. The story is also found in Ovid's *Heroides*, xvii and xix. It is also mentioned in *Amores* II, xvi, 31-32, which Marlowe himself had translated. For a study of this question see L. C. Martin's edition of Marlowe's poems (London, 1931).

counter of the two lovers, their immediate attraction to each other, and their passionate meetings. The drowning of young Leander and Hero's own tragic death, when she plunges from the tower to join the body of her dead lover, swiftly follow. To this simple account, Marlowe, following the new fashion begun by Lodge, added almost five hundred lines of decoration, including several narrative episodes that do not exist in the original. For this we need not apologize; they form the very essence of Marlowe. Through them the spirit of Ovid is reborn and pervades the whole of the poem.

Hero and Leander has been praised effusively for its great qualities, but it has also been severely censured for serious faults. It has been criticized by some scholars because of the incoherence of its conception and its lack of organic development. Others have been unable to understand how Marlowe could have fashioned an ending to the poem, befitting the dignified tragedy found in the original. In the final estimate of Marlowe such judgments must be considered, yet it seems hardly fair to bring a poet to account on the strength of an unfinished piece such as this. One must grant from the very beginning that the poem retains little of the Hellenic spirit, for it is gothic, both in conception and execution. But one must also assume from the very beginning that it is impossible to guess what parts of the poem would have been pruned or amplified before Marlowe sent it to the printer. For a certainty, in reading *Hero and Leander,* one is constantly aware of a feeling of incompleteness. There are many instances where one senses a quality of abruptness, especially in the transitions. The poem presents its component parts laid side by side but apparently not joined. Yet, we know that Marlowe was capable of good craftsmanship. Let us glance at a typical example from the second sestiad:

> Leander strived, the waves about him wound,
> And pull'd him to the bottom, where the ground
> Was strewed with pearl, and in low coral groves
> Sweet singing mermaids sported with their loves

On heaps of heavy gold, and took great pleasure
To spurn in careless sort the shipwrack treasure.
For here the stately azure palace stood,
Where kingly Neptune and his traine abode.
The lusty god embraced him, call'd him "love",
And swore he never should return to Jove.
But when he knew it was not Ganymede,
For under water he was almost dead,
He heav'd him up, and looking on his face
Beat down the bold waves with his triple mace.[4]

The italicized lines are placed there organically enough, but are fairly crying out for a smoothing hand. There is no transition, no manner of explanation for Neptune's wooing of Leander in a less abrupt manner. It seems hardly possible that the poet who could conceive lines such as:

Hero the fair,
Whom young Apollo courted for her hair,
And offered as a dower his burning throne,
Where she should sit for men to gaze upon,[5]

and countless others as beautiful, would consciously have left unpolished such obviously rough spots. Moreover, it is apparent that once Marlowe has warmed up to his task, the traces of awkwardness disappear, and the poem proceeds smoothly, with only occasional false lines to check its flow.

There are other flaws in the poem. It has become almost a commonplace to point out the presence of a certain amount of gnomic sentiment and the frequent anachronisms. These, however, seemed to rest easily on Marlowe's conscience. In other places, his characterization has a false ring, and from the lips of the virgin-priestess we hear phrases that Douglas Bush says, "might belong to Mrs. Pinchwife." Hero has been vowing her youthful love to Leander, expressing tender, maidenly sentiments, when she adds quite gratuitously,

. . . . .

[4] Marlowe, *Hero and Leander,* II, 159ff.
[5] *Ibid.,* I, 5ff.

A dwarfish beldam bears me company,
That hops about the chamber where I lie,
And spends the night that might be better spent
In vain discourse and apish merriment.[6]

Again, in the following lines, the sentiment is worthy of
Byron's *Don Juan;* it is almost burlesque:

She stayed not for her robes, but straight arose,
And drunk with gladness, to the door she goes,
Where seeing a naked man, she screeched for fear,
Such sights as this to tender maids are rare,
And ran into the dark herself to hide.[7]

It is impossible to believe that Marlowe would have retained
such incongruities in the final accounting of the poem.

Despite this mingling of the serious and mocking, despite its
lack of unity of conception, the poem offers long passages of
real beauty, where the imagery is sheer magic, so pervasive as
to efface all other emotions. This magic springs from Marlowe's characteristic fervor, his torrential emotion which
sweeps everything before it. For Marlowe, perhaps more than
any other Elizabethan, had the ability to plunge the reader into
the world of myth and legend, making him believe in it, despite his clothing these myths in the gay accoutrements of
Renaissance England. It is a quality which North and Golding
also had to an eminent degree. Marlowe may introduce an
episode, such as Neptune's courtship of Leander, which we
feel to be an intrusion, yet we know that all this is part of his
intense feeling for the mythological world.

Such absolute self-identification with the world of mythology gives Marlowe the power to infuse into his myths a warmth
and life that makes them welcome to us, in contrast to the cold
abstractions which we shall find in George Chapman. In this
quality, Marlowe surpasses even Edmund Spenser. Compare
his pictures of the temple of Venus (I, 139ff.) with some simi-

. . . . .

[6] *Ibid.,* I, 352ff.   [7] *Ibid.,* II, 235ff.

lar passages in Spenser or Ariosto! Granted that often such additions are irrelevant and inorganic, who would wish to delete the many Ovidian episodes of which the tale of Mercury and the country maid is typical? Conceits we also find in plenty, but they are forceful, like Donne's; they have none of the Petrarchistic sugariness of Lodge. There is life and imagination in his image of Leander as he "awaits the sentence of her scornful eyes." In general, the imagery of *Hero and Leander* follows the pattern of the plays. Very few of its images deal with daily life, for here, as everywhere else in his work, all is brilliance and airiness. Marlowe is writing with his head in the clouds, an eagle winging its way towards the sun.[8]

The date of *Hero and Leander* has been one of the problems which have defied solution.[9] Was the poem the fruit of the early years spent by Marlowe at Cambridge, when he was dipping into the Greek classics, translating Lucan and becoming interested in Coluthus?[10] Or was it the product of his last few months at Deptford, whither he had taken refuge during the plague which prevented him from presenting his plays on the London stage? Both theories are supported by eminent scholars; there is much to be said on either side. But in the end, the reader must throw up his hands. On the one side, we must admit that the amount of youthful material and Marlowe's

. . . . .

[8] For some significant remarks on Marlowe's imagery, see Caroline Spurgeon's *Shakesperian Imagery* (Cambridge University Press, 1935), p. 13ff.

[9] L. Chabalier, *Hero et Leandre* (Paris, 1911). This author presents the entire problem, but although he advocates an early date, he has been unable to draw any convincing conclusions.

[10] Marlowe is said by Warton (H. E. P., III, 350) to have translated Coluthus's *Rape of Helen* into English rhyme in 1587. He remarks that during the previous year, Thomas Watson had rendered the poem into Latin verse, and that this had probably given Marlowe the idea for his translation. However, the version is nowhere else recorded. There exists also a *Raptus I Helenae* by John Trussel (1593), which is characterized by its use of the meter of *Venus and Adonis*, with many of its phrases taken from this poem, although it is mainly an imitation of the *Rape of Lucrece*.

tendency to produce a quip, even at the height of the most serious moment, point to an early production and tend to show that Marlowe composed it at Cambridge, being perhaps prevented from finishing it by his other occupations and his allegiance to the theatre. Again, the erotic quality of the poem and the fact that young writers found it almost conventional to try their wings in this genre, argue for an early date. On the other hand, it seems hardly likely that Marlowe, busy though he was, would put aside a poem of popular nature like *Hero and Leander*. We must keep constantly in mind the fact that the Elizabethans considered this type of poem far more important than the plays.[11] In view of the popularity which the poem enjoyed in manuscript, it is hardly possible that Marlowe should not have finished it. Arguments have also been marshalled to prove that the poem is too mature in execution and philosophy to be the work of a university youth. Certainly, if we accept some of its imperfections as the result of its unrevised state, this last argument takes on much more importance.

Critics have also been puzzled by the fact that Chapman was chosen to complete *Hero and Leander*, even though he was by temperament totally unsuited to finish the highly erotic work of his predecessor. Again, we must keep in mind that by 1598, Chapman was known as a Greek scholar who had established somewhat of a reputation in this field. What was more natural than his finishing a version of the work of Musaeus? We, of course, are inclined to patronize Chapman, the pedant, but in his day, although not exactly popular, as he himself admitted, he still enjoyed respect as a serious poet, well versed in neo-platonic doctrine. This raises the question: did Marlowe ask Chapman to finish his work? Chabalier believes that since Chapman was well-known to Marlowe, the latter encouraged him to finish this half-complete poem. This French critic interprets some obscure but tantalizing lines in Chapman's

. . . . .

11 See Tucker Brooke, "The Reputation of Christopher Marlowe," *Transactions of the Connecticut Academy*, XXV (1922), 347ff.

continuation (III, 183ff.) to mean that Marlowe had shown Chapman the incomplete work and that, as his friend, he is now complying "with his late desires" and finishing the poem. The interpretation is tempting, but since it rests on a pair of obscure lines, unsound.[12]

Although not printed until five years after his death, Marlowe's poem was known earlier in manuscript and made a deep impression upon his contemporaries. Echoes of *Hero and Leander* reverberate throughout many of the poems written during this decade.[13] Its lines are heard in Nashe's *Jack Wilton;* they creep into Drayton's mythological poems and are echoed by the score in the works of Thomas Edwards, who set out consciously to imitate Marlowe. Thus it may safely be said that Marlowe took the mythological poem, introduced by Lodge, and brought it to a level comparable with the best of such efforts on the Continent. *Hero and Leander* achieved this eminence, despite the fact that it was known only through manuscript, and that when it was printed it must have had to

. . . . .

[12] The reader may judge for himself how much may be construed from Chapman's passage:

> Then thou most strangely-intellectual fire,
> That proper to my soul hast power t'inspire
> Her burning faculties, and with the wings
> Of thy unsphered flame visit'st the springs
> Of spirits immortal; now (as swift as Time
> Doth follow Motion) find th'eternal clime
> Of his free soul whose living subject stood
> Up to the chin in the Pierian flood,
> And drunk to me this half Musean story.
> Inscribing it to deathless memory:
> Confer with it and make my pledge as deep,
> That neither's draught be consecrate to sleep.
> Tell it how much his late desires I tender
> (If yet it know not) and to light surrender
> My soul's dark offspring, willing it should die
> To loves, to passions, and society.

[13] See Bush's article, "The Influence of Marlowe's *Hero and Leander* on Early Mythological Poems," in *MLN*, XLII (1927), 211ff. See also the notes to L. C. Martin's edition of the poems of Marlowe.

overcome the handicap imposed upon it by Chapman's continuation. But it is now time to turn briefly to this heavy-handed composition.

It was George Chapman's misfortune to have been born in an age studded with great poets; therefore, his gifts, which in any other company might have shone to better advantage, are perforce judged alongside those of his contemporaries. He suffers greatly as a result. His attempt to continue one of the great poems in English literature is even more detrimental to his fame, for the reader cannot escape making the obvious comparison between Marlowe's verse and Chapman's continuation of *Hero and Leander*. Consequently, his harsh and inchoate allegories have to stand beside the graceful and airy fantasies of Spenser; his crabbed, obscure verses compared with the mellifluous stanzas of the *Faerie Queene*; his turbid and grotesque conceits ranged side by side with the golden imagery of Marlowe. Small wonder that we disparage him and quite often unfairly.[14] If any censure of Chapman must be made, it will have to be on the grounds that he attempted too much; that along with his fiery imagination and far too profuse intellect, he was not also endowed with the ability to select and coordinate the material before him; and that he tried to combine indiscriminately, especially in his mythological poems, erotic material, voluptuous description, with a high and abstruse morality.

This confusion within Chapman's mind leaves its mark on a poem like *Ovids Banquet of Sense* (1595), which, even a sympathetic critic must term, *"une mélange de pedantisme grave et de subtile lascivité."* [15] Chapman's own Argument will suffice to outline the poem:

. . . . .

[14] The reader may turn to the brilliant, if effusive, essay on Chapman by Swinburne, prefacing his edition of Chapman's works in which he estimates the poet's worth. See also Bush's discerning criticism in his chapter on Chapman.
[15] F. L. Schoell, *Etudes sur l'Humanisme Continental en Angleterre, a la Fin de la Renaissance* (Paris, 1926), p. 38.

Auditus   Ovid, newly enamored of Julia, daughter to Octavius Augustus Caesar, after by him called Corinna,[16] secretly conveyed himself into a garden of the Emperour's court, in an arbour whereof Corinna was bathing, playing upon her lute and singing, which Ovid overhearing was exceedingly pleased with the sweetness of her voice, and to himself uttered the comfort he conceived in his sense of Hearing.

Olfactus   Then the odours she used in her bath breathing a rich savour, he expressed the joy he felt in his sense of Smelling.

Visus   Thus growing more deeply enamoured in great contentment with himself, he ventures to see her in the pride of her nakedness; which doing by stealth, he discovered the comfort he conceived in Seeing, and the glory of her beauty.

Gustus   Not yet satisfied, he useth all his art to make known his being there without her offence, or, being necessarily offended, to appease her, which done, he entreats a kiss, to serve for satisfaction of his Taste, which he obtains.

Tactus   Then proceeds to entreat for the fifth sense, and there is interrupted.[17]

The wooing of Corinna is like a cold debate; Ovid, the lover *par excellence,* advances his suit more as a learned pedant than as an Augustan Casanova.

> "Dear Mistress" answered Ovid, "to direct
> Our actions by the straitest rule that is,
> We must in matters moral quite reject
> Vulgar opinion, ever led amiss,
> And let autentic Reason be our guide." [18]

Unconvinced by his eloquence, when he requests a kiss, she haughtily recalls to him the difference in their stations; whereupon he batters down her arguments with a Popean couplet:

. . . . .

[16] As we may see, Chapman perpetuates the favorite error of identifying the daughter of the emperor with Corinna.
[17] Chapman, *op. cit.,* p. 22.   [18] *Ibid.,* p. 32.

Virtue makes honour, as the soul doth sense
And merit far exceeds inheritance.[19]

How different is this wooing from Marlowe's, where the lovers
have only to look into each other's eyes and clasp hands to
know that the fulfillment of their love must inevitably take
place! What a contrast between Marlowe's frank simplicity
and the pruriency of Chapman's lover who, as he prepares to
lay his hands upon Corinna's body, cannot repress a neo-Platonic discourse, only to have his designs frustrated by the intrusion of her ladies.

This tendency to produce a philosophical disquisition upon
any subject at hand sets Chapman apart from other mythological poets. He substitutes these neo-platonic discourses for the
series of vignettes that are conventional in the genre. Although
this overloading of his poem with learning is a serious artistic
flaw, nevertheless, it remains Chapman's primary intent. He
glories in his attitude, stating bluntly: "The profane multitude
I hate, and only consecrate my strange poem to those searching
spirits whom learning hath made noble, and nobility sacred." [20]
He feels that poetry is an arcanum for the elect, a mystery to
be appreciated by the few capable of such enjoyment. Again
he defends his methods, saying, "Obscurity in affection of
words and indigested conceits is pedantical and childish; but
where it shroudeth itself in the heart of his subject, uttered
with fitness of figure and expressive epithets, with that darkness I will still labor to be shadowed." [21]

But such digressions are only the result of the lack of design in Chapman's poems. Much of Chapman's laboring and
confusion comes from what Swinburne terms, "a substitution
of an intellectual for an ideal end"; he sees in almost every
page of Chapman

. . . . .

[19] *Ibid.*, p. 34.
[20] *Ibid.*, Epistle to Matthew Roydon, p. 21.
[21] *Ibid.*, p. 21.

The struggle and toil of a powerful mind, convulsed and distended as if by throes of travail in the effort to achieve something that lies beyond the proper aim and possible scope of that form of art, within which it has set itself to work.[22]

Most of this struggle is due to his eagerness to expound neoplatonic philosophy. He draws heavily from the moralized and allegorized mythology of Italy, especially Comes, Giraldi, and Marsilio Ficino.[23] In the final analysis, Chapman uses the poem merely as a framework upon which to weave his tortuous allegories. But then, this is in keeping with Chapman's own theory of poetry and his dictum that, "the sense is given us to excite the mind." But perhaps Bush is right when he accuses the poet of being afraid of the senses.[24] Let us take, for example, *Ovids Banquet of Sense*. Here Chapman was actually inventing another Ovidian episode. Yet, instead of picturing Ovid as frankly enjoying his Corinna, as the Roman poet actually described it (*Amores* V), Chapman goes off into a maze of philosophy and rescues himself only by introducing some of her tiring-maids. What a contrast between Chapman's puling description of Corinna-Julia's nakedness and Ovid's frank, appreciative appraisal of her lusty thigh, decribed as "the sweet fields of life which Death's foot dare not press."

One cannot help feeling, too, especially in reading his continuation of *Hero and Leander*, that the poet has no fundamental unity of purpose. One moment he is interested in neoplatonism, the next in feminine psychology or in depicting some vignette in the best Italianate fashion. In this respect, he differs sharply from Marlowe who rushes on without halt, all his incidents focussed upon the central idea. How different Chapman, who is quite willing to check the flow of his poetry in order to reflect on his aversion to a town gallant or to hurl

. . . . .

[22] *Ibid.*, p. lxvi.
[23] See Schoell, *op. cit.*, chapters on Chapman and Appendix I, where he treats the poet's relation to the Italian mythologists, especially Comes and Ficino. See also the chapter on Chapman in Bush.
[24] Bush, *op. cit.*, p. 204.

a gibe at some clergyman! As a result, at frequent intervals, he is forced to resume the lost thread of his story, labelling it "narratio" as if to aid the reader in following its tortuous course. After an interpolation of forty-five lines, casually dismissing his violation of the rules, he will merely say, "with this digression" and calmly proceed with his story. It is difficult also to discover the necessity of Hero's endless rationalizations in excusing her lapse from virtue. For a certainty, Chapman's substitution of his own anticlimactic death of Leander for the tragic end of the lovers as found in Musaeus only mars a beautiful story.[25]

. . . . .

[25] This perhaps overcritical examination of Chapman's technique as a narrator does not take into account several passages in *Hero and Leander* which would seem to belie the foregoing statements. This is all the more striking, as Chapman, at times, gives one the impression that he feels himself superior to Ovidian material and the neo-Ovidian vignette of the mythological poets. Yet how may we explain such clear-cut bits of description as the episode of the fox and the country maid (IV, 96ff)? How may we account for the swift moving tale of Teras (V, 65ff)? Here Chapman reveals latent powers for description and narration; he demonstrates an unwonted simplicity and the ability to steer away from the vapours of neo-platonism. Perhaps this may be an unusual lapse from his avowed purpose to clothe poetry with gravity, but a provocative note from Warton's *History of English Poetry* (III, 350) stirs the imagination: "I learn from Mr. Malone," says the venerable Warton, "that Marlowe finished only the first two Sestiads and about one hundred lines of the third. Chapman did the remainder." Whimsical though Warton may be, there are times when his information is uncannily reliable and in his statement may lie our explanation. It has already been advanced by Francis Cunningham (in his edition of Marlowe's works, London, 1912, Introd. xvii), that these 100 lines of Marlowe's poem "are not to be looked for in the place assigned them, but in the episode of Teras and other portions of the Fifth Sestiad where the higher hand of Marlowe is discernible." Since Chapman arranged the poem into sestiads, there was nothing to prevent him from juggling around whatever parts had been left in manuscript by Marlowe, especially such verse as had not been already incorporated in a definite section. It has already been advanced that Marlowe's work was not likely to have been in a finished state. It seems to me that the episode of the fox and the maid might be included in the scattered lines left by Marlowe.

Likewise in his function as a painter, we feel that Chapman has been overcome by a lack of clarity and his inability to select his materials. For a poet who dealt so much with Homeric verse, it is amazing to witness his failure to transfer the characteristic Greek concreteness to his own poetry. Hence, Ceremony's interminable pageant (III, 11off.); hence the intrusion of a reference to the contemporary military operations against Cadiz in *Hero and Leander*. Unlike Marlowe, Chapman is unable to present his images in simple, unforgettable characters. Consequently, he is forced to resort to bombast in describing Julia's pudic wrath:

> So straight wrapt she her body in a cloud
> And threatened tempests for her high disgrace,
> Shame from a bower of roses did unshroud
> And spread her crimson wings upon her face.[26]

This figure Musaeus renders infinitely more simply by telling us that in a like situation, Hero unconsciously wrapped her mantle more firmly about her thighs. Again, after reading Chapman's colorless vignette of Niobe's story carved upon the fountain, we can only imagine what a picturesque tableau Drayton would have presented given the same subject. But in Chapman's continuation, the scene resolves itself into a mere catalogue of names. Every critic has pointed out one of Chapman's attempts at neo-Ovidian description, his picture of Hero's scarf, which requires almost one hundred lines of verse. However, it is not luminous like Marlowe's or multicolored like Drayton's imagery. His clouded and confused metaphors render it opaque, and the reader must struggle constantly with Chapman's verse, as he tries to fit the various parts of his involved figures into the jig-saw puzzle. One feels that Chapman saw the world of the gods, but did not wholly believe or delight in it; hence his labored myths, totally unlike those of Ovid or Marlowe. Compare, for example, Chapman's fumbling image

. . . . .

[26] Chapman, *op. cit.*, p. 32.

of Neptune (VI, 244ff.), as the latter flings his mace at the Fates, wounding Lachesis and breaking Leander's thread of life, with Marlowe's almost identical figure (II, 210ff.), which is light and graceful.

But in all due justice to Chapman, we must balance the scales with what Swinburne calls "the rare flashes of high and subtle beauties." Passages such as:

> In a loose robe of tinsel forth she came,
> Nothing but it betwixt her nakedness
> And envious light. The downward-burning flame
> Of her rich hair did threaten new access
> Of venturous Phaeton to scorch the fields.[27]

Or occasional lines:

> Here Ovid sold his freedom for a look
> And with that look was ten times more enthralled.[28]

Or a truly beautiful picture:

> She lay, and seemed a flood of diamant
> Bounded in flesh, as still as Vesper's air,
> When not an aspen leaf is stirred with air.[29]

Passages such as these amply recompense the reader for the arduous journey through Chapman's tortured verse.

Hero and Leander was the subject of another curious continuation, Henry Petowe's *The Second Part of Hero and Leander* (1598), in which the poem is turned into a conventional verse romance. Some critics have seen in this an effort to popularize the legend for the middle classes.[30] Although this was in keeping with the contemporary tendencies, it seems strange, however, that much of the erotic element should be shorn from the story by an author who shortly afterwards was to write *Philochasander and Elanira*.[31] This version injects

. . . . .

[27] *Ibid.*, p. 23.   [28] *Ibid.*, p. 29.   [29] *Ibid.*
[30] Alice Crathern, "A Romanticized Version of *Hero and Leander*," *MLN*, XLVI (1931), 382ff.   [31] See above p. 175.

much irrelevant material into the myth. The course of true love is threatened when Duke Archilaus insists on wooing Hero on his own account:

> Duke Archilaus, cruell, voyd of pitie,
> Where Hero dwelt was regent of that citie,
> Woe worth that town where bloody homicides
> And tyrants are elected citie guides.[32]

Despite his guile and his threats, Hero will not yield. Leander is banished; whereupon he journeys to Delphos to consult the oracle. Meanwhile, the love-stricken tyrant having died, his brother Eristippus, eager to avenge Archilaus's death, decrees that Hero shall die, unless she find a champion within three months. Warned of danger by the oracle, Leander returns in disguise and puts the craven to death. Before leaving, he tests Hero's constancy by wooing her under his disguise. When she proves faithful, they are united. Feeling the compulsion of the Ovidian convention, Petowe causes them, after a long and happy life, to be transformed into trees:

> Their lives spent date and unresisted death,
> At hand to set a period to their breath,
> They were transformed by all divine decrees,
> Into the forme of two pine trees;
> Whose natures such the Faemale pine will die
> Unless the Male be ever planted by.[33]

From these verses, typical of the poem, one may appraise the poetic worth of Petowe's version. Not much can be said for his originality. He claims a source for his poem, since he "was inriched by a Gentleman friend of mine with the true discourse of those lovers further fortunes," but no one has taken these assertions seriously, ascribing them to the conventions of the time. The mediocrity of this work only serves to emphasize the superiority of Marlowe's creation.

. . . . .

[32] Henry Petowe, *The Second Part of Hero and Leander,* reprinted in Chabalier's *Hero et Leandre,* p. 187.
[33] *Ibid.,* p. 198.

Shakespeare and His Followers

Disregarding for the moment the aura of immortality wreathed about *Venus and Adonis* as one of the first poetic efforts by the young dramatist, Shakespeare, it must be granted that in the light of the Ovidian tradition it is one of the two or three choicest exemplars of mythological poetry in England. But at the same time, we must recognize that *Venus and Adonis* is endowed with all the faults, as well as the merits, of the genre. Along with *Hero and Leander,* it played an important part in the development of the Italianate mythological poem, not only by treating a favorite Ovidian theme within conventional lines, but also by focussing the attention on a genre which, after the first cultivation by Lodge and Spenser, was ready to bloom in Renaissance England.

Shakespeare's poem was tremendously popular in his own day, for, if to us it serves chiefly to presage the latent powers that were to flower in *The Tempest* and in *King Lear,* to his own contemporaries it revealed a new poet, skilled in the language of love and able to revive the spirit of the old Roman master. As Meres phrased it, "the sweete, wittie soule of Ovid lives in mellifluous and hony-tongued Shakespeare."[1] The poem appeared first in 1593, published by Richard Field, a native of Stratford, who had also come to London to make his fortune as a printer, and within ten years it had been reprinted six times. It received the meticulous attention of the young poet, for it was destined as an homage to the Earl of Southampton, whose patronage Shakespeare was seeking. Although the theory has been advanced that it was composed earlier in his youth, during his Stratford days, there is little to confirm such a view. It is more likely that the poem was a direct effort on Shakespeare's part to avail himself of the popularity of the new genre and was written by him during the lull in theatrical activity caused by the plague of 1593.

The origin of the tale takes little effort to divine, for the theme was a favorite Ovidian episode and had been treated extensively by other authors during the sixteenth century. We need only remember the numerous versions in Italy, in France and in Spain.[2] It is highly improbable that any of these influenced Shakespeare, especially since he had other sources more conveniently at hand. We know that the poet was familiar with the Latin text of Ovid, besides Golding's translation of the *Metamorphoses,* which was his *vade mecum.* There were, in addition, plenty of other English accounts of the myth readily accessible to anyone interested.

From what is known of Shakespeare's methods of using sources, it is apparent that his mind was a crucible in which materials of all sorts were collected, gathered from all quarters, refined, and finally shaped into Shakespeare's pure gold. Thus,

. . . . .

[1] Francis Meres, *Poetrie,* ed. D. C. Allen (Urbana, 1933), p. 76.
[2] In his edition of Shakespeare's Poems (Arden ed., 1927, Introd. xxix), C. K. Pooler lists versions by Minturno, Alciati and Sannazzaro in Latin; a translation of Bion's *Elegy* into Italian by Amomo, and other versions in the same language by Dolce, Tarcagnota, Parabosco and Marino. In France there were translations of Bion by St. Gelais and an *Adonis* by both Jean Passerat and Ronsard. In Spain, there were also several renderings in verse of the tale.

it is simple to detect traces of Ovidian lines, hints from Lodge's poem, imagery reminiscent of Marlowe and Golding.[3] These parallels have little significance, except insofar as they reflect a common Elizabethan practice of inserting verbatim an author's favorite passages in his own poems. Such resemblances are also largely due to the fact that these conceits were, in reality, commonplaces in the literary world. Excellent proof of this is the revealing manner in which the poet wove two or three myths into his tale, blending them into a unified whole that stands superbly as an artistic entity. In Ovid, Adonis is hardly a reluctant lover; consequently it is supposed that Shakespeare drew the hint for the obdurate Adonis from the well-known tale of Salmacis and Hermaphroditus (*Metamorphoses* IV), in which the youth is ardently pursued by the nymph. However, the poet could have gleaned many suggestions for the reluctance of Adonis from Marlowe, Greene or Fraunce's *Ivychurch*.[4] All these sources could have contributed to the myth of Venus's passionate wooing of the indifferent boy.

The very popularity of the poem brought upon it scathing attacks from contemporary reformers in numerous commentaries and epigrams of the day. We read of *Venus and Adonis* as the "true model of lascivious letcher."[5] For many years it was numbered among the objectionable erotic books which amorous youths used in their wanton pursuits. We have already seen that the book was to be found in a courtezan's library. But no stigma must be attached to the young poet because, if *Venus and Adonis* contains a great deal of eroticism, this was a definite characteristic of the genre. If it mars our

• • • • •

[3] For a study of the relationship of *Venus and Adonis* to Lodge's poem, see Pooler. On the relationship of the poem to *Hero and Leander*, see Bush's chapter on Shakespeare, and also *MLN*, XLII (1927), 211ff. The relation of Marlowe and Shakespeare is also discussed in *Notes and Queries*, Series 10, I (1904), 1ff.

[4] See above p. 216; also Bush, *op. cit.*, p. 145.

[5] Thomas Freeman, *Epigrams* (1614), Sig. K3ʳ.

appreciation of the poem, we can only accept it as a trait of its age, just as we recognize Richardson's sentimentality to be typical of his own day. Shakespeare may be regarded as the young poet, intoxicated with the senses, abandoning himself to beauty and the revelry of life. But in a certain sense, he differs from Marlowe, in that *Hero and Leander,* equally frank and sensuous, is the paean of youth. There is an inevitability, a joyous consummation of the love between the two young Grecians, whereas in *Venus and Adonis,* we are struck by a certain note of cold sensuality which not all of Shakespeare's artistry can efface.

Brought down to its fundamentals, Venus's hot pursuit of Adonis is the determined hunt of an inexperienced youth by a practised woman. It is an attempted seduction by an experienced wanton, who instantly reveals the sureness of her touch by the expertness with which she handles him. In a trice Adonis is off his horse, and Venus has him cornered. None of the boy's indifferent replies can discourage her lecherousness. His coolness has no effect upon her. She cannot perceive that Adonis is a peevish boy, whose immediate desire to go hunting has been frustrated, that he is a plainly bored youth, indifferent to the advances of the Queen of Love and concerned only with escaping from her unwelcome attentions and the heat of the sun. Nevertheless, she feeds on his panting breath and licks the moisture of his palm, pursuing the time-tried paths towards her goal, certain that they will not fail. And though Adonis unwillingly grants her a kiss merely to rid himself of her, in reading the poem we feel that only the boar has robbed her of her final victory, that in the end she would have overcome the youth's reluctance. One may see why *Venus and Adonis* enjoyed such popularity among a certain class of readers in England. A prelude to seduction, it summed up in elegant, beautiful language what was probably accepted *ars erotica,* conjuring up in breathless, iridescent pictures, the voluptuous and beautiful myth.

But it would be doing Shakespeare a rank injustice if one

left the impression that these are the only sensations conveyed by the poem, for we encounter in it the eternal plea of beauty for self-perpetuation, the world-old plea that youth lasts only a fleeting moment and that enjoyment of it should, therefore, be all the more imperative. As in the *Sonnets,* later on, Shakespeare pleads for the union of the flesh as a means of continuing the divine beauty, for,

> Torches are made to light, jewels to wear,
> Dainties to taste, fresh beauty for the use,
> Herbs for their smell, and sappy plants to bear;
> Things growing to themselves are growth's abuse:
>   Seeds spring from seeds and beauty breedeth beauty;
>   Thou wast begot; to get it is thy duty.[6]

The tastes of the age are reflected in the choice of language of the poem, as well as in its form. We have the popular sizain stanza, adopted from Lodge, which had also been used by Spenser in the *Shepherds Calender.* More than that, we have a decidedly Euphuistic tendency, brought about largely by the popularity of the sonnet and its stock phraseology. Of Venus, burning from her unquenched love, he says, "she bathes in water, yet her fire must burn." Her tears are

> The crystal tide that from her two cheeks fair
> In the sweet channel of her bosom dropped.

Yet, throbbing beneath all the Italianate language, we may feel the great latent power for metaphor that was to reveal itself in the plays. We realize that, like Donne, Shakespeare is too sinewy to reflect for long the Petrarchistic languorousness. Even though the nature of the subject itself required ease, mellifluousness of language, we have to look to Spenser and Drayton for such style, rather than to Shakespeare.

In passing from Marlowe to Shakespeare, the reader is struck by the very noticeable difference in the architecture of

· · · · ·

[6] *Venus and Adonis,* lines 163ff.

the two poems, by the organic arrangement of the various component parts of *Venus and Adonis* as contrasted to the other poem. Although we have already pointed out that it is hardly fair to make such a comparison in view of the unfinished state of *Hero and Leander*, still one may perceive here the dramatic genius of Shakespeare. Everything is held together; there are no loose strands; the beginning and the end are related units, even though one may feel that occasionally there is a regrettable introduction of extraneous material. In *Venus and Adonis*, there is no lingering; the reader is plunged at once into the very heart of the action as Venus immediately sets herself to the conquest of the desired youth. Numerous dramatic touches add a great deal to the poem. For example, the conventional description of the loveliness of the lady, the long Renaissance catalogue of her charms are omitted. Here Venus is made to describe herself; she holds herself temptingly before the indifferent youth, she, who has been the beloved of the dread God of War, she, the Queen of Beauty. Is she not fair? Is she not without blemish?

> Thou canst not see one wrinkle in my brow;
> Mine eyes are grey and bright and quick in turning;
> My beauty as the spring doth yearly grow,
> My flesh is soft and plump, my marrow burning.[7]

Shakespeare adds further dramatic value to his narrative when Venus, pausing after one of Adonis's interruptions, asks: "where did I leave?"

If we wish to find the real gold in the poem, it must be sought in the numerous word-paintings which the poet introduces into the rich tapestry that is *Venus and Adonis*. From all the recesses of his fancy, crystal-clear vignettes are called up, presaging the inexhaustible wealth of his imagery. It has become a commonplace to quote Shakespeare's scene of the hunting of the hare, and critics have waxed expansive over his

. . . . .

[7] *Ibid.*, lines 139ff.

naturalistic description of the encounter of the jennet and Adonis's mount. Such passages are typical, and they reveal that from his earliest poetic days, the well-springs of Shakespeare's poetry lay, not in the clouds, as was the case with Marlowe, or in the Pantheon, as in Chapman, but in the dells of the English countryside, in the earth, in the landscape of Stratford. He has the most sensitive awareness of the snail; he has a feeling for the most subtle shades of white, as he exhibits the beauty of Venus; or he can paint a graphic picture which has virility, as well as beauty. Here is Venus searching for Adonis:

> And as she runs, the bushes in the way
> Some catch her by the neck, some kiss her face,
> Some twine about her thigh to make her stay:
> She wildly breaketh from their strict embrace,
> > Like a milch doe, whose swelling dugs do ache,
> > Hasting to feed her fawn hid in some brake.[8]

Even at the risk of heresy, however, one must point out spots where the touch is not so sure. His conceits of the eagle devouring its prey, the lion walking along the hedge to watch the youth, are as incongruous in the lines of the poem as the animals themselves would have been on the English countryside he so effectively pictured. Again, the simile of Venus likening herself to a park, wherein Adonis shall find shelter and fondly graze on her lips, seems extravagant and lacking the usual clarity. One may question also the effectiveness of the picture created by Venus, standing Amazon-like beside Adonis's horse, flinging the reins over one arm and tucking her unwilling lover beneath the other! Even more serious against the canons of art is the intrusion in the heart of the action of the long, discursive controversy between Venus and the boy. It is the customary debate on chastity, with the usual arguments marshalled on both sides. The reasons advanced by the youth are like the replies of

. . . . .

[8] *Ibid.*, lines 871ff. For a detailed study of this phase of Shakespeare's art, see Caroline Spurgeon's *Shakespearean Imagery* (London, 1935).

an advocate, cold, logical, planned; they have not the fire nor the impetuousness of Hero's answer to Leander; there is none of the quality of yielding before an unanswerable argument as we have in Marlowe. Adonis is plainly vexed by her continual returning to the fray:

> "Nay, then" quoth Adon, "you will fall again
> Into your idle over-handled theme:
> The kiss I gave you is bestowed in vain,
> And all in vain you strive against the stream;
>   For by this black-fac'd night, desire's foul nurse,
>   Your treatise makes me like you worse and worse.
>
> If love have lent you twenty thousand tongues,
> And every tongue more moving than your own
> Bewitching like the wanton mermaid's song,
> Yet from thine ear the tempting tune is blown;
>   For know, my heart stands armed in mine ear,
>   And will not let a false sound enter there." [9]

Our poet is not above delivering a homily on jealousy nor above arraigning love, but after all, this aphoristic tendency was part of the poetical convention of the time and was to be found in abundance in all Renaissance poetry. These are faults which mar the artistic composition of *Venus and Adonis*, yet the poem remains a chant of the open air, the passionate exultation of a young man in love with words, with color, and with life; it is the paean of the young poet, singing the song, not of Ovid, but of his native countryside, a song of earth, the song of a new nation that has arisen about him, the song of youth, heralding the splendid maturity that is to come.

With the publication of *Venus and Adonis*, the floodgates of mythological poetry were released, and poet after poet hastened to follow the fashion. Among the more obvious imitations may be listed *Oenone and Paris* by T. H. in 1594. Its author is said to be Thomas Heywood, mainly on the strength

    . . . . .

[9] *Ibid.*, lines 769ff.

of similarity of the initials. The poem has been termed a "travesty of Shakespeare." [10] Actually, it is merely a frank imitation of *Venus and Adonis*, generously sprinkled with verbal passages selected from it. Some allowances may be made for the work, labelled by its author, "the first fruit of my indevors." To begin with he candidly acknowledged his borrowings, saying, "In the publishing of the little poem, I have imitated the painter, giving you this poore pamphlet to peruse, lurking meanwhile obscurely, till that hearing how you please to censure my simple work." [11] However, there is no evidence of any such treatment of *Venus and Adonis* as might be implied by the word "travesty." Mr. Parsons has collected many parallels; we take the liberty of quoting the first lines of the poem:

> When sun-bright Phebus in his fierie carre,
> Ended his passage through the vernal signes,

Cf. *Venus and Adonis*, which begins:

> Even as the sun with purple-colour'd face
> Had ta'en his last leave of the weeping morn.[12]

Again:

> His comely temples shadowed with his hatte
> Like frowning Juno in an angrie dumpe.

Cf. *Venus and Adonis*:

> And with his bonnet hides his angrie brow,
> Looke on the dull earth with disturbed minde.[13]

These hardly seem to be travesties, for if we accept such a verdict, then we must label all the later poems with that name. Moreover, there is hardly the need to point out the universality of Elizabethan plagiarism. A large percentage of every sonnet

. . . . .

[10] J. D. Parsons, *Notes and Queries*, Series 13, CLVII (1929), 39, 325ff.
[11] T. H., *Oenone and Paris* (1594), Epistle to the Reader.
[12] *Notes and Queries*, Series 13, CLVII (1929), 325.
[13] *Ibid.*, p. 326.

sequence consists of unacknowledged translations or paraphrases of sonnets taken from other collections.

Orpheus, his Journey to Hell and his Music to the Ghosts for the Regaining of Faire Eurydice, his love and New Spoused Wife (1595) is cast along the same lines. Its author, R. B., has been tentatively identified as Richard Barnfield, but the poem bears hardly a trace of the style of this lyric poet. Furthermore, in the preface to *Cynthia*, Barnfield cautioned his readers that this volume had been falsely ascribed to him.[14] The poem makes use of the popular sizain stanza and follows the conventional Ovidian pattern, leaving the reader pleasantly surprised to find that the usual effusive descriptions are subordinated to the narrative element. By way of innovation, the poet introduces several lyrics. These are the songs of Orpheus before the gods of the underworld, Pluto and Proserpine. They employ the familiar medieval refrain, *"Quod Amor vincit omnia"*; but they are undistinguished, as may be witnessed from the following stanza addressed to Pluto:

> Thou great Commaunder of this Court
> Triumphant victor over Death,
> To whom so many soules resort,
> When pale-fac'd death gins stop their breath,
> Witnes the truth of this I say,
> QUOD AMOR VINCIT OMNIA.[15]

Within recent years, another one of the host of mythological poems has been brought to light, John Trussel's *The First Rape of Fair Hellen* (1595). The poem is cast in the familiar sizain stanza and contains strong reminiscences of *Venus and Adonis*. There are also numerous resemblances to the *Rape of Lucrece*, from which a number of passages have been pilfered.

. . . . .

[14] R. B. McKerrow, Richard Barnfield's editor, feels that the initials affixed to this poem were merely a forgery by someone who attempted to capitalize on Barnfield's reputation.

[15] J. P. Collier, *A Bibliographical and Critical Account* (New York, 1886), I, 63n.

Attempts have been made to connect this John Trussel with the family by that name, located at Billesley, near Stratford, a family which must have moved in the same circles as some of Shakespeare's relatives, but such efforts are none too convincing.[16] The reader may also recollect another poem on the same subject, Richard Barnfield's *Hellens Rape*, a short, undistinguished composition in hexameters, which takes liberties with the Trojan story.

In the same year two poems came from Thomas Edwards, based directly on the Ovidian tradition, *Narcissus* and *Cephalus and Procris*. The first poem deserves mention only because of its excess of decoration and a constant tendency to misogyny, which may be due to the author's close imitation of the moralized versions of the tale. Edwards loses no opportunity to attack women. He subtly exposes their wiles, as they attempt to attract Narcissus, desiring him, yet wishing to play coy. The story follows the account in the *Metamorphoses*, but the author covers his original with a thick layer of descriptive material. Yet the story may be considered a good study in narcissism. In seeking to escape the cloying attentions of women while accepting their gifts, Narcissus falls in love with his own person. However, in the process of escaping from feminine advances, he becomes more coy than women themselves. He realizes his fatal passion for a shadow, but cannot resist its lure. On and on he is drawn, forgetting everything else, until he finally leaps into the spring for a final embrace and his subsequent metamorphosis.

Cephalus and Procris is an excellent example of the fate of the mythological poem fallen into unskillful hands. Written in pentameter couplets, the piece is obviously modelled upon its more distinguished predecessors, but it suffers immeasurably as a result of its moralizing and bourgeois attitude. In general, Edwards follows Golding's version of the *Metamorphoses*, with only slight variations. Golding, for example, concentrates

. . . . .
[16] For a discussion, see *TLS*, July 9, 16, 1931.

mainly on the description of Procris, whereas Edwards shows a predilection for the more fanciful account of Aurora. One cannot escape the numerous references to jealousy, the repeated attacks upon women's venality, and the power of gold over them.[17] Nor can one avoid a feeling of annoyance at his ridiculous prudery:

> Her garland deckt with many a pretie gemme,
> And flowers sweete as Maye, she gave to hem;
> Her feet (immodest dame) she bear'd to show him,
> And askt him, yea, or no, if he did know them,
> And therewithall, she whispers in his eare,
> Oh, who so long, is able to forbeare?[18]

This from a man who had the honest frankness of the *Amores* before him and the exultation of *Hero and Leander* ringing constantly in his ears!

However, for all his inability to express himself, Edwards is able to bring forth, upon occasion, felicitous bits of description and lines that have considerable beauty in them. There is a very lively picture of the hunt:

> The toylike dogges therewith do mainly runne,
> And having found their game, their Lord to come,
> They yelpe courageously as who would say,
> "Come maister come, the footing serves this way."[19]

But there is always the tendency to dissipate the atmosphere created by colorful pictures and characteristic mythological vignettes with digressions and invocations which serve only to destroy the mood.

. . . . .

[17] This might have been drawn from Pettie's version of the story of Cephalus, in which the two lovers are represented as living in Venice. Cephalus, under a disguise, tempts Procris with rare jewels, a temptation which she cannot withstand and which leads directly to the fatal accident in the wood.

[18] Thomas Edwards, *Works,* ed. W. E. Buckley (Roxburghe Club, 1882), p. 13.

[19] *Ibid.,* p. 14.

Edwards was a very frank imitator. Repeatedly he alludes
to contemporary poets who had preceded him in this genre.
Narcissus laments profusely, invoking Adonis's aid and calling
upon Leander to join him, although the latter would doubtless
have given him some sound advice about avoiding the opposite
sex. In Lenvoy to *Narcissus*, the poet invokes "Collyn, who
unlockt Albion's glory"; he refers to

> Adon deafly masking thro,
> Stately troupes rich conceited,

and alludes to Daniel, Drayton and Sackville.[20] Further on,
the poet deplores the deaths of Watson and Marlowe:

> Deal we not with Rosamund,
> For the world our own will coate,
> Amintas and Leander's gone,
> Oh deere sonnes of stately kings,
> Blessed by your nimble throates,
> That so amorously could sing.[21]

But even more convincing than this are the innumerable
verbal echoes that are to be found in Edward's poetry coming
from *Hero and Leander* and *Venus and Adonis*. They range
from marginal notes, copied exactly by Edwards, to actual
lines, transported into *Narcissus*. Sententious couplets and
colorful images are lifted bodily from Shakespeare and Marlowe to enrich the weaker vein of Edwards. The poet set out
consciously to imitate Marlowe and his pilferings are constant

. . . . .

[20] *Ibid.*, p. 335n. The passage which refers to the Earl of Dorset is not
quite clear, and other persons have been advanced. Buckley discusses
the various possibilities offered. At the end of the poem the poet promises another version of *Narcissus*, one perhaps with a gayer ending:

> And when all is done and past,
> Narcissus in another sort,
> And gaier clothes shall be plast
> Eke perhaps in good plight.
> p. 64.

[21] *Ibid.*, p. 62.

evidence of his efforts to bolster a weak poem. Edwards's attempts to reproduce the Ovidian description so felicitous in Marlowe, his arguments against chastity are only a few of the imitations from *Hero and Leander*. The same may be said with regard to *Venus and Adonis*, echoes of which are forever reverberating in Edwards's poetry. The luxuriant description, its images taken from daily life, the very theme of a youth pursued by an older, more experienced woman all resemble Shakespeare's details. Aurora's pursuit of Procris, her blandishments, her concupiscence make her an exact counterpart of Venus. Cephalus wails against her attentions and plaintively wishes to go hunting, just as Adonis repulses his importunate pursuer with a bored, "Fie, no more love!"

Drayton, Barnfield, etc.

AT THE VERY HEIGHT OF THE POPULARITY OF the mythological poem, Michael Drayton chose to swerve from the accepted path of presenting Ovidian incident and with *Endimion and Phoebe* (1595) lifted his narrative into the pure, if rather cold, heights of the neo-platonic world. Perhaps he recalled that he could hardly surpass the efforts of his predecessors, even though Marlowe's poem was still circulating only in manuscript; perhaps his nature was repelled by the erotic effusions of Marlowe and Shakespeare. If so, he chose a theme well-suited to his moral disposition, for no subject could be more irreproachable than that of his poem. If this is the case, it may explain his failure to allude to these two poets in *Endimion and Phoebe*. Drayton mentions only Spenser by his literary name, "Colin," Daniel as "Musaeus," and Lodge as "Goldey." Whatever the reason for this change of mood, *Endimion and Phoebe* does not seem to have been popular, since it was not reprinted within the lifetime of the poet. Drayton himself recast it in 1606 as *The Man in the Moone,* retaining only a few of the essential parts. Evidently, readers did not take too kindly to his neo-platonizing of their favorite myths, even though the practice had been prevalent in former decades. Perhaps the reading public missed the conventional Ovidian atmosphere and turned elsewhere for it. For it must be admitted that, as a result of Drayton's valiant efforts to purify the Ovidian vein, his poem lacks inspiration, and one willingly returns to the sensuous but highly poetic strains of Marlowe and Shakespeare.

The poem deals with the familiar tale of Phoebe's love for the shepherd, Endimion, who has pledged himself to serve her. Phoebe descends to his mortal haunts on Mount Latmus, woos him under the guise of a nymph, only to be repelled by his declaration that he is faithful to his goddess. Nevertheless, he is strangely moved by her and is overjoyed when, at a later visit, she reveals herself to be his Phoebe. The piece ends with the triumphal ascent of the shepherd to the abode of the gods, where he is to dwell forever in her company.

Drayton is constantly searching for the vein of purity; everywhere we hear him reiterate that Phoebe's love is chaste, that she is motivated only by pure desires in her love for Endimion. She repeatedly assures him that: "Nor wanton nor lascivious is my love." When one examines this situation, so similar to that in *Venus and Adonis,* it is astonishing to observe the lack of eroticism in Drayton's tale. The description of Phoebe's charms is very proper; there is not the slightest hint of the flesh; the body and its beauty are only mentioned in the process of evolving the neo-platonic view that material beauty must be restricted solely to bringing about the contemplation of absolute or spiritual beauty. There is frequent mention of the "heavenly secrets," the revelation of which, however, never materializes beyond a recital of the cant of neo-platonism, much like the verbiage of modern psychoanalysis. In fact, much of the poem is given over to this technical jargon, in which he speaks of

One only powerfull faculty,
yet governeth a multiplicity,
being essentiall, uniforme in all,
not to be severed nor individuall,

> But in her function holdeth her estate,
> By powers divine in her ingenerate.[1]

This language is as obscure as it is unpoetic. Consequently, the poem, especially in its final stages, becomes largely a treatise of astronomical information, in which we learn much about the motion of the planets and the whimsical properties of the sacred number three.

Much of this neo-platonic lore was derived from the popular handbook by Natalis Comes, although Drayton might have been influenced by the French Protestant poet, Du Bartas, whose religious epics were very popular in England. The latter's Uranie could very easily have served as the model for Phoebe, even though much of the material was, in reality, poetic commonplace.[2] Spenser's very potent influence also must have contributed to his choice and treatment of the subject. Indeed, the whole poem might be termed in Drayton's own words a

> gorgious arras in rich colours wrought
> With silks from Affricke or from Indies brought.

It borrows much from Spenser, especially in the description of Mount Latmus, which bears a strong resemblance to the Gardens of Adonis or the Bower of Bliss in the *Faerie Queene*.

Despite Drayton's remarkable assimilation of his sources, for nowhere is any one influence dominant, we may track down special borrowings.[3] Here and there, we hear echoes from *Venus and Adonis* or from *Hero and Leander*, especially in Drayton's use of maxims such as: "simples fit beauty, fie on drugs and art." Lodge's poem may have suggested the change in Endimion, who, at first, is unresponsive to the advances of the disguised Phoebe, but later relents. The device of the god-

. . . . .

[1] Michael Drayton, *Endymion and Phoebe*, lines 516ff.
[2] See Bush, *op. cit.*, p. 159.
[3] See J. W. Hebel's edition of *Endimion and Phoebe* (Boston, 1925), Introduction; also Bush's chapter on Drayton; and Oliver Elton, *Michael Drayton* (London, 1905).

dess disguising herself to woo a man who already loves her seems to have no specific source, but we meet it frequently, especially in the romances, where it is used as a ruse to test the fidelity of lovers. Phoebe's courtship of Endimion is exactly parallel to the wooing in *Venus and Adonis,* yet it is treated most differently. Whereas, in the earlier poem the mood is one of unbridled passion and desire, in Drayton, the relationship is of the chastest sort, cold and proper. Phoebe wanders from tree to tree, carving her beloved's name, but when she meets him, her arguments are of the purest tenor. True, like Venus, she tries to bribe him with a dazzling display of the world's treasures, but there is not the slightest hint of impropriety on her part. Like Venus, however, she expresses the age-old argument that youth must seize the moment at hand:

> O thou art young and fit for love's profession,
> Like wax, which warmed quickly takes impression.[4]

And like Adonis, the youth petulantly objects to her interference with his sport—in this case, fishing—reminding her to stand aside, for the fish have been frightened away by her shadow. But excluding a few such touches, there is little dramatic value in *Endimion and Phoebe.*

The poem is a well-planned composition, noticeable for the quiet monotony of its verse and the even regularity of its beauty. Written in a pastoral vein, it offers long catalogues of flowers and precious stones. These, though good examples of Drayton's skill as a versifier, can hardly be termed great poetry. The lengthy description of the pageant, interesting, but hardly vital to the tale, might well have served as a typical court entertainment. Some of these descriptions are of inordinate length, one of them occupying nearly a quarter of the poem. This lack of brevity causes Drayton to mar scenes of considerable beauty. The metamorphoses described in *Endimion and*

. . . . .

[4] Drayton, *Endimion and Phoebe,* lines 277ff.

Phoebe can hardly compare with Marlowe's vignettes. It is hardly an inspired Muse which accompanies Drayton as he describes Phoebe in all her glory or as he pictures her triumphant birth. Like Chapman, Drayton goes to Olympus for his gods; he calls upon them often and loudly, but never can make them come to life.

If Drayton succeeds in anything, it is in presenting a rich and colorful description, in decking out a brave pageant of finery which allows his imagination to run rampant. His use of color is astonishing; in a few lines, we encounter all the hues of the palette. He seems to revel in the very cataloguing of rich and strange hues, in the mention of gorgeous stuffs. He has the true Renaissance love for opulent display, for cambric, and embroidery, and web-like ruffs. Nowhere does he achieve this better than in the triumph of Endimion. Trains of Oriades, their flaxen hair wreathed with silken fillets, follow lightly upon the footsteps of their sisters, the Hamadriads, who emerge shyly from their shady bowers; all the denizens of the world of fancy, all the gods from legendary Olympus are there to attend the deification of the fortunate mortal, upon whom the goddess has bestowed her favor. These are the instances when the Muse touches Drayton with her magic and, for a brief while, he achieves great poetry:

> She layd Endimion on a grassy bed,
> With sommers Arras ritchly over-spred,
> Where from her sacred Mantion next above,
> She might descend and sport her with her love,
> Which thirty yeeres the Shepheards safely kept,
> Who in her bosom soft and soundly slept;
> Yet as a dreame he thought the tyme not long,
> Remayning ever beautiful and yong,
> And what in vision there to him be fell,
> My weary muse some other time shall tell.[5]

. . . . .

[5] *Ibid.*, lines 983ff.

Pity that he never kept his promise or that this vein did not continue!

During the same year, appended to Richard Barnfield's volume of short lyrics, *Cynthia*, there appeared a longer mythological poem, *The Legend of Cassandra*. It starts in the conventional manner, but, perhaps under the influence of Shakespeare's *Rape of Lucrece*, it changes its tone and becomes more and more like a *complaint*. Its beginning, however, is very much in the mood of *Venus and Adonis*:

> Upon a gorgious gold embossed bed,
> With tissue curtaines drawne against the sunne,
> Which gazers eies into amazement led,
> So curiously the workmanship was donne,
> Lay faire Cassandra in her snowy smocke,
> Whose lips the Rubies and the pearles did locke.[6]

In this version of the familiar Greek myth, young Phoebus, rising from the East, spies her as she sleeps, becomes radiant, and steals a kiss from her. Having been so abruptly awakened, the startled Cassandra wounds him with one of the darts from her eyes. Phoebus changes himself into one of Venus's crew. Gayly attired as a Renaissance gallant, he woos her; first reminding her, however, of the fate which has befallen her reluctant predecessors, such as Daphne, who was transformed into a laurel. Since Cassandra has no intention of suffering a like fate, she feigns to welcome his suit, extracting from him a promise to grant her a boon. This turns out to be the demand for the gift of prophecy. Then, once Phoebus has sworn, she changes her tune and "chastely counterchecks love's hot alarms," leaving a disillusioned god behind her. The enraged Phoebus grants her demand, but with the condition that she will not be believed. Then follow the Trojan disasters, Cassandra's prophecies to Priam, the downfall of the city and her capture by Agamemnon, who wishes to make her his leman.

. . . . .

[6] A. M. Bullen, *Some Longer Elizabethan Poems* (London, 1903), p. 213.

Even though he learns from her of his fate at the hands of
Aegisthus, he will not place credence in her foretelling. He returns to Greece with her, takes the fatal robe from Clytem-
nestra, and is slain by her lover. Cassandra herself is imprisoned
in a tower, where she is fed the body of the slain king. She
ends her woes by plunging a knife into her breast.

It is only natural that a tale less than five hundred lines in
length must dispose hurriedly of some of the details. We are
conscious of the change in mood from the beginning, as the
opulence of color and description gives way to the atmosphere
of the *complaint*. For example:

> I lived quoth she to see Troy set on fire:
> I lived to see renowned Hector slaine:
> I lived to see the shame of my desire,
> And yet I live to feel my grievous paine:
> Let all young maides example take by me,
> To keepe their oathes and spotless Chastity.[7]

Barnfield is not at his best, although some of the vignettes he
paints are creditable. His marked aptitude in the use of color-
words may be traced directly to his fondness for the lyric. The
influence which Shakespeare's poems have had on the *Legend
of Cassandra* has been repeatedly pointed out, echoes of
Lucrece being especially noticeable.[8] We frequently encounter
tiresome, sententious couplets, such as

> Only chaste thoughts, virtuous abstinence
> Gainst such sweet poyson is the surest defence.[9]

Despite the change in mood towards Puritanism in the last
decade of Elizabeth's reign, a number of mythological poems
retain this moralizing strain to a marked degree. They exhibit
a bourgeois tone which is reminiscent of the spirit of the verse

• • • • •

[7] Bullen, *op. cit.*, p. 225.
[8] See Pooler's analysis in his edition of Shakespeare's poems, Introd.
ixff; also Bush, p. 310.
[9] Bullen, *op. cit.*, p. 221.

romance and were probably written to cater to the tastes of the lower classes. Typical among them are an anonymous *Legend of Orpheus and Eurydice* and Peter Colse's *Penelope's Complaint or a Mirrour for Wanton Minions* (1596). Based on the Homeric tale, this poem records mainly the tearful wailings of Penelope, when she finds herself increasingly unable to cope with her importunate suitors. There are moments when she wonders whether it might not be wiser to yield to their offers, as she ponders over her lonely bed, the darksome nights, and all the troubles besetting her. But her conjugal devotion and her loyalty to Ulysses win out in the end. Haughtily Penelope replies to her suitors that she is well able to care for herself and wishes to mourn for her husband undisturbed. This does not prevent her from expressing to her maids her practical views upon marriage, chastity, and the state of widowhood. Her suitors attempt to convince Telemachus to turn her out and seize the land; whereupon he scornfully answers:

> Your company I well could spare:
> Pardon me if I fret and fume,
> I see right little do you care,
> How you my father's goods consume:
> Except you better you behave
> Your absence shortly let me crave.[10]

Throughout all these trials, Penelope refuses to write to her husband, feeling that he must have enough worries of his own:

> No, no my gemme, my sweetest joy,
> Thou shalt not need for me to care,
> Thou business has enough at Troy,
> Looke wisely to thy owne welfare,
> For Troy yeeldes many a dogged lad
> Which makes me sighing sit thus sad.[11]

. . . . .

[10] Colse, *Penelopes Complaint*, Sig. C2ᵛ.
[11] *Ibid.*, Sig. C3ᵛ.

To put an end to this situation, Ulysses returns, under the guise of a palmer, vanquishing the suitors through the stratagem of the bow. As a literary production, *Penelopes Complaint* is very mediocre, and its torturing of both the spirit of Homer and Ovid's *Heroides*, from which the letter to Ulysses is taken, by no means improves the piece. The style, repetitious, full of needless apostrophes and alliteration, is in keeping with the general tenor of the poem.[12]

A little known version of Orpheus and Eurydice is appended to one of the numerous collections of sonnets composed during this period by an unknown young poet, who timidly offered this "infant of my Muse" to the public without revealing his name.[13] The work is entitled: *Of Loves Complaint with the Legend of Orpheus and Eurydice* (1597). The volume consists of a series of sonnets to the poet's mistress and a longer poem, as was conventional with such compilations.[14] There is little to distinguish the shorter lyrics from the flood of other amatory poems. They represent the swooning sighs of the young lover, expressed in extravagant conceits. But, as is invariably the case, the sonnet sequence ends on a note of disappointment, a fit prelude to the mood of the accompanying piece.

The Legend of Orpheus and Eurydice opens with the usual astrological beginning, by way of setting, placing the action in spring. Orpheus and Eurydice are pictured for us in the extravagant terms of the sonnets; soon Eurydice is torn from this earth, for

. . . . .

[12] The piece has been brought into the Shakespearean controversy concerning *Willobies Avisa*, because of a statement in the Dedication to Lady Horsey, attacking the latter poem. For a discussion, see G. B. Harrison's edition of *Willowbies Avisa*, and also Bush, p. 310.

[13] This poem was evidently unknown to Julius Wirl, for it is not mentioned in his work, *Orpheus in der Englischen Literatur*, *Wiener Beitrage* XL (1913). It was only recently reproduced through the kindness of the Modern Language Association.

[14] See *ante* p. 70ff.

Myrrour of beauty, quaintest work of nature,
And heavens image in an earthly creature.
Image it only was and, therefore, fraile,
The reason why it past so soone away.[15]

And now, where happiness once reigned, deepest woe comes
to enclose the soul. Death comes to exile beauty to her eternal
night,

For faire Eurydice, the fairest faire,
That ever yet did blaze her Orient shine,
Or from a virgin-breast drew purest ayre
To death doth all her graces now resigne.[16]

The myth is very baldly told; there is little elaboration, little
of the verbal luxuriance customary in this genre. The story
follows the conventional lines of Virgil and Ovid as Orpheus
pursues his wife to Hell, and comes to grief through his impetuousness. But the author was not content to cease here. He adds
a tearful lament in which the desolate Orpheus wails over
beauty:

Tell how Beautie is a bitter sweet,
Whose getting care, whose losing greater woe,
And with our eares it soone away doth fleete,
And when Age commeth how it backe doth goe,
And then the faire, o'recome by beauties foe,
Can onely weeping say, we have been so.[17]

As he wanders over the hills, singing, while all Nature stands
ravished by his music, Orpheus rails bitterly against women,
delivering a sermon on their wiles. All this invective hurled at
women is difficult to digest, especially when put into the
mouth of Orpheus of all characters, but it may have been
planned as a definite link to the sonnet portion of the volume,
as a tirade against an over-cruel mistress. Even that, however,
hardly excuses its incongruity. It is clear that the presence of

. . . . .

[15] *The Legend of Orpheus and Eurydice*, Sig. C6ᵛ.
[16] *Ibid.*, C6ᵛ.   [17] *Ibid.*, Sig. E3ʳ.

this superfluous moralization stamps our unknown as one of the host of moralizing poets whom we have so frequently encountered delivering moral lessons through popular genres.

To counterbalance this moralizing strain, there were always the numerous compositions directly carrying on the spirit of Marlowe and Shakespeare, the mood of Nashe's *Choice of Valentines* and Petowe's *Philochasander and Elanira*. Typical of such poems are Cutwode's *Caltha Poetarum* and Dunstan Gale's *Pyramus and Thisbe* (1596). Gale's poem treats the familiar story from Book IV of the *Metamorphoses* in the conventional manner, with only a few deviations. In Golding, the attacking animal is a lioness, whereas Gale changes it into a lion; in this poem, the lion, being sated after devouring a lamb, merely wishes to steal a kiss. There are several such important changes. The usual abundance of outrageous conceits and the conventional language of the sonnets—antitheses and lengthy similes—is also present. But the author never achieves the trenchant phrases that characterize his worthier predecessors, whom he is obviously trying to copy. Bush has already pointed out the evident parallel to Hero in the account of Thisbe's arraying herself for the tryst. In *Hero and Leander* (I, 103ff.) there is also a similarity to the admiration provoked by Thisbe as she walks along, while the grass tries to kiss her feet.[18]

The resemblances to *Venus and Adonis* are just as striking; for example, like the boar in Shakespeare's poem, the lion merely wanted a kiss. The tone of some of Gale's passages is very reminiscent of the atmosphere in *Venus and Adonis*. There is a light, almost anacreontic feeling, especially during the early parts of this poem, with just a faint suggestion of banter on the author's part. But one gathers the impression that, although Gale is describing childish sport between the two children, he derives a certain amount of lascivious satisfaction, as he indulges in asides and dwells far too long on certain details. One can almost see the satyr's pointed ears:

. . . . .

[18] Bush, *op. cit.*, MLN, XLII (1927), 211ff.

Oft he would take her by the lillie hand,
Girdling her middle straight as any wand,
And cast her downe, but her her lie alone,
For other pastymes Pyramus knew none.[19]
Then up she starts and takes him by the necke,
And for that fall gives Pyramus a checke.
Yet at the length she chanst to cast him downe,
Though on the green she never gaind a gowne;
But rose againe and hid her in the grasse,
That he might tract that place where Thisbie was,
And finding her (as children use) imbrace her
For being children, nothing could disgrace her.[20]

One of the outstanding licentious poems found in the bon-
fire ordered by the Bishops in 1599 was Thomas Cutwode's
Caltha Poetarum (1599). This poem shows to perfection the
Italianate manner, the cloyed style, the over-abundance of
description and the lascivious strain which caused its doom to
the flames. On the other hand, it has undeniable merits, a
wealth of sensuous description, which is the very essence of
Renaissance poetry and that gay, anacreontic mood which
reaches its height in the poetry of Robert Herrick.

Caltha Poetarum abounds in brilliantly sensuous descriptions, redolent with the sweet smells of the countryside. The
poet paints lovingly and at great length a picture of colorful country gardens, dwelling on each flower, on "the blew
cornuted Collumbine," on "the kingcup, with sops in wine
that every heart delights." He loves to linger on pictures of
Venus, dallying with her infant son; and he is unusually
successful in evoking the true Ovidian atmosphere, where

. . . . .

[19] These parenthetical expressions remind one of Marlowe's lines I,
61ff.

> Albeit Leander rude in love and raw,
> Long dallying with Hero, nothing saw
> That might delight him more, yet he suspected
> Some amorous rites or other were neglected.

[20] Dunstan Gale, *Pyramus and Thisbe*, Sig. A4ʳ.

goddesses and mortals sport and dally. The story centers about
Venus's decision to right matters between the Woodbine and
Caltha, a marigold, who has been spurning her wooer for a
long time:

> How oft comes he with kingcups full of gold,
> And as a present offereth to this flower,
> And riches in great handful he doth hold,
> Rayning upon her lap an Orient shower,
> Of pearle, which mongst faire women have much power,
> But all as naught her nicitie neglects them,
> And even as rags most rudely she rejects them.[21]

Venus proposes to accomplish this by requesting her archer-son
to wound the proud lady. Unfortunately, the blind Cupid
strikes instead a bumble-bee who is searching for honey:

> He came but lately from the damaske rose,
> Unto my marygolde that shines so sunnie
> And got him there a pair of yealow hose
> Of virgin waxe, all wet about with hunnie.[22]

Venus is wroth with the lovely blunderer, who pertly reminds
her that the harm is done. Having fallen in love with the Lady
Caltha, the Bee repairs to his hive, where he establishes a cult
of the lady, erecting altars to her, offering sacrifices in her
honor, to the great chagrin of the jealous Venus.

She summons the spiders with their webs and subtle engines
to set a snare in which the unfortunate Bee is caught. Given to
Cupid as a plaything, he succeeds in escaping, wounding his
jailer in the bargain. Venus swears revenge upon Caltha, but
Proserpine now comes to the marigold's rescue:

> She comes to Caltha to her broidered bed,
> And taketh holde upon her tender stalke,
> This done, she layes her hand upon her head,
> And mumbels in her mouth with whisper talke.
> And there in circle wise about did walke,

. . . . .

[21] Cutwode, *Caltha Poetarum*, stanza 34.   [22] *Ibid.*, stanza 38.

As Tragetours for spirits set their spels,
To conjure up the Fairies or the Elves.[23]

Caltha is placed under her protection and made one of Diana's companions. Her plans foiled, Venus decides to avenge herself upon Primula, Caltha's sister. She plants a mandrake nearby, for Primula to view. Despite the fact that her new neighbor is a loathsome creature, Primula is moved to laughter and not above playing peek-a-boo with him.

Meanwhile the Bee is heartbroken at his failure to find Caltha, and becomes a hermit:

> He made himself a pair of holy beads,
> The fiftie aves were of gooseberries,
> The paternosters and the Holy Creeds
> Were made of red and goodly fair ripe cherries.[24]

In this guise he begs his way through the Kingdom of Cantharides, where he eventually finds Caltha in Diana's train. Once his woeful tale is heard, he is quickly transformed into a man. We shall have to pass over the subsequent descriptions, because Cutwode takes a decided turn for the bawdy, revelling in details which brought down upon him the Bishops' censorship. Suffice it to say that since the Bee had left his sting in Cupid, he is forced to wander about without the corresponding part of the human anatomy, to the great amusement of the ladies of the Court. Diana repairs the damage with a thorn from a hawthorn bush; then, giving him a viol and a fiddle, she names him Musaeus. Diana's curiosity sends the Bee back to ascertain Primula's fate; during this visit, he witnesses her wedding to Mandrake.

Having told him of her fear of reprisals, Venus sets the disguised Bee to watch over her. Meanwhile, he sings a song to lull her, and she falls asleep. Now comes his moment for revenge. Cutwode spares no detail of the Bee's efficient ravishing of the sleeping goddess. In his mischievous vein he adds:

. . . . .

23 *Ibid.,* stanza 92.   24 *Ibid.,* stanza 116.

Now whether that this Lady slept or no,
Or winked wild as little wantons use
There will I leave you, for I do not know,
Judge of it as you list, for you may chuse,
And me I pray you heartily excuse.
But there the fidler found an instrument
That makes him mirth and much mad meriment.[25]

Suddenly Venus awakens and begins to shout, "The Bee! The Bee!"

Help Fidler, for the Bumble hath stung me,
Then quoth Musaeus, all our quarel ends
And let us kis good madam and be friends.[26]

There is no doubt that the overly frank description, the undisguised pleasure with which Cutwode lingers over ribald passages would bar it from inclusion in a college anthology; nevertheless, he possesses an undeniable power of myth-making, and many of the vignettes which decorate the poem are among the freshest found in this genre. The pictures of the wedding of Primula, the description of Diana's court are really very charming. Cutwode shows also an ease of versifying and a feeling for color, unusual even in this last decade of the waning century. His gayety, his mocking, add verve to the poem and give rise to some very lively scenes, such as that of Caltha and Diana, exchanging gossip and enjoying Venus's discomfiture with true feminine maliciousness.

Another piece which unites some of the characteristics of the pastoral romance and the mythological poem is John Weever's *Faunus and Melliflora* (1600). In tone it resembles closely Spenser's episode of Sir Calidore and Pastorella in Book IV of the *Faerie Queene*, but it makes definite use of some of the motifs from the mythological genre, including the Ovidian transformation at the end. Prince Faunus encounters a gathering of shepherds in a quiet, idyllic valley and takes part in their

. . . . .

[25] *Ibid.*, stanza 176.   [26] *Ibid.*, stanza 179.

innocent sports. While playing Barlinbreake, he spies Melliflora and, encouraged by her frank, simple acceptance of his suit, falls in love with her. Deiopeia, another nymph, also conceives a fancy for the handsome Faunus, thus providing the proper dramatic touch. There follows the usual sighing courtship, in true sonnet fashion, during which Faunus

> If once on Melliflora he did thinke
> He wet his paper both with tears and incke.

Having persuaded her to renounce her vows to Diana, Faunus marries her in spite of his father's remonstrances. Venus, thereafter, transforms Picus into a black bird; on the other hand, to revenge herself for the broken vow, Diana changes Melliflora's child into the satyr who later gives rise to the race of Latinus. The piece is marked by a certain languid grace, with pleasing tableaux, full of color and luxuriant landscape, reminiscent of Drayton. We are plunged deeply into the mythological world of the later Renaissance—a world of unreality and fancy.

Not inconspicuous among the large number of mythological poems is the translation of an Italian poem on chess to be found in a treatise on the game, published in 1597. *Ludus Scacchiae: Chesse Playe. a Game, Bothe Pleasant, Wittie and Politicke: With Certaine Briefe Instructions Thereunto Belonging: Translated out of the Italian into the English Tongue. Containing also Therein a Pretie and Plasant Poeme of a Whole Game Played at Chesse. Written by G. B.* The author of the Italian poem was Marco Girolamo Vida, Bishop of Alba. The translation, curiously enough for a composition of this type, is in fourteener couplets, but it achieves a degree of liveliness, despite the lumbering measure in which it is cast.

After a conventional prologue which announces epic battles to be fought between soldiers "framed of box," we are shown the gods arriving to attend the wedding of Oceanus to Tellus. The host brings out a chess board for the amusement of his guests. The poem explains the various positions and the play of each piece. A game is then arranged, with Apollo choosing white and Mercury the opposing side.[27]

There are thrusts and counter-attacks; Mercury feints with a pawn:

> And that his Queene he might surprise,
> A pawne he doth presente,
> Which nathlesse the suttle God
> Doth seeme for to repente.
> The Archer then for right side seekes
> The white Queen to entangle,
> Which heedless foe not marking, thrust
> A pawne in left side angle.
> When Venus faire foresaw the losse
> That thereby should ensue,
> She warning gave to Phoebus milde,
> By signs and tokens true.
> Apollo thus admonished
> Did cast his eyes about,
> And viewed the camp, and sodainely
> He spied among the rout,
> One of his foes that ready was
> To swallow up the pawne,
> And checke the Queene, he with his hand
> Did pull him in againe.[28]

Foiled in his ruse, Mercury attempts to claim the game, precipitating an argument among the gods. There are many such dramatic incidents. Phoebus, the guileless, proudly announces that he is aware of Mercury's craftiness; all the gods laugh and the battle rages on. Mars, who is Mercury's friend, secretly tries to help the latter and even attempts to place back on the board a black rook and a pawn, but he is detected by Mulciber,

· · · · ·

[27] Lest chess enthusiasts be disappointed if they hunt down this piece, no actual game seems to be played out; at least it is impossible to determine one from the beginning of the game. There is no doubt that in the end-game, the author did have a definite plan of attack in mind and was not merely trying to retire the sides.

[28] *Ludus Scacchiae*, Sig. C3v.

Juno's lame son, and the pieces are banned. Though possessing a decided advantage, White forgets the ultimate objective in the pursuit of a diversion, and Mercury mates the white King. As a reward, he receives from Jove the Caduceus, symbol of control over the magic arts. Subsequently, Mercury teaches the game to the men of Italy and, having fallen in love with the nymph Scacchis, names the game after her to requite her courtesies.

The poem shows a good deal of dramatic force. There is no tendency towards repetitiousness, and the action is vigorously carried out, for the author keeps in mind the dramatic aspects of the game at all times.

It is the fate of all things to flourish and decay, so with the mythological poem. It flourished, but eventually, perceiving in it an apt medium for satire, writers used it to mock the swarm of amatory poetasters who had overrun England during this decade. Thus John Marston chose this type as his springboard into the poetic world, employing it, however, as a means of protest against the entire host of imitators in the Ovidian tradition, the "lewd Priapians," who sighed and swooned and prostrated themselves before their mistresses, gushing forth protestations that had been stale for fifty years. His poem, *The Metamorphosis of Pygmalion's Image,* ostensibly made use of the Ovidian transformation from Book X of the *Metamorphoses.* Actually, the piece was a travesty of the genre, written in the vein of "melting poesy," using all the known tricks and devices of the amorists in order to ridicule them. It was all the more ironical that his purpose should be mistaken, not only by his contemporaries, but by later critics,[29] and that his verses should be condemned to the fire along with *Caltha Poetarum* and other licentious works by order of Bishop Whitgift in 1599. It is not unreasonable to suppose that the censors may have considered the remedy worse than the cure, for, in

. . . . .

29 John Marston, *The Works,* ed. A. H. Bullen (London, 1887), Introduction.

his zeal to imitate those whose style he had been trying to ridicule, Marston displayed a frankness not often encountered in the poems of Marlowe and Shakespeare. This misunderstanding of the poem's intent, continuing well into the next century, even caused it to be included, along with Barkstead's *Myrrha* and *The Scourge of Venus,* in a collection of licentious poetry.

One cannot read Marston's poem, however, without detecting definite signs of his satiric purpose. We have, it is true, the development of the tale along the familiar Ovidian lines; we are regaled with a definite amount of prurient detail, a minute description of the statue's charm, and Pygmalion's rather too passionate fondling of it. Marston dwells overlong on the sensuous details, but the true purpose of such inclusions becomes apparent when we view the multitude of satirical allusions and interpolations with which the poem fairly bristles.

At the very beginning, the author pens a highly ironical epistle, "to the World's mighty monarch, Good Opinion." It is fulsome praise, and one may read its parallels in the numberless other dedications penned to Queen and noblemen. The same tone is continued in the Dedication, "To his mistresse," a tone which is conveyed through mocking asides, encountered throughout the poem, *e.g.,*

> For having wrought in purest ivory
> So faire an image of a woman's feature
> That never yet proudest mortality
> Could show so rare and beateous a creature
> (Unlesse my mistress' all-excelling face,
> Which gives to Beauty beauty's only grace.[30]

There are numberless resemblances to the other mythological poems; the list of parallels industriously gathered by commentators bears witness,[31] but we are far from the mood of Dray-

. . . . .

[30] *Ibid.,* III, 251.
[31] Bush, p. 180n., lists a good many such resemblances; see also the notes to Martin's edition of *Hero and Leander.*

ton or Lodge. Marston has described in detail Pygmalion's
enjoyment of his statue's charms—head, neck, breasts:

> Until his eye descended so far down
> That it descried Love's pavilion
> Where Cupid doth enjoy his only crown,
> And Venus hath her chiefest mansion:
> > There would he wink and winking look again,
> > Both eyes and thought would gladly there remain.

> Whoever saw the subtil city-dame
> In sacred church when her pure thoughts should pray,
> Peer through her fingers, so to hide her shame,
> When that her eye, her mind would feign bewray:
> > So would he view and wink, and view again:
> > A chaster thought could not his eye retain.[32]

Again, having regaled his readers with the titillations they so
eagerly looked for, he says mockingly:

> And now methinks some wanton, itching ear,
> With lustful thoughts and ill attention,
> List to my muse, expecting for to hear,
> The amorous description of that action
> Which Venus seeks, and ever doth require,
> When fitness grants a place to please desire.[33]

Throughout the poem there are like touches from Marston,
as he mocks the "gaping ears" that eagerly await further details from the pen from which some "loose lines have slipped."
But as if not content with all this display of irony, Marston
followed it up with a piece, *The Author in Praise of the Prece-
dent Poem*, in which he satirizes the poetic vogue. He asks to
be crowned with bays, for has he not followed the common
Muse? Has he not glorified his mistress in the accepted fashion? Has he not sighed and prostrated himself before her? Are
not his lines "written right in the swaggering humor of these
times?" Has he not like a Paphian, wantonly displayed

. . . . .

[32] Marston, *op. cit.*, III, 253.   [33] *Ibid.*, III, 259.

The Salaminian titillations
Which tickle up our lewd Priapians?

Marston was to preserve this contempt for amatory literature, and in his satires there are frequent sneers at swooning
lovers. He asks indignantly if his interlocutors dare class him
with the "Paphian shows," or if they conceive that he will
stoop to the common vogue:

Thinkst thou that I in melting posey
Will pamper itching sensuality? [34]

He heaps scorn upon the common run of poetasters who call
upon Colin Clout whenever they set out to write a poem; he
is indignant at the suspicion that he might have written
Pygmalions Image in "sad seriousness." [35] But all this may be
mere rhetoric and, as one critic suggests, Marston, like many
other censors, may have derived a certain amount of vicarious
gratification from detailed accounts of the very vices he attacked. [36]

Though many mythological poems were written during the
following century, after Marston's travesty the genre experienced a very definite decline. Having achieved its ripeness,
the mythological poem withered and fell through natural
causes.

Thus was the cycle brought to completion. The Italianate
poem, which saw its rise in the early mythological accounts,
died of natural exhaustion when the springs that provided its
strength ran dry. We have seen its early beginnings in the attempts to allegorize and introduce the moralizing element into
Ovidian material. Gradually, such interpretations were shed,
and there was a more natural rapprochement to the original
feeling of the *Metamorphoses* and the Italian mythological
poem, even though the change was effected through native
forces, rather than through Continental imitation. But there
was always present a strong tendency on the part of the

. . . . .

[34] *Ibid.*, III, 340.   [35] *Ibid.*, III, 339.   [36] Bush, *op. cit.*, p. 179.

Puritans to moralize Ovid's pagan myths. Even as they had utilized the *mirrors* and the verse romances, these zealots chose the mythological narrative as a means of spreading their doctrines. Although the check given by Elizabeth to their program brought a momentary halt to this tendency, nevertheless, throughout Elizabeth's reign, there was always evident the undeclared but definite war between the forces of strict morality and those which advocated a more natural frankness. But as the Queen increased her hold upon the throne, as the Renaissance feeling gathered strength, the natural reaction set in, and mythological poetry shone forth once more in all its honest nakedness. The paganism of Italy triumphed over the godly mood. This change brought a new stress on form and pictorial effects; the mythological poem shifted its emphasis from mere narration to sensuous, voluptuous description. Drawing its inspiration in Spenserian color and word-painting and vitalized by the tremendous strength of Shakespeare and Marlowe, the genre reached its ultimate perfection in *Hero and Leander* and in *Venus and Adonis*. After this, poets must content themselves with imitating or playing variations on the themes set by these two great poems. What might have proved a fruitful innovation was attempted by Drayton, but it met with little success and was practically ignored by his contemporaries, who continued to write in the conventional manner. Before long, the mood of fresh exuberance and frankness found in the mythological poetry of the early nineties was converted more and more into an excuse for licentiousness, as the appetites became jaded and no new ideas were brought into the type. Eventually, the lasciviousness of these compositions brought the wrath of the Church upon them; they became the butts of satirists, and their popularity waned. The world of mythology was exchanged for the shady pastures of literary shepherds; the *Metamorphoses* gave way to Donne's impassioned sermons; and the world of the gods vanished beneath the cold glare of the skeptical seventeenth century.

X X I I

Conclusion

WHATEVER CONCLUSIONS MIGHT BE DRAWN
from this examination of Elizabethan narrative poetry must
have already been impressed upon the reader in the preceding
pages. Though the number of narrative poems produced during this period was considerable, it must have become evident
by now that only a fraction of them possess any genuine literary distinction. But, as has already been frequently pointed
out, that was not their aim. They laid little claim to poetic
value. Most of these narrative poems were employed for other
purposes, and those they amply fulfilled. Their chief function
was to provide entertaining stories which the common people
read voraciously and with little critical judgment, but which
furnished a lively reading fare to relieve the tedium of their
daily lives. They introduced a measure of romance into the
existence of the god-fearing middle class readers who went
faithfully about England's prosaic tasks.

In perusing these accounts, the reader is struck once again
by the tremendous intellectual ferment which seized England
during the Elizabethan age. Although this was true of all
social strata, it was especially noticeable in the burgher class.

Raised to a position of importance and affluence by the downfall of the old nobility, the tradesmen of England made good
use of their new-found wealth and leisure. They explored
every recondite corner of the world. Those who could travel
journeyed to Europe; if not, they sailed with Drake and Frobisher to plunder Spanish galleons; those who could go off to
the wars took part in the campaigns against Spain in the
Netherlands. The remainder, the workaday world, stayed
home and read about these exploits in news-letters, relations of
voyages, prose novels, laudatory poems and an incredible number of other accounts. Narrative poems, dealing with every
conceivable subject, supplied some of this reading matter. As
the Renaissance passion for learning and discovery widened
the horizon for the Englishmen of this time, they became engrossed with every aspect of life. All subjects interested them.
As a result, narrative poetry records the most varied events and
treats the most widely divergent topics. In it we may watch
evolve some of the most significant changes which took place
in Elizabethan England. Through these narrative poems, we
may observe the development of social ideals. Through them
is preached the gospel of the middle class: Thrift, work and
morality.

Since history was a prized subject during the Renaissance,
a large portion of this poetry deals with historical narratives.
The all-important *Mirror for Magistrates,* which formed the
vanguard of many such chronicles, focussed the attention of
Englishmen upon their past. Its repeated editions, expanded
and elaborated, brought before the English public the examples to be drawn from the conduct of former rulers. For, above
all, during this time, history must be useful. History conveyed
to the people moral and political lessons. It glorified the national heroes, stressing the valor of Englishmen to a populace
eager for such accounts. History buttressed their vanity, as
they sought a pedigree which would place them on an equal
footing with older and stronger nations in Europe. More than
that, from history they learned invaluable political lessons,

which aided them in shouldering their responsibilities as citizens. History taught the English people morality and obedience to their God-appointed sovereign. *Mirror* after *mirror* held up examples of evil doers being brought to justice, thus warning those who contemplated crimes against the state that they could not carry out with impunity their nefarious designs. Hundreds of *mirrors* and chronicles repeated this lesson. In addition, the *Mirror for Magistrates* and all its imitations furnished the playwrights of England with a rich mine of historical fact. It educated the public in legendary history and acquainted it with characters and events, thus making possible the success of many plays, the subject matter of which would otherwise have been unfamiliar to the English audiences.

In the fictional element of narrative poetry, we are again enabled to observe significant social tendencies at work. Though they designed them for the amusement of the reading public, English authors of the verse romances warped the original intent of the works they translated, coating their tales with a layer of sententious moralizing. Consequently, the lessons of thrift and godly behaviour dominate throughout the fictional material. As the heirs of the medieval romances of chivalry, the popular verse romances were useful vehicles for conveying such didacticism. For it is clear that England appreciated and expected such motives; it was the same attitude that made Englishmen appreciate and demand those terrifyingly lengthy sermons which today appall us. By this process, a twofold purpose was achieved; the important works of European writers were translated for Englishmen, at the same time that their venom and paphian licentiousness were removed.

Elizabethan authors did not confine themselves narrowly in their search for material, but ranged over all European literature. Tales of Spanish and Greek origin intermingled with medieval *fabliaux*. By far the most popular sources, however, were the collections of Italian *novelle*, especially Boccaccio's and Bandello's. Yet the frank, satirical tales of Boccaccio were sedulously avoided, unless they could be used to denounce the lewdness and the wiles of Popery. Usually, writers showed a preference for tales of violence or stories of love ending in tragic fashion. In depicting the miserable fate of unfortunate lovers, the poets usually jumped at the opportunity to draw a moral lesson, eager to show that the impetuousness of lovers or their unwillingness to wait for parental consent inevitably precipitated tragic consequences.

All this resulted from the desire of the Puritan element to reform the old order in England. Not long after Elizabeth assumed the crown, however, the Puritans realized that their hopes were to be blasted. Utopia could not be established in England as it had been at Geneva. Their attempts to gain political recognition defeated, the Puritans were forced to recede. But their vanquishers gained only a Pyrrhic victory. In spite of their setbacks, the reformers had gained such a foothold in England that they continued to spread their gospel to the common people until it finally won over the middle classes, the lawyers and the merchants, the country squires and the humble tradesmen. It was these beliefs which created the social revolution of the next century; many of them color the attitude of Englishmen to this day. The program was largely accomplished through their writings, for, though momentarily checked politically, the Puritans continued to write their books. In their program of action, narrative poetry was not the least of their weapons. Though generally lacking in literary merit, it played its humble, yet effective part, in spreading the necessity of obedience to God and Queen, in presenting the lessons of work and godliness.

The encroachment of moralizing upon this genre is widespread. But in mythological narratives, it is possible to observe the definite reaction to this tendency; it is possible to watch the drama between the forces of godliness and Renaissance paganism unfold. This is especially true during the last decade of the century after the check given to Puritan aspirations brought their reform movement to a temporary standstill. As a result, the mythological accounts, which in previous decades had been heavily moralized, emerged in a state which more truly conveyed the original classical feeling. Gradually, the vitiated interpretations of Ovid were cleared away, and the influence of morality on myth was dissipated. The great poems of Marlowe, Shakespeare and Spenser made their appearance without the accretion of moralization. But it was not long before the authors of mythological poems replaced the frankness of the *Metamorphoses* with mere licentiousness; eventually, the popular reaction to such lewdness brought many of these poems under public and official displeasure. Still, although for the moment paganism was rampant, with few exceptions, this body of poetry always lacked the spontaneity and abandon to be found in the Italian mythological poem. Because of this, the genre soon died of natural causes, giving way to the newer, stronger moods of the seventeenth century.

In spite of all its faults and deficiencies, the narrative poem was eminently popular in England. It furnished the people amusement, edification and historical knowledge. Sometimes, it stealthily introduced even a measure of ribaldry, over which the good subjects of Queen Elizabeth could enjoy a hearty chuckle. The common people of England may have lacked critical ability, but they knew enough to applaud Shakespeare and to make a place for his poems among their books. They read Marlowe and his imitators fervently. They avoided the frigid personifications of Chapman and turned a cold shoulder to Drayton's platonized myths. Above all, they demanded a story. Though they took it larded with didacticism and garnished with moralizing, they clamored for a narrative spiced with plenty of incidents and action. Narrative poems gave them all this; hence their popularity.

Bibliography

THE FOLLOWING BOOKS AND ARTICLES REPRESENT a selective list of secondary works and texts which contain useful critical material. In some cases primary sources are given to aid the reader in locating certain inaccessible material. All other sources will be found by referring to the text.

The following is a partial list of the more common abbreviations used in this bibliography:

DNB — Dictionary of National Biography
EETS — Early English Texts Society
MLA — Modern Language Association
MLN — Modern Language Notes
MP — Modern Philology
N&Q — Notes and Queries
PMLA — Publications of the Modern Language Association of America
PQ — Philological Quarterly
RES — Review of English Studies
SP — Studies in Philology
STC — Short Title Catalogue
TLS — Times Literary Supplement

ACHELLEY, THOMAS, *A Most Lamentable History Containing the Tyranny Which Violenta Executed Upon Her Lover*. London, 1576.
ARBER, EDWARD, ed., *A Transcript of the Registers of the Company of Stationers of London* (1554-1649). London, 1875-77.
ARIOSTO, LODOVICO, *Orlando Furioso* (ed. S. Debenedetti). Bari, 1928.

ASCHAM, ROGER, *The Scholemaster*. (Arber's Reprints), London, 1570.

AVERILL, WILLIAM, *An Excellent Historie Discoursing of the Death of Charles and Julia*, 1581. MLA Rotograph 408 F.

——, *A Dyall for Dainty Darlings Rockt in the Cradle of Securitie*. London, 1584.

B. R., *Orpheus His Journey to Hell and His Music to the Ghosts*. London, 1595.

BANDELLO, MATTEO, *Opere* (ed. F. Flora). Milano, 1934.

BELLONI, ANTONIO, *Il Poema Epico e Mitologico*. Milano, 1912.

BERDAN, JOHN M., *Early Tudor Poetry*. New York, 1920.

BEVERLEY, PETER, *The Historie of Ariodanto and Jeneura* (1566?). MLA Rotograph 413 F.

BOCCACCIO, GIOVANNI, *Il Decamerone* (ed. A. F. Massera). Bari, 1927.

BRADNER, LEICESTER, *Edmund Spenser and the Faerie Queene*. University of Chicago Press, 1948.

BROOKE, ARTHUR, *The Tragicall Historie of Romeus and Juliet* (ed. J. J. Munroe). New York, 1908.

BROOKE, C. F. TUCKER, "The Reputation of Christopher Marlowe." *Transactions of the Connecticut Academy of Arts and Sciences*, XXV (1922), 347ff.

BULLEN, ARTHUR H., *Some Longer Elizabethan Poems*. London, 1903.

BUSH, J. DOUGLAS, "Hero and Leander and Romeo and Juliet." *PQ*, IX (1930), 396-99.

——, "The Influence of Marlowe's *Hero and Leander* on Early Mythological Poems." *MLN*, XLII (1927), 211ff.

——, *Mythology and the Renaissance Tradition in English Poetry*. Minneapolis, 1932.

——, "Notes on Hero and Leander." *PMLA*, XLIV (1929), 760ff.

CAMPBELL, LILY B., "The Suppressed Edition of *The Mirror for Magistrates*." *Huntington Library Bulletin*, No. 6 (1934), 1ff.

——, *Tudor Conception of History and Tragedy in the Mirror for Magistrates*. Berkeley, 1936.

CARPENTER, F. I., *A Reference Guide to Spenser*. University of Chicago Press, 1923.

CASTIGLIONE, BALDASSARE, *The Courtier* (Tudor Translations). London, 1900.

CAVENDISH, GEORGE, *The Life of Cardinal Wolsey* (ed. S. W. Singer). London, 1825.

CAXTON, WILLIAM, *Recueyll of the Historyes of Troye* (ed. W. O. Sommer). London, 1894.

Certain Worthy Manuscript Poems, 1597. MLA Rotograph 409 F.

CHABALIER, L., *Hero et Leandre*. Paris, 1911.

CHAPMAN, GEORGE, *The Works of George Chapman: Poems and Minor Translations* (ed. A. C. Swinburne). London, 1875.

CHURCHYARD, THOMAS, *Churchyards Challenge*. London, 1593.

——, *The First Part of Churchyardes Chippes*. London, 1575.

———, *A Generall Rehearsal of Warres Called Churchyards Choice.* London, 1579.

———, *A Mirror of Man.* London, 1594.

———, *The Miseries of Flanders.* London, 1579.

———, *The Tragedie of Shores Wife.* London, 1593.

CHUTE, ANTHONY, *Beawtie Dishonored.* London, 1593.

COLLIER, JOHN P., *A Bibliographical and Critical Account of the Rarest Books in the English Language.* New York, 1866.

———, *The History of English Dramatic Poetry to the Time of Shakespeare, and Annals of the Stage to the Restoration.* London, 1831.

———, *Illustrations of Early English Popular Literature.* London, 1864.

———, *The Poetical Decameron.* Edinburgh, 1820.

COLSE, PETER, *Penelopes Complaint or a Mirror for Wanton Minions.* London, 1596.

COMPARETTI, DOMENICO, *Virgilio nel Medioevo.* Firenze, 1896.

COTTON, ROGER, *A Spirituall Song; Contayning an Historical Discourse from the Infancy of the World.* London, 1596.

COURTHOPE, WILLIAM J., *History of English Poetry.* New York, 1895.

CRAIG, HARDIN, *The Enchanted Glass.* New York, 1936.

CRANE, R. S., *The Vogue of Medieval Chivalric Romances during the English Renaissance.* Menasha, Wisconsin, 1919.

CRATHERN, ALICE, "A Romanticized Version of *Hero and Leander.*" *MLN*, XLVI (1931), 382ff.

C. T., *A Notable History of Nastagio and Traversari.* London, 1569.

CUTWODE, THOMAS, *Caltha Poetarum.* London, Roxburghe Club, 1815.

DANIEL, SAMUEL, *The Works of Samuel Daniel* (ed. A. Grosart). London, 1885.

DOWRICHE, ANNE, *The French Historie,* 1589. MLA Rotograph 406 F.

DRAYTON, MICHAEL, *Endymion and Phoebe* (ed. J. W. Hebel). Boston, 1925.

———, *The Works of Michael Drayton* (ed. J. W. Hebel). Oxford, 1931.

DROUT, JOHN, *A Pityful Historie of Two Loving Italians,* (ed. J. P. Collier). London, 1844.

DUNN, ESTHER G., *The Literature of Shakespeare's England.* New York, 1936.

EDWARDS, THOMAS, *The Works of Thomas Edwards* (ed. W. D. Buckley). (Roxburghe Club) London, 1882.

ELTON, OLIVER, *Michael Drayton.* London, 1905.

ELVIDEN, EDMUND, *The Most Pleasant Historie of Pesistratus and Catanea.* London (1570?).

ELYOT, SIR THOMAS, *The Boke Called the Governour* (ed. H. H. S. Croft). London, 1883.

ESDAILE, ARUNDELL, J. K., *A List of English Tales and Prose Romances Printed Before 1740.* London, 1912.

Ewig, Wilhelm, "Lucrece, Eine Litterar Historische Untersuchung," *Anglia*, XXII (1899), 1f., 343ff., 393ff.

Farnham, Willard, *The Medieval Heritage of Elizabethan Tragedy.* Berkeley, The University of California Press, 1936.

——, "England's Discovery of the *Decameron*," PMLA, XXXIX (1924), 123ff.

Feasey, Evelyn, "The Licensing of *The Mirror for Magistrates.*" *The Library*, Ser. 4, III (1923), 177ff.

Fenne, Thomas, *Fennes Frutes.* MLA Rotograph 403 F.

Fenton, Geoffrey, *Certain Tragicall Discourses of Bandello, Translated into English by Geoffrie Fenton* (ed. R. L. Douglas). London, 1896.

Fitzgeoffrey, Charles, *The Life and Death of Sir Francis Drake.* Oxford, 1596.

Flamini, Francesco, *Studi di Storia Letteraria.* Livorno, 1895.

Fletcher, Giles, *Licia, with the Rise to the Crowne of Richard III.* London, 1593.

Forrest, William, *The History of Grisild the Second* (ed. W. D. Macray). Roxburghe Club, 1875.

——, *The Notable History of the Most Chaiste Innocent Ioseph.* MLA Rotograph 308.

Fraunce, Abraham, *The Countess of Pembroke's Emanuell.* London, 1591.

——, *The Third Part of the Countess of Pembroke's Ivychurch— Entituled, Amintas Dale,* 1592. MLA Rotograph 75.

French, Robert D., *A Chaucer Handbook.* New York, 1927.

Fulwell, Ulpian, *The Flower of Fame.* (Harleian Miscellany, IX), London, 1808-11.

Fulwood, William, *The Enemie of Idlenesse, Teaching How to Endite Epistles.* London, 1568.

Furnivall, F. J., ed., *Robert Laneham's Letter.* London: Chatto and Windus, 1917.

Gale, Dunstan, *Pyramus and Thisbe,* 1596. MLA Rotograph 400 F.

Garter, Bernard, *The Tragicall and True Historie Which Happened Betweene Two English Lovers,* 1568. MLA Rotograph 447 F.

Gascoigne, George, *The Works of George Gascoigne* (ed. J. W. Cunliffe). Cambridge, 1907.

G. B., *Ludus Scacchiae.* London: Harding and Wright, 1810.

Genouy, Hector, *L'Element Pastoral dans la Poesie Narrative et le Drame en Angleterre de 1579-1640.* Paris, 1929.

God, John, *A Discourse of the Great Crueltie of a Widow Towardes a Young Gentleman,* 1569-70. MLA Rotograph 410 F.

Gottfried, Rudolf B., "Spenser and the Myths of Locality." SP, XXXIV (1937), 107ff.

Grosart, A. B., ed., *Miscellanies of the Fuller Worthies Library.* London, 1870.

GROVE, MATTHEW, *The Most Famous and Tragicall Historie of Pelops and Hippodamia* (ed. A. Grosart). 1878.

HALLER, WILLIAM B., *The Rise of Puritanism*. New York, 1938.

HARDYNG, JOHN, *The Chronicles of John Hardyng* (ed. Henry Ellis). London, 1812.

HAZLITT, WILLIAM C., *Handbook to the Popular, Poetical, and Dramatic Literature of Great Britain*. London, 1867.

———, *Remains of the Early Popular Poetry of England*. London, 1866.

HILARIE, HUGH, *The Resurreccion of the Masse*, 1554. MLA Rotograph 411 F.

HOGARDE, MILES, *The Assaulte of the Sacrament of the Altar*, 1554. MLA Rotograph 404 F.

HOLLAND, ROBERT, *The Holy Historie of Our Lord Jesus Christ into English Meeter*, 1594. MLA Rotograph 446 F.

HOLME, WILFRED, *The Fall and Evill Success of the Rebellion*, 1572. MLA Rotograph 401 F.

HOWELL, THOMAS, *The Poems of Thomas Howell* (ed. A. B. Grosart). London, 1879.

HUNNIS, WILLIAM, *Hunniss Recreations*, 1595. MLA Rotograph 468 F.

———, *A Hyvefull of Hunnye*, 1578. MLA Rotograph 407 F.

I. O., *A Lamentation of Troy for the Death of Hector*. London, 1594.

JEFFERY, VIOLET M., *John Lyly and the Italian Renaissance*. Paris, 1928.

JELLINEK, MAX H., *Die Sage von Hero und Leander in der Dichtung*. Berlin, 1890.

JENYNGES, EDWARD, *The Notable History of Two Faithful Lovers Named Alfagus and Archelaus*, 1574. MLA Rotograph 402 F.

JIRICZEK, O. L., *Specimens of Tudor Translations from the Classics*. Heidelberg, 1923.

JOHNSON, RICHARD, *Nine Worthies of London*. (Harleian Miscellany, VIII), London, 1808-11.

JONES, H. S. V., *A Spenser Handbook*. New York, 1930.

KELSO, RUTH, *The Doctrine of the English Gentleman in the Sixteenth Century*. Urbana, University of Illinois Press, 1929.

KNAPPEN, M. M., *Tudor Puritanism*. University of Chicago Press, 1939.

KOEPPEL, EMIL, "Die Englische Tasso-Ubersetzungen des XVI jahrhunderts." *Anglia*, XIII (1891), 1ff.

———, "Studien zur Geschichte der italienischen Novellen in der englischen Litteratur des sechzehnten Jahrhunderts." *Quellen Und Forschungen*, LXX (1892).

KYTTES, G., *The Unluckie Firmentie*, (1585?). MLA Rotograph 479 F.

The Lamentation of Troy for the Death of Hector, 1594. MLA Rotograph 414 F.

LEWICKE, EDWARD, *The History of Titus and Gesippus*. London, 1562.

LINCHE, RICHARD, *Diella* (ed. A. B. Grosart). London, 1877.

LODGE, THOMAS, *The Complete Works of Thomas Lodge*, (ed. E. Gosse). Hunterian Club, 1883.

Of Loves Complaint; with the Legend of Orpheus and Eurydice, 1597. MLA Rotograph 412 F.

LYDGATE, JOHN, *The Fall of Princes* (ed. Henry Bergen). EETS, 1924.

MARBECKE, JOHN, *The Holie Historie of King David*, 1579. MLA Rotograph 461 F.

MARLOWE, CHRISTOPHER, *The Poems of Christopher Marlowe* (ed. L. C. Martin). New York, 1931.

MARSTON, JOHN, *The Works of John Marston* (ed. A. H. Bullen). London, 1887.

MATTHIESSEN, FRANCIS O., *Translation, An Elizabethan Art*. Cambridge, Mass., 1931.

MENENDEZ Y PELAYO, M., *Antologia de Poetas Liricos y Castellanos*. Madrid, 1919.

MERES, FRANCIS, *Palladis Tamia* (ed. D. C. Allen). New York, 1938.

MIDDLETON, CHRISTOPHER, *The Legend of Humphrey, Duke of Glocester*. London, 1600. (Harleian Miscellany, X) London, 1808-11.

MIDDLETON, THOMAS, *The Ghost of Lucrece* (ed. J. Q. Adams). New York, 1937.

The Mirror for Magistrates (ed. Lily B. Campbell). Cambridge, 1938.

The Mirror for Magistrates (ed. Joseph Hazlewood). London, 1815.

Mirror for Magistrates, Parts Added to the Mirror for Magistrates (ed. Lily B. Campbell). Cambridge, 1946.

MORE, THOMAS, *The English Works of Sir Thomas More* (ed. W. E. Campbell). London, 1931.

NASHE, THOMAS, *The Choice of Valentines*. London, 1899.

OLDYS, WILLIAM, *The Harleian Miscellany*. London, 1808-11.

OVIDIUS NASO, PUBLIUS, *Shakespeare's Ovid, Being Arthur Golding's Translation of the Metamorphoses* (ed. W. H. D. Rouse). London, 1904.

PAINTER, WILLIAM, *The Palace of Pleasure* (ed. Joseph Jacobs). London, 1890.

PALMER, HENRIETTA R., *A List of English Editions and Translations of Greek and Latin Classics Printed Before 1641*. London, 1911.

PARADISE, BURTON N., *Thomas Lodge; The History of an Elizabethan*. New Haven, 1931.

PARKS, THOMAS, ed., *Heliconia, Selections of English Poetry*. London, 1815.

PARTRIDGE, JOHN, *The Most Famous and Worthy History of the Worthye Ladye Pandavula*. London, 1566.

PATCH, H. R., *The Goddess Fortuna in Medieval Literature*. Cambridge, Mass., 1927.

PEELE, GEORGE, *The Works of George Peele* (ed. A. H. Bullen). London, 1888.

PEEND, THOMAS, *The Most Notable Historie of John, Lord of Mandosse*, 1565. *MLA* Rotograph 469 F.

PETOWE, HENRY, *Philochasander and Elanira*, 1599. *MLA* Rotograph 415 F.

PETTIE, GEORGE, *A Petite Pallace of Pettie his Pleasure* (ed. Sir Israel Gollancz). London, 1908.

PHILLIPS, JOHN, *The Life and Death of Sir Philip Sidney*, 1587. *MLA* Rotograph 465 F.

POLLARD, A. F. AND REDGRAVE, G. R., eds. *A Short Title Catalogue of Books Printed in England, Scotland, and Ireland and of English Books Printed Abroad, 1475-1640*. London, The Bibliographical Society, 1926.

PRUVOST, RENE, "The Source of George Turberville's *Tragicall Tales*." *RES*, X (1934), 29ff.

RAND, E. K., "Editor's Preface." *Speculum*, I (1926), 3ff.

———, *Ovid and His Influence*. Boston, 1925.

RICK, LEO, *Ovids Metamorphosen in der englischen Renaissance*. Munster i.w., 1915.

ROBINSON, RICHARD, *The Golden Mirror* (ed. T. Corser). Manchester, 1857.

ROLLINS, HYDER E., *An Analytical Index to the Ballad Entries (1557-1709) in the Registers of the Company of Stationers of London*. Chapel Hill, N. C., 1924.

———, *A Gorgeous Gallery of Gallant Inventions*. Cambridge, Mass., 1926.

———, "New Facts About George Turberville." *MP*, IV (1918), 129ff.

———, ed. *The Paradise of Dainty Devices*, Cambridge, Mass., 1927.

SABIE, FRANCIS, *Adams Complaint*, 1596. *MLA* Rotograph 416 F.

———, *The Fisherman's Tale*. London, 1595.

SACKVILLE, THOMAS, *The Complaint of Henry Duke of Buckingham* (ed. Marguerite Hearsey). New Haven, 1936.

SCHEVILL, RUDOLPH, *Ovid and the Renascence in Spain*. University of California Publications, Berkeley, 1913.

SCHIAVO-LENA, A., *La Poesia Mitologica nel Secolo XIV, XV, XVI*. Caltagirone, 1907.

SCHIRMER, WALTER F., *Antike, Renaissance und Puritanismus*. München, 1933.

SCHOELL, F. L., *Etudes sur l'Humanisme Continental en Angleterre a la Fin de la Renaissance*. Paris, 1926.

SCOTT, JANET, *Les Sonnets Elizabethains, les Sources et l'Apport*. Paris, 1929.

SCOTT, MARY A., *Elizabethan Translations from the Italian*. Boston, 1916.

SPENCER, HAZELTON, "Shakespeare's use of Golding in *Venus and Adonis.*" *MLN,* XLIV (1929), 435ff.

SPURGEON, CAROLINE, *Shakesperian Imagery.* Cambridge University Press, 1935.

STORER, THOMAS, *The Life and Death of Thomas Wolsey, Cardinal.* In *Heliconia,* Vol. II (ed. T. Parks). London, 1815.

T. H., *The Fable of Ovid Tretin of Narcissus, Translated into English Mytre.* London, 1560.

T. H., *Oenone and Paris.* London, 1594.

TAYLOR, H., *Topographical Poetry in England during the Renaissance.* University of Chicago, Abstracts of Theses, Humanistic Series, V (1926-7).

THALER, ALWIN, "Churchyard and Marlowe." *MLN* XXXVIII (1923), 89ff.

THOMPSON, GUY A., *Elizabethan Criticism of Poetry.* Menasha, Wisconsin, 1914.

TICKNOR, GEORGE, *History of Spanish Literature.* Houghton Mifflin Company, 1888.

TILLEY, ARTHUR, *The Literature of the French Renaissance.* Cambridge, 1904.

TOFTE, RICHARD, *Two Tales Out of Ariosto.* London, 1597.

TRENCH, W. F., *The Mirror for Magistrates: Its Origin and Influence.* Edinburgh, 1898.

TURBERVILLE, GEORGE, *Epitaphs, Epigrams.* London, 1570.

——, *Tragicall Tales.* Edinburgh, 1837.

TWYNE, THOMAS, *The Scholemaster or Teacher of Table Philosophie.* London, 1576.

VALLANS, WILLIAM, *A Tale of Two Swannes* (Reprinted in John Leland's *Itinerary,* ed. T. Hearne, 1711).

WARTON, THOMAS, *A History of English Poetry* (ed. W. C. Hazlitt). London, 1840.

WEEVER, JOHN, *Faunus and Melliflora.* London, 1600.

WELLS, JOHN E., *A Manual of the Writings in Middle English.* New Haven, 1916.

WHETSTONE, GEORGE, *The Rocke of Regard* (ed. J. P. Collier). London, 1867.

WILLIAMS, RICHARD, *The Complaynte of Anthonye Babington* (ed. F. J. Furnivall). 1868.

WIRL, JULIUS, *Orpheus in der englischen Literatur, Wiener Beitrage.* XL (1913).

WITZ, E., *Die englische Ovidübersetzungen des XVI Jahrhunderts.* Leipzig, 1915.

WRIGHT, LOUIS B., *Middle Class Culture in Elizabethan England.* Chapel Hill, University of North Carolina Press, 1935.

——, "The Reading of Renaissance English Women." *SP,* XXVIII (1931), 671ff.

Index

297